European Yearbook of International Economic Law

EYIEL Monographs - Studies in European and International Economic Law

Volume 50

EYIEL Monographs is a subseries of the European Yearbook of International Economic Law (EYIEL). It contains scholarly works in the fields of European and international economic law, in particular WTO law, international investment law, international monetary law, law of regional economic integration, external trade law of the EU and EU internal market law. The series does not include edited volumes. EYIEL Monographs are peer-reviewed by the series editors and external reviewers.

Jens Hillebrand Pohl

Arbitration of Disputes related to National Security Screening of Foreign Investments

Springer

Jens Hillebrand Pohl
Helsinki Geoeconomics Society
Helsinki, Finland

ISSN 2364-8392 ISSN 2364-8406 (electronic)
European Yearbook of International Economic Law
ISSN 2524-6658 ISSN 2524-6666 (electronic)
EYIEL Monographs - Studies in European and International Economic Law
ISBN 978-3-032-26341-4 ISBN 978-3-032-26342-1 (eBook)
https://doi.org/10.1007/978-3-032-26342-1

This Springer imprint is published by the registered company Springer Nature Switzerland AG.
The registered company address is: Gewerbestrasse 11, 6330 Cham, Switzerland

Acknowledgements This dissertation was written during my doctoral research at Maastricht University and reflects several years of intellectual exploration at the intersection of international law, geoeconomics, and global investment governance. I am deeply grateful to the many individuals and institutions who supported this journey.

First and foremost, I would like to express my sincere gratitude to my supervisors. Professor Peter Van den Bossche provided invaluable guidance, intellectual rigor, and encouragement throughout the doctoral process. His deep expertise in international economic law and his thoughtful engagement with my research were instrumental in shaping this dissertation. I am equally grateful to Dr. Denise Prévost for her careful supervision, insightful comments, and constant support during the development of this work.

I also extend my appreciation to my co-supervisor, Dr. Iveta Alexovicova, whose advice and feedback contributed significantly to refining the analytical framework and argumentation of the dissertation.

My thanks also go to the members of the assessment committee—Professor Anselm Kamperman Sanders, Professor David Collins, Professor Krista Nadakavukaren Schefer, and Professor Bas van Zelst—for their time, expertise, and willingness to engage with my work.

Part of this research was conducted during my time as a visiting researcher at the Max Planck Institute Luxembourg for International, European and Regulatory Procedural Law. I am grateful to the Institute for providing an intellectually stimulating environment and access to exceptional research resources.

Over the years, I have benefited from discussions with many colleagues, scholars, and practitioners working in international economic law, arbitration, and geoeconomics. Their insights helped sharpen many of the ideas developed in this dissertation.

Finally, I wish to thank my family and friends for their patience, encouragement, and unwavering support throughout the years of research and writing that culminated in this dissertation.

Any remaining errors or shortcomings are, of course, entirely my own.

Jens Hillebrand Pohl

Competing Interests The author has no competing interests to declare that are relevant to the content of this manuscript.

About This Book

This monograph, titled "Arbitration of Disputes Related to National Security Screening of Foreign Investments," explores the complexities arising at the intersection of international law, state sovereignty, and global commerce. The core focus is on how international arbitration can be employed to resolve disputes stemming from the national security screening of foreign direct investments (FDI).

The flow of FDI has been integral to global economic development, yet it has increasingly attracted scrutiny from national governments. This scrutiny has intensified due to geopolitical tensions and concerns over control of critical infrastructure and sensitive technologies. As states aim to balance the economic benefits of FDI with the need to protect national security, conflicts between state actions and international investment agreements have grown more complex.

International arbitration, particularly through investor-state dispute settlement (ISDS), represents a crucial forum for resolving these disputes. The arbitration process involves navigating between upholding international treaties and respecting the legitimate security concerns of states. This dissertation provides a detailed examination of how ISDS mechanisms can address these disputes, the legal principles involved, and the broader implications for international law and global investment governance.

The study aims to contribute to the ongoing discourse on harmonizing national security needs with the standards of protection promised under international investment law. It critically analyzes the role of arbitration in resolving conflicts arising from national security screenings, offering insights into how arbitral tribunals balance state sovereignty with investor protection. Additionally, it explores potential improvements to the arbitration process to enhance its fairness and efficiency in handling these high-stakes disputes.

Contents

About the Author

Jens Hillebrand Pohl FRGS, is President and Secretary-General of the Helsinki Geoeconomics Society and Editor-in-Chief of the Helsinki Geoeconomics Monitor (HeGeMon). His work focuses on international economic law, economic security, and geoeconomics.

His professional experience spans legal practice, multilateral diplomacy, and academic research. After studying law at the universities of Stockholm and Uppsala, he served as a judicial clerk at the Stockholm High Court and later practiced law in Stockholm and New York, including at Paul, Weiss, Rifkind, Wharton & Garrison LLP, where he worked on the Lehman Brothers bankruptcy. He subsequently advised on the establishment of the European Stability Mechanism and has practiced and argued cases before U.S. federal courts in New York and before the Court of Justice of the European Union in Luxembourg. He has held research and teaching positions at Maastricht University, the United Nations University, and the Finnish Institute of International Affairs, and has been a visiting researcher at the Max Planck Institute Luxembourg for International, European and Regulatory Procedural Law and the World Trade Institute. He is also Series Editor-in-Chief of *Springer Studies in Law & Geoeconomics*.

Dr. Pohl holds a Ph.D. in Law from Maastricht University, an LL.M. from Harvard Law School, and an M.Sc. in Economics and Business from the Stockholm School of Economics. He is admitted to legal practice in New York, England and Wales, and Ireland. He is a Fellow of the Royal Geographical Society.

Chapter 1
Introduction

Abstract This chapter introduces the central problem addressed in this dissertation: the growing tension between national security screening of foreign investment and the protections afforded to investors under international investment law. As geopolitical tensions intensify and states increasingly invoke national security to scrutinize or block foreign investments, conflicts with obligations under international investment agreements have become more likely. This chapter outlines the purpose and significance of the study, which is to examine the role of international arbitration in resolving disputes arising from such screenings. It formulates the core research questions concerning the extent of investor protection under international law, the legitimacy and scope of national security exceptions, the evaluation of national security risks by host states, and the criteria used by arbitral tribunals to balance investor rights with sovereign regulatory authority. The chapter also defines the scope and delimitations of the research, focusing on arbitration under international investment law from approximately 2000 onward, and explains the doctrinal methodology employed in the study. By situating the research within broader debates on sovereignty, investor protection, and dispute settlement, this chapter establishes the analytical framework for examining how arbitration mediates the relationship between national security policies and international investment obligations.

1.1 Introduction

In the increasingly interconnected world of global finance and investment, the flow of foreign direct investment (FDI) across borders has become a cornerstone of economic development and international economic relations. However, as this capital flow continues to intensify, so does the scrutiny it attracts from national governments, particularly through mechanisms designed to screen investments for

J. H. Pohl, *Arbitration of Disputes related to National Security Screening of Foreign Investments*, EYIEL Monographs - Studies in European and International Economic Law 50,
https://doi.org/10.1007/978-3-032-26342-1_1

national security concerns. This dissertation explores the arbitration of disputes related to the national security screening of foreign investments, an area at the nexus of international law, state sovereignty, and global commerce.

The practice of screening foreign investments for national security purposes is not new, but its prominence and regulatory scope have expanded significantly in recent years. This rise is attributed to increasing geopolitical tensions and growing concerns over the control of critical infrastructure, sensitive technology, and other strategic concerns. As states seek to balance the economic benefits of open capital markets with the imperative to protect national security, conflicts between state actions and international investment agreements have become more pertinent and complex.

Arbitration, particularly under the framework of investor-state dispute settlement (ISDS), has emerged as a pivotal forum for resolving such conflicts. The arbitration of these disputes involves difficult legal questions and significant political considerations, which reflect the broader tensions between the principles of state sovereignty and the regime of international investment law. These tensions manifest in legal proceedings where arbitrators must navigate between upholding the sanctity of international treaties and respecting the legitimate security concerns of sovereign states.

This introductory chapter sets the stage for a detailed examination of how international arbitration is employed in disputes arising from national security screening measures. It outlines the mechanisms of ISDS, the legal principles at play, and the broader implications of these disputes for international law and global investment governance. By investigating this intersection, the dissertation aims to illuminate the challenges and opportunities that lie ahead in harmonizing the needs of national security with the standards of protection promised under international investment law. Through this exploration, the study seeks to contribute to the ongoing discourse on the appropriate balance between protecting national interests and maintaining an open, predictable legal environment for foreign investors.

1.2 Purpose

The primary purpose of this study is to critically analyze the role of international arbitration in resolving disputes that arise from the national security screening of foreign investments. As global economic dynamics evolve, the frequency and complexity of these screenings have increased and given rise to significant legal and policy challenges. This research seeks to explore these challenges through the lens of arbitration particularly by focusing on how international law accommodates the dual imperatives of safeguarding national security and protecting foreign investors.

This investigation is of paramount importance due to the increasing instances where national security measures implemented by host states potentially conflict with the obligations under international investment treaties. These potential conflicts can lead to claims of discrimination, unfair treatment, and indirect expropriation by foreign investors, who may seek redress in arbitral tribunals. With over 2,500 international investment agreements currently in force, the potential for such disputes is significant and growing.[1] These agreements typically include provisions for the settlement of disputes by international arbitration, which makes them a critical area of study.

Moreover, this study aims to provide a comprehensive understanding of how arbitral tribunals navigate the delicate balance between the protection of foreign investments and the enforcement of national security measures. The arbitration process offers a unique perspective on the interaction between state sovereignty and global economic rules while highlighting broader issues of international law, state authority, and investor rights.

Another key objective of this research is to examine whether and how the existing frameworks of international arbitration are equipped to handle the specific challenges posed by national security considerations in investment screening. This objective involves analysis of the arbitral decisions, the interpretation of treaty provisions, and the application of legal standards in the context of national security. Therefore, this study investigates various arbitration cases in which comparable issues of vital national interests have been central by analyzing the reasoning and outcomes to discern patterns and principles that can guide future disputes.

Ultimately, this dissertation seeks to analyze existing practices and contribute to the discourse on potential improvements in the arbitration process regarding disputes over national security screening. By identifying the strengths and limitations of the current system, the study aims to suggest ways in which international arbitration can better serve its role as a fair, efficient, and balanced mechanism for resolving such disputes. This contribution can be particularly valuable for policymakers, legal practitioners, and scholars engaged in the fields of international investment and security law.

1.3 Problem Statement

The intersection of national security concerns and international investment has increasingly become a significant area of tension in global economic relations. As states continue to invoke national security to scrutinize or block foreign investments, the potential for conflict with established norms of international investment law escalates, which raises critical questions about the adequacy of existing legal frameworks to manage these disputes. This tension forms the core problem addressed in this dissertation: the extent of any inconsistency between national

[1] United Nations Conference on Trade and Development (UNCTAD), Investment Policy Hub database, available at http://www.investmentpolicyhub.unctad.org.

investment screening regimes and international investment law remains largely undefined despite their growing importance and frequency.

National security screening mechanisms, designed to protect a country's sensitive sectors and critical infrastructure, often operate with a high degree of discretion. This discretion can sometimes lead to actions that foreign investors perceive as arbitrary or discriminatory because they may breach international legal standards designed to protect investments. Such breaches can include violations of fair and equitable treatment, non-discrimination, and expropriation clauses typically found in international investment agreements. The increased scope and intensity of investment screening raise the likelihood of such conflicts and heightens the risk of compensation claims by foreign investors against host states. These claims, if substantiated, can lead to substantial financial liabilities for states and deter future foreign investment.

The problem is exemplified by the case of *Global Telecom v Canada*, the first arbitral award related to national security screening within the context of international investment treaties.[2] In this case, the arbitral tribunal had to navigate the complexities of a treaty that included specific clauses excluding certain types of national security decisions from its scope.[3] Despite these exclusions, the tribunal found that the particular screening decision—triggered by a share conversion—did not fall within these exclusions.[4] However, it concluded that the screening did not violate the substantive investment protection standards of the treaty, notably the obligation to afford fair and equitable treatment.[5] This case highlights the politically sensitive and often convoluted nature of legal interpretations required in such contexts and emphasizes the need for clarity and predictability in how national security considerations are integrated into the international investment law framework.

Furthermore, investment treaty obligations potentially breached by national security screening measures encompass a broad array of protections, including non-discrimination (national and most-favoured-nation treatment), fair and equitable treatment, prohibitions against expropriation without compensation, and adherence to performance requirements and umbrella clauses that may include stabilization provisions found in investment contracts and national legislation. Hence, each obligation must be carefully balanced against the legitimate security interests of host states, which requires a legal and ethical balancing act that poses significant challenges for arbitral tribunals.

This dissertation seeks to address these issues by exploring how international arbitration serves as a mechanism for resolving disputes arising from national security screening measures. It examines whether arbitration can effectively mediate between the sovereign right of states to protect their

[2] Global Telecom Holding SAE v Canada (Award) (ICSID Case No ARB/16/16, 27 March 2020).

[3] Global Telecom v Canada para. 334.

[4] Global Telecom v Canada para. 331–333.

[5] Global Telecom v Canada para. 647.

national security and the protection rights granted to foreign investors under international law. Moreover, it investigates the mechanisms through which arbitral tribunals can adjudicate these sensitive and often politically charged disputes without compromising the procedural justice owed to states and investors.

In summary, the central problem of this study revolves around the critical need to delineate the boundaries between national security measures and the protections afforded to foreign investors to ensure that the arbitration process can handle such disputes with fairness, efficiency, and respect for the delicate balance between competing legal and national interests.

1.4 Research Statement

The uneasy intersection between national security imperatives and the protections guaranteed to foreign investors under international law necessitates a deeper inquiry into the role of arbitration in resolving disputes arising from national security screening measures. This dissertation aims to address several pivotal questions that explore the core of this interaction, each designed to illuminate the broader implications for international investment law and arbitration practices. The following research questions are integral to guiding the investigation:

What is the degree of protection promised to foreign investors under international investment agreements in the context of national security screening measures? This question seeks to clarify the expectations set by international treaties regarding the treatment of foreign investments, especially related to the rights of investors when their investments are subjected to national security measures. It involves examining the legal obligations that host states have towards foreign investors and how they are articulated in the face of national security exceptions.

To what extent is it legitimate for investors to expect that their protection under international law will be subjugated to a host state's national security interests? Here, the inquiry focuses on the legitimacy and scope of national security as a defence against claims of treaty violations. The question seeks a critical analysis of how international arbitral tribunals interpret and apply the necessity and national security exceptions within the broader framework of international investment law.

What constitutes a manageable level of national security risk for a host state regarding foreign investment, and how should these risks be evaluated? This question aims to understand the thresholds and criteria used by states to define and evaluate national security risks in the context of foreign investment. It seeks to explore how these definitions align with international legal standards and the implications for state sovereignty and investor security.

According to what criteria and which procedures should the opposing interests of host states and foreign investors be weighed in arbitration? This question addresses the procedural aspects of arbitration, specifically how tribunals balance the state's right to protect its national security with the investor's rights under international law. It involves examining the methods and approaches used by arbitrators to adjudicate claims that involve national security considerations.

Can international arbitration effectively and fairly resolve disputes arising from national security screening measures of foreign investments? Finally, this overarching question seeks to evaluate the effectiveness and fairness of international arbitration as a dispute resolution mechanism in cases involving national security concerns. It involves assessing whether the arbitration process provides a balanced resolution that respects the rights and obligations of both parties involved.

By answering these questions, this dissertation aims to contribute to a clearer understanding of how international arbitration can navigate the challenging waters of national security and foreign investment while potentially offering recommendations for improving the coherence and fairness of arbitral outcomes in these high-stakes disputes.

1.5 Scope and Delimitations

This dissertation specifically focuses on the arbitration of disputes arising from the national security screening of foreign investments, a topic that sits at the intersection of international arbitration law and national security considerations. This focus was chosen due to the increasing prevalence of national security as a justification used by states to scrutinize or reject foreign investments and the consequential legal disputes that often invoke international arbitration as a resolution mechanism.

1.5.1 Scope

The study seeks to examine how international arbitration addresses these disputes, with particular attention to how arbitral tribunals interpret and apply international investment agreements in the context of national security. It investigates the balance arbitral tribunals strike between upholding the legal rights of foreign investors and respecting the sovereign rights of states to protect their national security. This investigation includes an analysis of the legal arguments presented by states and investors, the decisions of arbitral tribunals, and the implications of these decisions for international investment law.

1.5.2 *Delimitations*

While the scope of this study is broad in terms of legal analysis, several delimitations are necessary to maintain a clear focus:

1.5.2.1 Exclusion of Related Legal Fields

The research primarily considers international investment law but does not extensively cover related areas such as international trade law, European Union law, or international human rights law, except where these areas intersect significantly with the main focus of the study.

1.5.2.2 Geographical and Jurisdictional Limits

The study does not focus on a specific geographical region but instead considers a range of cases and legal frameworks from various jurisdictions to maintain a global perspective.

1.5.2.3 Temporal Scope

The dissertation focuses on developments in international arbitration related to national security screening measures, primarily from the early 2000s to the present, to reflect the surge in relevant disputes and legal developments during this period.

1.5.3 *Rationale for Delimitations*

These delimitations seek to ensure that the study remains manageable and focused while providing comprehensive coverage of the key issues at hand. By concentrating on arbitration within the realm of international investment law, the dissertation aims to provide a detailed examination of a complex yet specific area of international law that is of growing importance in today's geopolitical climate. The exclusion of certain legal fields and the broad geographical scope allow for a concentrated analysis of the core issues without dilution of the primary research objectives. These boundaries ensure that the dissertation remains a focused academic inquiry into how international arbitration navigates the tensions between national security and the protection of foreign investments.

The dissertation aims to provide a coherent and historically grounded framework for analysing the evolution of international arbitration in the context of national security and foreign investments. The rationale behind using the year 2000 as the cut-off date for the assessment is grounded in the observed increase in political and legal developments related to national security screening of foreign investments during this period. These developments are central to the types of disputes—both potential and materialised—that this study focuses on. The early 2000s marked the beginning of a significant rise in geopolitical tensions and heightened awareness of national security issues, leading to more frequent invocation of national security justifications by states in scrutinising foreign investments. Although this surge did not commence precisely on 1 January 2000, the early 2000s broadly represent the onset of a new era in the regulatory landscape and international arbitration concerning national security. This period saw the implementation of more stringent investment screening mechanisms and a corresponding increase in ISDS cases, making it a logical starting point for this study.

1.5.4 Availability of Primary Sources

The scope of this study is also shaped by the availability of primary sources, particularly ISDS awards. While efforts have been made to access a comprehensive range of arbitration awards and relevant documents, it is acknowledged that not all ISDS awards rendered since 2000 may be accessible. This limitation arises from several factors:

1.5.4.1 Confidentiality of Awards

Some ISDS awards are confidential and not publicly available due to the sensitive nature of the disputes or the confidentiality agreements between the parties involved.

1.5.4.2 Incomplete Public Records

There may be instances where awards have been rendered but not published or fully disclosed in public databases, often due to parties choosing not to disclose the outcomes.

1.5.4.3 Restricted Access to Arbitral Archives

Access to archives and databases that house these awards can be restricted by subscription or membership requirements, which might not cover all relevant cases.

1.5.4.4 Varied Publication Practices

Different arbitration institutions have varied practices regarding the publication of awards. Some institutions may routinely publish awards, while others may do so selectively or not at all.

1.5.4.5 Jurisdictional Restrictions

Certain jurisdictions may have legal or procedural restrictions on the disclosure of arbitration awards, further limiting access to these documents.

1.5.4.6 Technological and Logistical Barriers

In some cases, older awards or those from less prominent arbitral institutions may not be digitised or readily accessible through modern research tools.

Despite these constraints, the study utilises a robust selection of accessible ISDS awards and related legal documents to ensure a representative and thorough analysis of the issues at hand. Where direct access to primary sources is not possible, secondary sources and summaries provided in legal commentaries and scholarly articles are used to fill the gaps and provide necessary context.

These limitations are considered in the analysis to maintain the rigour and integrity of the study. By acknowledging the potential gaps in primary data, the dissertation remains transparent about its scope and provides a realistic understanding of the challenges faced in researching this complex area of international arbitration and national security.

1.6 Methodology

This dissertation employs a doctrinal research methodology, which is foundational in legal academic studies, especially when the aim is to clarify legal principles and assess their application within arbitration decisions. This methodology involves a comprehensive analysis of legal norms, principles, and statutes that govern international arbitration and investment law, particularly related to national security issues. AI-assisted tools were used for text refinement, citation formatting, and summarization. All interpretations, analyses, and conclusions are the author's own.

1.6.1 Primary Sources

The primary sources for this study include international investment agreements (IIAs), such as bilateral investment treaties (BITs) and multilateral frameworks that encompass provisions for arbitration in cases involving national security exceptions. Arbitration awards and decisions, where tribunals have addressed national security as a factor in their deliberations, form a critical part of the primary data. These documents provide direct insights into how legal principles are applied in practice and help identify the judicial reasoning and legal standards used by arbitrators.

Official documents and legal texts that define the procedural rules for arbitration, such as the UNCITRAL Arbitration Rules and the ICSID Convention, are also examined. These sources are crucial for understanding the structural framework for making legal arguments and rendering decisions.

Below follows a detailed overview of the investment arbitration cases analysed in this dissertation, categorized into ISDS cases, PCIJ and ICJ cases, WTO and other international cases, EU cases, and domestic cases. Each case is listed with the year of the decision, the court or tribunal that handled the case, and the type of ISDS case where applicable.

The cases selected for analysis represent a broad spectrum of investment arbitration disputes, focusing on those that involve national security considerations. The ICSID cases are chosen due to their prominence and the comprehensive legal frameworks they provide under the Washington Convention. Non-ICSID cases, such as those under the New York Convention, offer insights into different procedural and enforcement challenges. Other international cases, particularly those from the EU, are included to reflect the region-specific legal developments and judicial interpretations. Lastly, domestic cases are incorporated to illustrate the interplay between national laws and international arbitration principles.

The following Tables 1.1, 1.2, 1.3, 1.4 and 1.5 categorize the cases into their respective types and provide key details for each.

1.6.2 Discussion on Representativeness of Cases Assessed

The selected cases provide a representative sample of the broader landscape of disputes involving national security screening measures. They encompass a variety of jurisdictions, legal frameworks, and geopolitical contexts, ensuring that the analysis captures the multifaceted nature of these disputes. It is important to note the governing conventions:

Table 1.1 ISDS cases

Name of case	Year	Court or tribunal	Type of ISDS case
SPP v Egypt	1988	ICSID	ICSID
Fedax v Venezuela	1997	ICSID	ICSID
CSOB v Slovakia	1999	ICSID	ICSID
Metalclad Corporation v United Mexican States	2000	ICSID	ICSID
SD Myers v Canada	2000	UNCITRAL	Non-ICSID
Emilio Agustín Maffezini v Kingdom of Spain	2000	ICSID	ICSID
Waste Management Inc. v United Mexican States (I)	2000	ICSID	ICSID
Mihaly v Sri Lanka	2002	ICSID	ICSID
SGS Société Générale de Surveillance SA v Pakistan	2002	ICSID	ICSID
CMS v Argentina	2003	ICSID	ICSID
Nagel v Czech Republic	2003	SCC	Non-ICSID
Zhinvali v Georgia	2003	ICSID	ICSID
Técnicas Medioambientales Tecmed S.A. v Mexico	2003	ICSID	ICSID
Occidental Exploration and Production Company v Ecuador	2004	UNCITRAL	Non-ICSID
PSEG v Turkey	2004	ICSID	ICSID
Enron Creditors Recovery Corporation (formerly Enron Corporation) and Ponderosa Assets LP v Argentina	2004	ICSID	ICSID
MTD Equity Sdn. Bhd. and MTD Chile S.A. v Republic of Chile	2004	ICSID	ICSID
Siemens v Argentina	2004	ICSID	ICSID
Waste Management Inc. v United Mexican States (II)	2004	ICSID	ICSID
Petrobart v Kyrgyz Republic	2005	SCC	Non-ICSID
LG&E Energy Corp., LG&E Capital Corp., and LG&E International Inc. v Argentine Republic	2006	ICSID	ICSID
Champion Trading Company and Ameritrade International Inc. v Egypt	2006	ICSID	ICSID
Inceysa Vallisoletana S.L. v Republic of El Salvador	2006	ICSID	ICSID
Saluka Investments BV v Czech Republic	2006	UNCITRAL	Non-ICSID
Thunderbird v Mexico	2006	UNCITRAL	Non-ICSID
Sempra Energy International v Argentina	2007	ICSID	ICSID
BG Group Plc v Argentina	2007	UNCITRAL	Non-ICSID

(continued)

Table 1.1 (continued)

Name of case	Year	Court or tribunal	Type of ISDS case
Parkerings-Compagniet AS v Lithuania	2007	ICSID	ICSID
Continental Casualty v Argentina	2008	ICSID	ICSID
Nordzucker v Poland	2008	Ad hoc	Non-ICSID
Plama Consortium Ltd. v Republic of Bulgaria	2008	ICSID	ICSID
Rumeli Telekom A.S. v Republic of Kazakhstan	2008	ICSID	ICSID
Cargill Incorporated v Mexico	2009	ICSID	ICSID
UPS v Canada	2009	UNCITRAL	Non-ICSID
Joseph C. Lemire v Ukraine	2010	ICSID	ICSID
Frontier Petroleum Services Ltd. v Czech Republic	2010	UNCITRAL (PCA)	Non-ICSID
Chevron Corporation and Texaco Petroleum Corporation v Ecuador	2010	UNCITRAL	Non-ICSID
CEMEX Caracas Investments B.V. and CEMEX Caracas II Investments B.V. v. Bolivarian Republic of Venezuela	2010	ICSID	ICSID
Suez, Sociedad General de Aguas de Barcelona S.A. and Vivendi Universal S.A. v Argentine Republic	2010	ICSID	ICSID
Impregilo S.p.A. v Argentine Republic	2011	ICSID	ICSID
El Paso Energy International Company v Argentine Republic	2011	ICSID	ICSID
White Industries v India	2011	UNCITRAL	Non-ICSID
Mamidoil Jetoil Greek Petroleum Products Societe Anonyme S.A. v Albania	2011	ICSID	ICSID
Bosca v Lithuania	2013	SCC	Non-ICSID
Ioan Micula and others v Romania	2013	ICSID	ICSID
Gold Reserve Inc. v Venezuela	2014	ICSID	ICSID
Flughafen Zürich A.G. v Bolivarian Republic of Venezuela	2014	ICSID	ICSID
Von Pezold v Zimbabwe	2015	ICSID	ICSID
William R. Clayton Bilcon of Delaware and others v Canada	2015	UNCITRAL (PCA)	Non-ICSID
Mesa Power Group LLC v Canada	2016	UNCITRAL (PCA)	Non-ICSID
Crystallex International Corporation v Venezuela	2016	ICSID	ICSID
Philip Morris Brand Sàrl (Switzerland) and others v Uruguay	2016	ICSID	ICSID
China Heilongjiang International Economic & Technical Cooperative Corp et al. v Mongolia	2017	PCA	Non-ICSID

(continued)

Table 1.1 (continued)

Name of case	Year	Court or tribunal	Type of ISDS case
Beijing Urban Construction Group Co. Ltd. (BUCG) v Yemen	2017	ICSID	ICSID
Deutsche Telekom v India	2017	PCA	Non-ICSID
Achmea B.V. v Slovakia	2018	UNCITRAL	Non-ICSID
Chevron Corporation and Texaco Petroleum Corporation v Ecuador	2018	UNCITRAL	Non-ICSID
Marfin v Cyprus	2018	ICSID	ICSID
Unión Fenosa Gas S.A. v Arab Republic of Egypt	2018	ICSID	ICSID
Global Telecom Holding SAE v Canada	2020	ICSID	ICSID
RWE v Netherlands and Uniper SE et al. v Netherlands	2020	ICSID	ICSID

Table 1.2 PCIJ and ICJ cases

Name of case	Year	Court or tribunal
Certain German Interests in Polish Upper Silesia (Germany v Poland)	1926	PCIJ
Corfu Channel Case (United Kingdom v. Albania)	1949	ICJ
Barcelona Traction, Light and Power Company, Limited (Belgium v. Spain)	1970	ICJ
Military and Paramilitary Activities in and against Nicaragua (Nicaragua v United States of America)	1986	ICJ
Gabčikovo-Nagymaros Project (Hungary v Slovakia)	1997	ICJ

1.6.2.1 ICSID Cases

These cases are governed by the Washington Convention (ICSID Convention), providing a comprehensive framework for arbitration and enforcement of awards under the International Centre for Settlement of Investment Disputes.

1.6.2.2 Non-ICSID Cases

These cases are typically governed by the New York Convention, setting out the framework for the recognition and enforcement of foreign arbitral awards in contracting states. This category includes ad hoc arbitrations and those conducted under other institutional rules.

Table 1.3 WTO and other international cases

Name of case	Year	Court or tribunal
Jesse Lewis (UK v US)	1921	UK–US Arb. Trib.
Paul Donin de Rosiere v Iran	1986	Iran–US Claims Tribunal
United States–Shrimp	1998	WTO Appellate Body
United States–Gambling	2005	WTO Appellate Body
Brazil–Retreaded Tyres	2007	WTO Appellate Body
Certain Questions of Mutual Assistance in Criminal Matters (Djibouti v France)	2008	ICJ
United States–Clove Cigarettes	2012	WTO Appellate Body
United States–Certain Measures on Steel and Aluminium Products	2018	WTO Panel Report
Russia–Traffic in Transit	2019	WTO Panel Report
Certain Iranian Assets (Islamic Republic of Iran v United States of America)	2023	ICJ

1.6.2.3 Other International Cases

These include cases from various international frameworks such as the ICJ, WTO, and EU, highlighting the broad scope of international law and its impact on national security and investment disputes.

1.6.2.4 Domestic Cases

These cases reflect how national legal systems handle issues related to investment and national security, providing insight into domestic legal frameworks and their interaction with international norms.

However, certain limitations in representativity must be acknowledged:

1.6.2.5 Availability of Awards

Not all ISDS awards are publicly accessible, and some cases remain confidential. This limitation may affect the comprehensiveness of the dataset.

Table 1.4 EU cases

Name of case	Year	Court or tribunal
IBM v Commission	1981	ECJ
Campus Oil v the Minister for Industry and Energy	1984	ECJ
Mitsubishi Motors Corp. v Soler Chrysler-Plymouth Inc.	1985	U.S. Supreme Court
Rankin v Republic of Iran	1988	USCT
Zafiro I-USCT Short v Islamic Republic of Iran	1988	USCT
Technische Universität München v Hauptzollamt München-Mitte	1991	ECJ
G. SA v V. SpA et Tribunal Arbitral	1992	Swiss Federal Tribunal
Société Labinal v Société Mors et Société Westland Aerospace Ltd.	1993	Cour d'appel de Paris
Fincantieri-Cantieri Navali Italiani S.p.A. & Oto Melara S.p.A. v Ministry of Defence Armament & Supply Directorate of Iraq et al.	1994	Court of Appeal of Genoa
Belship Navigation Inc v Sealift Inc	1995	US District Court for the Southern District of New York
France-Aviation v Commission	1995	ECJ
Lisrestal v Commission	1996	ECJ
Primex Produkte v Commission	1998	ECJ
Association Eglise de Scientology de Paris and Scientology International Reserves Trust v The Prime Minister	2000	ECJ
Commission v Belgium	2002	ECJ
Commission v France	2002	ECJ
Aalborg Portland v Commission	2004	ECJ
Spain v Commission	2007	ECJ
Franchet and Byk v Commission	2008	ECJ
Commission v Violetti	2010	ECJ
Marcuccio v Commission	2011	ECJ
Solvay v Commission	2011	ECJ
ZZ v Secretary of State for the Home Department	2013	ECJ
Bank Melli Iran v Council	2013	ECJ
Commission v Kadi	2013	ECJ
Ralls Corp. v Committee on Foreign Investment in the United States (CFIUS)	2014	U.S. Supreme Court
First Islamic Investment Bank v Council	2015	ECJ

Table 1.5 Domestic cases

Name of case	Year	Court or tribunal
Government and Ministries of the Republic of Iraq v Armamenti e Aerospazio S.p.A. et al.	2015	Supreme Court of Cassation of Italy
Russian Federation v Veteran Petroleum Ltd	2016	The Hague District Court
Anatolie Stati, Gabriel Stati, Ascom Group SA and Terra Raf Trans Trading Ltd v Kazakhstan	2017	UK Commercial Court
Vidya Drolia v Durga Transport Corporation	2019	Supreme Court of India

1.6.2.6 Geographical Representation

While the study includes cases from multiple jurisdictions, certain regions may be underrepresented due to the lower availability of public arbitration records.

Despite these limitations, the dataset is robust and diverse, providing a solid foundation for analysing the key issues at the intersection of national security and international arbitration. The findings derived from these cases offer valuable insights and contribute to a deeper understanding of the complex dynamics at play.

1.6.3 Secondary Sources

The secondary sources comprise scholarly articles, books, and commentary on international arbitration and national security in foreign investments. These works are instrumental in framing the theoretical contexts of the study by offering critiques of existing legal approaches and providing comparative analyses that enrich the understanding of how different jurisdictions handle similar issues.

Legal databases such as Westlaw, LexisNexis, and JSTOR provide access to a wide range of legal literature and case law necessary for a comprehensive doctrinal analysis. These resources are invaluable for tracking developments in the field, understanding the evolution of legal thought, and obtaining authoritative interpretations of difficult legal issues.

1.6.4 Analytical Approach

The analytical component of the methodology involves a critical evaluation of how arbitral tribunals balance state interests in national security with the protections afforded to foreign investors under international law. This analysis looks at several key aspects:

1.6.4.1 The Interpretation of Treaty Provisions

How do tribunals interpret the scope and limitations of national security exceptions in IIAs?

1.6.4.2 The Application of Legal Standards

How consistent are the legal standards applied in different cases involving national security? This question examines the principles of fair and equitable treatment, non-discrimination, and expropriation.

1.6.4.3 Deference to State Authority

To what extent do arbitral tribunals defer to the judgments of states regarding what constitutes a national security threat?

1.6.5 Methodological Challenges

Employing a doctrinal research methodology presents several challenges that must be navigated to ensure a comprehensive and balanced analysis. One key challenge is the interpretation of arbitration decisions and legal texts, which must be accurate and reflective of broader legal principles. Arbitral awards must be analysed at face value and within the context of the international legal framework and the specific circumstances of each case. Another challenge is the potential for bias in interpreting ambiguous legal texts and arbitral decisions, which necessitates a careful and balanced approach to analysis.

To overcome these challenges, several strategies have been employed throughout this dissertation:

1.6.5.1 Use of Multiple Sources

Ensuring a broad and diverse range of sources helps mitigate potential bias and provides a more rounded perspective. This includes primary sources such as international investment agreements and arbitral awards, as well as secondary sources including legal commentaries and scholarly articles.

1.6.5.2 Contextual Analysis

Interpreting arbitration decisions within the broader context of international law and specific case circumstances ensures that conclusions drawn are well-grounded and reflective of the legal environment.

1.6.5.3 Peer Review and Feedback

Engaging with peer reviews and seeking feedback from experts in the field helps to identify and correct potential biases or misinterpretations. This collaborative approach enhances the rigour and reliability of the analysis.

1.6.5.4 Transparent Methodology

Clearly articulating the methodological approach, including the limitations and challenges encountered, ensures transparency and allows for a critical evaluation of the findings.

1.6.5.5 Triangulation of Data

Using multiple data points and sources to confirm findings helps to enhance the validity and reliability of the research outcomes. This method reduces the reliance on any single source of information and provides a more comprehensive view.

Despite these measures, it is important to acknowledge that certain limitations remain. The availability of primary sources, such as confidential ISDS awards, can pose a significant challenge. Efforts have been made to access a comprehensive range of arbitration awards and relevant documents; however, not all ISDS awards rendered since 2000 are publicly accessible. This limitation arises due to confidentiality agreements, incomplete public records, restricted access to arbitral archives, varied publication practices, jurisdictional restrictions, and technological and logistical barriers. Where direct access to primary sources is not possible, secondary sources and summaries provided in legal commentaries and scholarly articles are used to fill gaps and provide necessary context.

These methodological considerations are integrated into the analysis to uphold the study's rigour and credibility. By transparently discussing these challenges, the dissertation offers a realistic view of the complexities involved in researching the intersection of international arbitration and national security.

1.6.6 *Outcome of the Methodological Approach*

The expected outcome of this methodology is an improved understanding of how international arbitration addresses disputes over national security screening measures of foreign investments. By systematically analysing the legal arguments, tribunal decisions, and the application of international law, this study aims to contribute valuable insights into the effectiveness of arbitration as a dispute resolution mechanism in this complex intersection of law and international relations.

1.7 Significance

The significance of this dissertation lies in its timely exploration of the intricate balance between national security and international investment protections, an increasingly pertinent dynamic in today's globalized economy. As governments intensify scrutiny over foreign investments for security reasons and international investment continues to proliferate, understanding how these trends intersect through the lens of international arbitration is critical. This study offers substantial contributions to theoretical and practical dimensions of international law, arbitration practices, and policy formulation.

1.7.1 *Theoretical Contributions*

Theoretically, this research enriches the academic discourse on the application of international investment law in contexts that invoke national security. By dissecting and analysing arbitration decisions and treaty provisions, the study clarifies the legal principles and criteria that guide arbitral tribunals when confronting national security issues. This analysis contributes to a deeper understanding of the legal constructs of "necessity" and "proportionality" in international law, particularly how they are interpreted and applied in disputes involving complex geopolitical considerations. Furthermore, it addresses a significant gap in the literature by systematically compiling and critiquing arbitration outcomes related to national security to provide a consolidated resource for future academic and legal work.

1.7.2 *Practical Implications*

Practically, the findings of this dissertation are intended to aid arbitrators, legal practitioners, and policymakers in navigating the legal challenges presented by national security considerations in foreign investments. By offering detailed analyses of how existing legal norms are applied, the study aids in understanding arbitration outcomes in similar contexts to enhance the predictability and transparency of arbitral decisions. This understanding is crucial for investors and states alike, as it provides clearer expectations and guidelines for protecting investments and enforcing national security policies.

Moreover, the study's insights into the effectiveness and limitations of arbitration in resolving such disputes can inform policy adjustments and treaty reforms. Understanding where current arbitration mechanisms fall short allows for targeted improvements to ensure that states' sovereignty and investors' rights are maintained in a balanced manner. This understanding is particularly relevant for states looking to attract foreign investments while safeguarding critical national interests.

1.7.3 Policy Relevance

Finally, the research has significant policy implications because it offers empirical evidence and legal analysis to support the crafting of more policy relevant and effective investment treaties. By identifying the conditions under which arbitration effectively resolves disputes involving national security, the study provides a foundation for future treaty negotiations and policy formulations, which can better accommodate the evolving landscape of international security and economic cooperation.

In sum, this dissertation seeks to advance an academic understanding of a complex and urgent field of international arbitration while serving as a practical guide for stakeholders engaged in navigating the challenges at the intersection of national security and international investment law.

1.8 Structure

This dissertation is structured into five main chapters, each dedicated to exploring different aspects of the relationship between international investment law, national security, and FDI screenings. The structured analysis is designed to build a comprehensive understanding of how geopolitical strategies influence economic policies and the resulting legal implications.

Chapter 2: Investment Treaties and the Challenge of Weaponized Investments

This chapter introduces the concept of geoeconomic risk associated with FDI and how it has evolved into a tool of geopolitical strategy.[6] It discusses how economic interdependencies, once seen as beneficial, are now viewed as vulnerabilities to be exploited in geoeconomic strategies. The chapter further explores how host states use

[6] The term "weaponized investment" refers here to the strategic use of foreign direct investment (FDI) by states or state-affiliated entities to achieve geopolitical objectives. This includes using

investment screening as a defence mechanism against these risks and how investment treaties can sometimes mitigate the geoeconomic risks posed by host states' overreach. The conclusion calls for further research to develop a better understanding of balancing economic sovereignty with legal protections in the global economic arena.

Chapter 3: National Security as Subject Matter of Investment Arbitration
This chapter examines the legal challenges to examine how national security concerns are arbitrated under international law. It critically explores the absence of a clear rule precluding arbitration for disputes involving national security and discusses public policy challenges under major international conventions like the New York and Washington Conventions. The analysis shows that disputes affecting national security often fall within the arbitral tribunal's jurisdiction unless explicitly excluded, which highlights tribunals' capabilities to handle sensitive issues by balancing state sovereignty with obligations under international investment law.

Chapter 4: Investment Screening and Jurisdiction Under Investment Treaties
This chapter focuses on the jurisdictional issues related to investment screening, particularly the standing of sovereign-driven investors and the implications of screening mechanisms on the jurisdiction of arbitration panels. It discusses how investment screenings, especially those implemented ex ante, affect the jurisdictional reach of international arbitration and the need for clearer treaty definitions to guide tribunals in differentiating between commercial and governmental activities of sovereign investors.

Chapter 5: National Security-Related Defences and Treaty Exceptions Applied to Investment Screening
This chapter investigates the application of the necessity defence and treaty exceptions in investment screenings to examine how these legal constructs are utilized to justify national security measures within the framework of international investment law. It analyses the complexity of these legal defences and their application in arbitral case law while emphasizing the need for a case-by-case approach in international investment dispute resolution to maintain a balance between state sovereignty and legal obligations.

Chapter 6: Investment Screening and the Right to Regulate Investments
The final chapter explores the balance between national security considerations and the substantive application of international investment treaties by focusing on how they allow host states to regulate FDI. It explores the challenges of maintaining

---

investments to exert influence over critical infrastructure, technology, or other strategic assets in the host country. It can also involve restricting outbound investments to control or punish other states economically. Weaponized investments are typically characterized by their intention to gain leverage, control, or influence in ways that go beyond purely economic interests, often intersecting with national security concerns. For a more detailed discussion, see Chap. 2, "Investment Treaties and the Challenge of Weaponized Investments."

procedural transparency in investment arbitration, particularly in security-sensitive matters, and discusses strategies to balance confidentiality with the need for transparency in national security screening measures.

Each chapter of this dissertation builds on the previous ones to develop a layered analysis of how international investment law interacts with national security considerations in the context of globalization and heightened geopolitical tensions. The comprehensive structure is designed to provide clarity and depth to the discussion, which can contribute to a better understanding of the legal and economic dynamics at play in the modern globalized economy.

1.9 Preliminary Literature Review

The intricate relationship between national security and FDI under the scope of international investment law has been increasingly scrutinized in contemporary scholarly literature. This preliminary literature review outlines the key themes and discussions that have shaped the academic discourse on this topic to provide a foundational understanding for the subsequent chapters of this dissertation.

1.9.1 Geoeconomic Risks and FDI

Scholars have increasingly focused on the concept of geoeconomic risks associated with FDI, particularly in the context of global geopolitical tensions. Baldwin (1985) first introduced the idea of economic security, which has since evolved to encompass the vulnerabilities that states face due to economic interdependence. More recently, scholars like Blackwill and Harris (2016) and Farrell and Newman (2019) have discussed how states use economic tools to achieve geopolitical ends and labelled these strategies as "weaponized interdependence" (see Chap. 2).

1.9.2 National Security and Investment Screening

The literature on national security implications for FDI screening has expanded significantly. For instance, Jensen et al. (2012) explored how political risk and national security concerns influence foreign investment approvals. They argued that host states have increasingly viewed FDI through a security lens, especially in sectors deemed critical for national interests. This argument is supported by work from Wellhausen (2015), who examined the regulatory frameworks that govern these screenings and suggested a trend towards stricter controls and more rigorous screening processes.

1.9.3 Investment Treaties and State Sovereignty

A central theme in the literature is the tension between state sovereignty and the protections offered to foreign investors under international treaties. Much of the scholarly debate has centred on the balance that needs to be struck between these two often conflicting interests. Scholars like Schill (2009) and Salacuse (2010) have debated the extent to which IIAs should permit exceptions for national security purposes without undermining the security and predictability that these treaties provide to investors.

1.9.4 Arbitration and National Security Concerns

The arbitration of disputes involving national security issues has become a hotly debated topic. Franck (2005) discussed the challenges arbitrators face when various defences, such as national security, are cited as a reason to deviate from usual treaty obligations. Similarly, Miles (2013) focused on how tribunals interpret national security exceptions by often relying on a narrow interpretation to ensure that such exceptions are not abused. Moreover, Alvarez (2011) critiqued the lack of transparency and consistency in arbitral decisions involving national security and called for clearer guidelines to aid arbitrators in these difficult cases.

1.9.5 Jurisdictional Challenges and Investment Screening

Jurisdictional issues in the context of investment screening are particularly problematic when dealing with investments that may not yet be fully realized or are in their preliminary stages. Dolzer and Schreuer (2008) discussed the challenges of defining "investment" in such contexts by questioning the traditional notions of what constitutes an investment under international law. Bjorklund (2013) further explored the concept by analysing the standing of sovereign and state-owned entities in bringing claims under investment treaties. The author noted the unique challenges posed by these types of investors.

1.9.6 Balancing Economic Interests and National Security

A growing body of literature has focused on finding a balance between protecting economic interests and addressing national security concerns. Ma (2019) suggested that while investment screenings are essential for protecting national security, they must also be fair and not unnecessarily restrictive to avoid deterring beneficial foreign investment. Sauvant and Sachs (2009) had earlier echoed this idea and laid the groundwork for assessing the proportionality of national security measures in investment screenings.

In summary, the existing literature provides a robust framework for understanding the complex dynamics at play in the intersection of national security and international investment law. However, further research is needed to develop more nuanced approaches to balancing economic sovereignty with legal protections in an increasingly interconnected and tense global economic environment. This dissertation aims to contribute to this area by offering a deeper analysis of how these issues are currently addressed and proposing ways to enhance the effectiveness and fairness of the arbitration process in disputes involving national security screening measures.

1.10 Conclusion

This dissertation explores the intricate interplay between national security concerns and international investment law, particularly in the context of FDI screening. The forthcoming examination across several chapters illuminates how states have increasingly leveraged investment screening mechanisms to mitigate geoeconomic risks while striving to adhere to their international legal commitments to protect foreign investments.

The analysis in this dissertation underscores the need for a delicate balance between safeguarding national security and ensuring a favourable environment for international investors. The findings reveal that while investment screenings are crucial for protecting national interests, they must be conducted within a framework that respects the legal rights of investors, as defined by IIAs. The discussions highlight the need for clarity and consistency in how investment screenings are implemented and how national security exceptions are interpreted within the arbitration process.

Moreover, the dissertation contributes to a broader understanding of the role of arbitration in resolving disputes that arise from national security screening measures, which suggests that arbitration can serve as an effective means of adjudicating these complex disputes. Therefore, it advocates for enhanced transparency and procedural fairness in arbitration proceedings to ensure that states and investors participate on equal footing.

In conclusion, as geopolitical tensions continue to influence economic policies globally, this dissertation calls for ongoing research and dialogue to refine the legal frameworks governing FDI screening. This investigation can protect national security and promote sustained international investment by upholding principles of fairness and justice in international economic relations.

References

Alvarez JE (2011) The public international law regime governing international investment. Hague Academy of International Law

Baldwin DA (1985) Economic Statecraft. Princeton University Press

Bjorklund AK (2013) The role of counterclaims in rebalancing investment law. Lewis Clark Law Rev 17:461

Blackwill RD, Harris JM (2016) War by other means: geoeconomics and statecraft. Harvard University Press

Dolzer R, Schreuer C (2008) Principles of international investment law. Oxford University Press

Farrell H, Newman AL (2019) Weaponized interdependence: how global economic networks shape state coercion. Int Secur 44(1):42–79

Franck SD (2005) The legitimacy crisis in investment treaty arbitration: privatizing public international law through inconsistent decisions. Fordham Law Rev 73(4):1521–1625

Jensen N, Biglaiser G, Li Q, Malesky E, Pinto P, Pinto S, Staats J (2012) Politics and foreign direct investment. University of Michigan Press

Ma J (2019) International investment and national security review. Vanderbilt J Transnatl Law 52:899

Miles K (2013) *The origins of international investment law: empire, environment, and the safeguarding of capital*. Cambridge University Press

Sauvant KP, Sachs L (2009) *The effect of treaties on foreign direct investment: bilateral investment treaties, double taxation treaties, and investment flows*. Oxford University Press

Salacuse JW (2010) The law of investment treaties. Oxford University Press

Schill SW (2009) The multilateralization of international investment law. Cambridge University Press

Wellhausen RL (2015) *The shield of nationality: when governments break contracts with foreign firms*. Cambridge University Press

Chapter 2
Investment Treaties and the Challenge of Weaponized Investments

Abstract This chapter explores the evolving role of FDI as a critical element of global geopolitical strategies and illustrates its shift from straightforward economic activities to significant tools of geopolitical influence. As great power rivalries have heightened, economic interdependencies, once viewed as mutually beneficial, have been viewed as potential vulnerabilities exploitable in geoeconomic strategies. Host states have increased their use of rigorous inbound FDI screening processes to protect national security and maintain economic independence. Meanwhile, investment arbitration serves to mitigate risks posed by host states to foreign investors, which highlights the tensions between national security measures and international investment protections. This chapter calls for further research to develop a nuanced understanding of these dynamics to balance economic sovereignty and legal protections in the global economic and political arena.

2.1 Introduction

For more than half a century, states have signed investment treaties guaranteeing certain basic protection for foreign investors and their investments, which have included the right to have disputes heard by international arbitrators.[1] During much of this period, states have liberalized and opened their markets for foreign capital while rolling back or abolishing earlier restrictions on capital transfers and foreign exchange transactions.

[1] See Newcombe and Paradell (2009) 45.

J. H. Pohl, *Arbitration of Disputes related to National Security Screening of Foreign Investments*, EYIEL Monographs - Studies in European and International Economic Law 50,
https://doi.org/10.1007/978-3-032-26342-1_2

A significant shift began around 2016, with states increasingly instituting mechanisms to screen foreign investments for national security threats.[2] This change reflected a broader resurgence in geoeconomic rivalry, further intensified by the COVID-19 pandemic, which highlighted vulnerabilities[3] due to economic interdependence[4] and accelerated the shift towards a more confrontational global economic stance—a trend starkly evident during the Trump administration in the United States.[5]

This period also saw the "weaponization" of investments, where foreign direct investments (FDI) are strategically used by states or state-affiliated entities to achieve geopolitical objectives. Weaponized investments involve using investments to gain leverage over critical infrastructure, secure access to sensitive technology, or exert economic control over strategic assets in the host country. For example, state-owned enterprises (SOEs) may invest abroad to secure technologies or data beneficial to their home countries. Sovereign wealth funds (SWFs) might invest in infrastructure that supports strategic economic frameworks. Additionally, governments may subsidize domestic firms' mergers and acquisitions overseas to align with national strategic directives. These activities highlight how investments, traditionally seen as purely economic transactions, are now leveraged for strategic geopolitical gains.

Furthermore, states may block investments from other countries as a form of economic sanction, a practice that became prominent with the extensive sanctions against Russia following its 2022 invasion of Ukraine. Such measures, termed "investment embargoes," restrict adversarial states' access to necessary FDI. Similarly, outbound investment screening, where countries prohibit investments in certain states or strategically sensitive contexts, is another facet of weaponized investment, underscoring the multifaceted nature of this concept.

This chapter explores how these weaponized investments, amplified by recent global events, represent a new category of geoeconomic risk. This risk arises from the deep economic interconnections that now serve as potential threats rather than mutual safeguards. Economic interdependencies, once heralded as a barrier to conflict, have recently turned into a currency of power. These interdependencies have been leveraged for strategic ends to feed a geoeconomic chain reaction, with states applying broader economic controls out of concern for their economic autonomy.[6] This new paradigm compels states to reevaluate and sometimes counteract these dependencies with policies previously antithetical to free-market principles.

The practice of "weaponizing" FDI has been central to this transformation in several respects. First, overseas investments can be strategically used to enhance influence. For instance, SOEs may invest abroad to secure access to crucial technologies, products, or

---

[2] See OECD (2021). Investment Policy Developments in 62 Economies Between 16 October 2020 and 15 March 2021. 3, 5.

[3] Ibid. See also Sinkkonen and Ruokamo (2022); Saari (2021b).

[4] See, e.g. Leonard (2021); Farrell and Newman (2019).

[5] Farrell and Newman (2020).

[6] Choer Moraes and Mikael Wigell (2022).

data beneficial to their home countries.[7] SWFs are known to invest in infrastructure that bolsters the economic framework of the host countries while often gaining strategic negotiation advantages in return. Additionally, governments may subsidize domestic private firms' mergers and acquisitions overseas while expecting these firms to adhere to strategic directives when necessary (e.g. halting the production or supply of essential resources during crises such as vaccines, financial services, and media outputs during the COVID-19 pandemic).[8] This scenario exemplifies how control over vaccine supplies became a significant tool of geoeconomic influence, with the potential withholding of vaccines or conditional supply granting unprecedented leverage to vaccine-producing countries and their host states.

Second, the weaponization of investments extends beyond the act of investing. A state's ability to block another state's investment opportunities can serve as a tool of geoeconomic leverage. This blockage is particularly relevant to the investment capabilities of nationals of the targeted state, which are construed under international law as individuals and companies. Furthermore, states may impose economic sanctions as a form of "investment embargo" to deprive an adversarial state of necessary FDI. The extensive economic sanctions implemented by Western countries against Russia after its 2022 invasion of Ukraine serve as a stark example.[9] These sanctions significantly curtailed Russian investment opportunities globally. The expansion of investment screening mechanisms in Western countries also reflects a strategic move to restrict foreign investments from potential adversaries more selectively.[10]

Third, FDI can also be utilised as an instrument of economic statecraft by restricting investments from one state's nationals to another, particularly in strategically sensitive contexts. Countries may prohibit investments in certain states or employ outbound investment screening to prevent domestic investments in adversarial environments.[11] These actions underscore that FDI transcends simple economic transactions to embody a complex array of geoeconomic applications.

This chapter asks how these weaponized investments, amplified by recent global events, represent a new category of geoeconomic risk.[12] This risk stems from the deep economic interconnections that now serve as potential threats rather than mutual safeguards. This new paradigm compels states to reevaluate and sometimes counteract these dependencies with policies that once seemed antithetical to the principles of free-market economics.

---

[7] See, e.g. Esplugues Mota (2018).

[8] Another illustrative example of the importance of control (through investment) of a critical resource is the speculated acquisition of German vaccine manufacturer CureVac by U.S. interests. https://www.politico.eu/article/germany-confirms-that-donald-trump-tried-to-buy-firm-working-on-coronavirus-vaccine/.

[9] Schott (2023); Raik et al. (2023).

[10] OECD. (2022). Framework for Screening Foreign Direct Investment into the EU Assessing Effectiveness and Efficiency; Bauerle Danzman and Meunier (2021).

[11] Hanemann et al. (2022); Brennan and Vecchi (2021).

[12] OECD. (2020). Investment screening in times of COVID-19 and beyond. OECD Policy Brief. See also Wigell et al. (2022a); Pohl (2020a).

Geoeconomic risk emerges from the extraordinary economic interdependence and interconnectedness that defines today's global system. This interconnectedness, especially highlighted in the aftermath of the pandemic, has been increasingly perceived as a vulnerability and a potential threat to economic stability.[13] Consequently, nations are compelled to mitigate this precarious dependency on international entities by implementing economic policy measures previously deemed extraordinary. These measures often challenge the traditional market-driven principles that have shaped economic policies and international relations for years. As a result, they strain the established rules and norms of the global economy while introducing significant new risks for economic actors worldwide.

This chapter explores two primary questions: (a) How do government concerns regarding weaponized investments and the associated geoeconomic risks influence state treatment of inbound FDI amidst the resurgence of great power rivalry? (b) How do international legal frameworks, especially BITs, address and adapt to state behaviours driven by geoeconomic considerations? The chapter utilises a phenomenon-based research approach[14] to provide a comprehensive set of responses to these inquiries that elucidate the implications for international investment law and policy.

The chapter begins by exploring economic interdependencies as potential vulnerabilities that are central to geoeconomic risk (2.2). It details various methodologies for conceptualizing the uncertainties associated with these vulnerabilities potentially leading to adverse outcomes. The discussion progresses to the recognition, assessment, and measurement of such risks. Furthermore, the chapter looks into the implications of awareness of geoeconomic risks within the framework of inbound FDI screening by analysing how such awareness influences governmental actions (2.3). By evaluating geoeconomic strategies through different investment-related policy instruments, the chapter assesses the utility of geoeconomic risk as an analytical concept. Subchapter 2.4 looks at investment screening as a mitigant against geoeconomic risks associated with inbound FDI. Subchapter 2.5 explores the limits and capabilities of geoeconomic risk analysis in explaining host state behaviour towards FDI by focusing on legal frameworks that moderate geoeconomic strategies, which include standards of non-discrimination and relative treatment found in BITs, alongside factors that constrain these mechanisms. The chapter concludes (2.6) by summarizing key observations and proposes directions for further research.

[13] European Commission. (2023). Joint Communication to the European Parliament, the European Council and the Council on "European Economic Security Strategy". JOIN/2023/20 final; Choer Moraes and Wigell (2022).

[14] von Krogh et al. (2012).

2.2 Conceptualizing Geoeconomic Risk

FDI drives economic interdependence and serves as a tool within geopolitical frameworks. The analysis below is structured into several sections; each addresses various aspects of FDI's impact on global economic and political landscapes. The point of departure is to explore the basic relationship between the investor's home state and the host state in the context of how FDI fosters economic ties that can influence national stability and policies (Sect. 2.2.1). Next, how these economic connections can become vulnerabilities to be exploited in global power strategies is considered by highlighting the complexities of economic dependency and strategic vulnerability (Sect. 2.2.2). The subsequent discussion compares various methodologies for understanding and quantifying the uncertainties tied to international economic interactions (Sect. 2.2.3). Finally, a strategy of balancing dependence is presented as a method to manage and mitigate risks associated with economic interdependence amid global competition (Sect. 2.2.4).

2.2.1 FDI and Economic Interdependence

Fundamentally, FDI forms a connection between two countries: the investor's home country and the host country where the investment occurs. Although this relationship does not necessarily require governmental involvement from the respective states, it inherently fosters economic interdependence via market dynamics. While a solitary FDI transaction may have a minimal impact on this interdependence, collectively, FDI can lead to significant interdependence on a national scale.

The interconnected nature of FDI transactions may not be immediately evident. Initially, an FDI transaction places the investor in a position of economic reliance on the host state in subjection to the host state's legal and regulatory framework.[15] Hence, the host state has substantial power to economically impact the investor, potentially through expropriation or limiting profit repatriation, even if such action is not explicitly sanctioned by law. Conversely, the host state becomes economically dependent on foreign investors collectively, not necessarily on any single investor.[16] Host state actions perceived as illegal, arbitrary, or otherwise hostile can lead to severe economic repercussions, such as difficulty in accessing international capital markets, retaliatory trade restrictions, and facing international legal challenges.[17]

Two distinct types of asymmetric interdependencies arise from FDI. First, foreign investors often supply essential capital at lower costs than domestically

[15] Busse and Hefeker (2007).

[16] McMillan (1999) 1–22; London and Ross (1995).

[17] Cutler (2000).

available capital.[18] This competitive funding benefits the host state by reducing overall capital costs and indirectly supporting economic sectors like the labour market, which enhances socio-economic stability. Thus, a sudden withdrawal of this capital can dramatically increase funding costs and destabilize the economy and political climate of the host state.

Second, the transfer of technology, data, and know-how from foreign investors introduces another layer of dependency.[19] While the host state risks theft of this technology, retaliatory measures by investors can also pose risks. For example, investors may hesitate to locate sensitive operations within the host state's jurisdiction or pursue legal actions for forced technology transfer under protections offered by BITs.[20] Thus, the host state faces the potential loss of future technological benefits, which deepens its reliance on foreign technological inputs.

These economic interdependencies are inherently asymmetrical. The dependencies that constitute these interdependencies are diverse and differ in their importance between the host state and the home state(s) of the foreign investors. Moreover, these economic interdependencies are not static, as well illustrated in the case of global value chains (GVCs). Indeed, staying connected to a GVC provides many economic benefits to a host state, yet the prospect of being excluded becomes a source of vulnerability.[21] However, the host state may also attain a level of bargaining power within a GVC by being positioned to disrupt it. These chains require significant resources to build up and maintain, which creates leeway for negotiation through the threat of disruption. This potential power play between host states and foreign investors is nothing new; it goes back to the very nature of FDI.[22] How it plays out considerably depends on the level of global policy coordination and cooperation.[23]

During the heyday of international economic multilateralism, the prospect of a swift and coordinated retaliatory response by the international community put contours around host states' adventurism.[24] International institutions, governments, and the international business community acted in solidarity against a host state's violation of the rule of law. The proliferation of investor-friendly BITs, which increased rapidly from the 1980s onwards, and the opening up of national banking and capital markets to international competition contributed to imposing "market discipline" globally.[25] The consequences for a host state that

[18] Kaczmarczyk (2023); Hymer (1960).

[19] Liu (2008); Blomström and Kokko (1996).

[20] Bonnitcha (2019).

[21] Carroll (2023); Moon (2022).

[22] Kaushal (2009); Lall and Streeten (1977).

[23] Aaltola et al. (2021).

[24] Alter (2020).

[25] Gourinchas and Jeanne (2002).

stepped out of line are richly illustrated by the case of the Argentinian sovereign debt crisis of 2002 and the ensuing saga,[26] as well as by the Greek sovereign debt crisis a decade later.[27]

However, with increasingly imperfect policy coordination and eroding policy cooperation, this type of global solidarity weakens. As a result, foreign investors lose the safety mechanism that a globally coordinated institutional action ensures, while the economic power balance between host states and foreign investors shifts in favour of the host states. In these instances, foreign investors cannot rely on the protection of a global "community response", so they must discover new protection infrastructures, such as falling back on the protection of their home states.[28]

When the protection of foreign investors' economic interests falls mainly on the investors' home states, these interests are easily commingled with the policy interests and concerns of the home states' governments.[29] These home state governments may sacrifice investors' interests for another policy advantage or exploit investors' claims as a diplomatic bargaining chip in exchange for host state concessions on a different policy issue. As a result, FDI becomes enmeshed in the home state's economic and non-economic interests, particularly its vital or critical interests, which are chiefly security interests.

2.2.2 *Economic Interdependencies as Geoeconomic Vulnerabilities and Risks*

In the absence of strong global policy coordination and cooperation, FDI provides an instrument for geoeconomic contestation and diplomacy. The preceding subsection illustrated how the interdependencies created by FDI can result in economic harm to the home and host states. These potential sources of harm are referred to as "geoeconomic vulnerabilities", where the subjects of vulnerabilities are threats directed by one state (the coercer) against the economic security of another state (the target).[30]

The nature of a vulnerability is that of potentiality: the potential for successful economic coercion.[31] Vulnerabilities are not economic security threats but open up the possibility of such threats by exposing a weakness or a mechanism through

[26] Grimson and Kessler (2014); Moran (2004).

[27] Bruff (2014).

[28] Polanco (2019).

[29] Casey (2020).

[30] This terminology was inspired by Greenhill et al. (2018).

[31] The present analysis focuses on coercion as the principal strategy of geoeconomics. Coercion is used here to describe one actor's behaviour (the coercer's) that influences another actor's (the target's) behaviour by manipulating the latter's intentions and resolve using negative incentives. When positive incentives are used, it becomes "negative coercion" or more appropriately "inducement". The arguments made in this chapter largely apply to coercion and inducement, but for the sake of simplicity, the focus is on the former.

which harm can be inflicted or leveraged. Exploiting a target state's vulnerability requires a coercer's capabilities, intent, and resolve. In this context, one can talk of geoeconomic risk (i.e. the degree of uncertainty as to whether negative outcomes will emerge from such vulnerabilities).

The term "geoeconomics" has become increasingly popular to describe the transformation in the logic underpinning global economic relations. Governments have turned to policies that integrate economic and security rationales at the regional and national levels at the expense of global economic policy coordination.[32] This change is exemplified by the EU's policy of "open strategic autonomy". The EU has adapted to geopolitical competition in the economic arena through a panoply of new policy measures, which range from new trade defence and anti-coercion tools, sanctions, and export controls to the screening of security threats and state-sponsored subsidies in the context of foreign investments, carbon border adjustment, supply chain due diligence, and a new industrial strategy.[33]

In this effort, the EU has reacted to similar moves by other major powers, notably the United States and China. Over the past decade, the United States has strengthened its national security review (i.e. screening) of inbound investments and enhanced its application of existing trade laws to respond to new geoeconomic risks, which includes the novel use of Section 232 investigations into steel and aluminium exports to determine their effect on national security. The United States is considering new instruments, as demonstrated by the 2022 CHIPS and Science Act and the Casey-Cornyn legislative proposal for screening outbound U.S. investment destined for other countries.[34] China's geoeconomic strategy is evident in efforts in the 14th Five-Year Plan of 2021 to secure critical technologies and data through national security oversight and control.[35] China has embraced geo-regulation by using technical standards as instruments to advance strategic goals, such as the Made in China 2025 strategy.[36] The COVID-19 pandemic demonstrated the breadth of sectors that are critical to the survival of the state, notably pharmaceutical expertise and technology.

Emerging from the practice of geoeconomic strategies, economic interdependencies are thus reappraised as geoeconomic vulnerabilities that give rise to geoeconomic risks. In the context of FDI, vulnerabilities arise from economic interdependencies. A host state may be vulnerable to the extent of its economic dependency on international capital flows or access to foreign critical resources, mainly technology, know-how, and data. Conversely, foreign investors or their home states are vulnerable to the extent of their invested capital in the host state and their access to host-state-controlled critical resources that are capable of being "weaponized" (i.e. exploited for coercive ends).

---

[32] Wigell et al. (2018); Roberts et al. (2019); Gertz and Evers (2020); Drezner et al. (2021); Babić et al. (2022).

[33] Gehrke (2021); Lavery et al. (2022); Helwig and Wigell (2022); Pohl (2023).

[34] Pohl (2023).

[35] Grünberg and Brussee (2021).

[36] Wigell et al. (2022a, 2022b).

2.2.3 Conceptualizing and Measuring Geoeconomic Risk

In general, geoeconomic risk describes the uncertain prospect of economic harm suffered by a state or non-state actor (i.e. target) due to a coercive measure adopted by another state or non-state actor (i.e. coercer).[37] The contemporary notion of risk originates in the work of American economist Frank H. Kright, who in 1921 conceptualized the role of uncertainty in economic activity, distinguishing "risk" as "measurable uncertainty".[38] This preliminary, proto-theoretical definition serves as a point of departure that can accommodate several conceptual approaches.

First, from the perspective of a target being a foreign investor in the context of FDI, the concept of geoeconomic risk can be understood to capture several unwelcome potential consequences of the host state's inherently uncertain future treatment of the foreign investor. These consequences result from the exercise of legal powers of the host state government, which in many jurisdictions include (a) the suspension of an investment transaction during an investment screening process that causes a delay, (b) placing conditions on the consummation of the transaction to alter the terms anticipated by the parties, and (c) blocking a transaction altogether or ordering its unwinding. Of even greater practical importance are the factual powers wielded by the host state. Hence, public knowledge of pending or ongoing review of an investment transaction can lead to an investor's withdrawal from a transaction altogether, while the target company may consequently face a significant loss of market value or be denied screening approval due to the review.

Second, a foreign investor may be mobilized as a geoeconomic agent of its home state, being used as a pawn in the home state's power competition by combining geostrategic interests with economic dynamics.[39] From this perspective, geoeconomic risk is associated with economics being used by states for political power objectives. Target states shore up their resilience against geoeconomic power politics by increasing their control over businesses in strategic sectors of the economy. This effort manifests in the panoply of

[37] This construct can be expressed as the product of the probability of the risk event occurring (geoeconomic threat) and the expected magnitude of losses in the event that it does (expected loss given the risk event). In theory, "[R]isk is a condition in which there is a possibility of an adverse deviation from a desired outcome that is expected or hoped for" (Vaughan and Vaughan (1996) 5, for alternative definitions 13–17). Conceptually, risk is commonly understood as modellable uncertainty about a future outcome, as distinguished from uncertainty proper, which is not capable of being the object of a conceptual model (Knight (1921) 19).

[38] Knight ibid. 233. There are numerous, more recent, and more or less granular, definitions of risk. At a high level of abstraction, the International Organization for Standardization (ISO) guide ISO 31000:2018 "Risk Management—Guidelines" defines "risk" as the "effect of uncertainty on objectives" [emphasis added] and provides the following notes: (1) "An effect is a deviation from the expected. It can be positive, negative or both, and can address, create or result in opportunities and threats." (2) "Objectives can have different aspects and categories, and can be applied at different levels". (3) "Risk is usually expressed in terms of risk sources", "potential events", "their consequences", and "their likelihood".

[39] Fjäder et al. (2021) 314.

new means of trade and export controls, investment screening mechanisms, data localization measures, sanctions, and subsidies.[40]

Third, geoeconomic risk can be conceptualized as a particular form of political risk. There have been many efforts to define political risk.[41] In the context of FDI and from the perspective of a foreign investor and its home state, political risk can be thought of as comprising (a) the risk of nationalization, expropriation, and confiscation of property, (b) the risk of host state exchange restrictions, (c) the risk of political violence, and (d) the risk of sovereign breach of contract.[42] However, political risk is often used as an omnibus term for a more fundamental and far-reaching concept, which covers the uncertain possibility of losses attributable to any political event, including instances where state powers are exercised.[43]

Today, no unified model of geoeconomic risk incorporates the various prisms outlined above. This model should accommodate various constellations of targets and coercers—home states, host states, foreign investors, and domestic enterprises—while being agnostic concerning the direction of influence and the balance of capabilities and vulnerabilities among them.

2.2.4 *Balancing Dependence as Geoeconomic Risk Management*

Analysing the elements of coercion (i.e. vulnerability, capabilities, intent, and resolve) is appropriate to understand the logic underpinning geoeconomic competition and the uncertainty it engenders. While the latter two factors are inherently subjective and difficult to ascertain, the former two are more readily susceptible to objective assessment and measurement. In a sense, they are also related. While vulnerability expresses the weaknesses of the target, capability expresses the strength of the coercion. Thus, both express the potential for successful coercion.

Geoeconomic risk takes the target's perspective by focusing on potential adverse outcomes arising out of uncertainty as a result of vulnerability to economic coercion. This vulnerability is a function of the degree of economic interdependence. Therefore, a solution presents itself, whereby a target can manage (i.e. minimize or optimize) its geoeconomic risk situation by adapting its level of economic interdependence to reduce its vulnerability—or, expressed equivalently, increase its economic resilience. The notion of balancing dependence captures this management of the level of economic interdependence.

Inspired by the balance of power theory, balancing dependence is a model of geoeconomic competitive behaviour that recognizes that geoeconomic actors integrate into the global flows of capital, data, goods, and resources while

[40] Choer Moraes and Wigell (2020).

[41] See, e.g. Protopsaltis (2019) 299; Hobér and Fellenbaum (2015) 1519; Yackee (2014) 479.

[42] Protopsaltis (2019), cf. Hobér and Fellenbaum (2015).

[43] See Ascari (2010).

simultaneously protecting their economic autonomy.[44] In this model, how actors weigh integration versus autonomy is contingent on the nature of interdependent relations. In practical terms, economic interdependence has been increasingly instrumentalized for political power ends as the geoeconomic competition between the West, China, and Russia has intensified.[45] As such, it is assumed to precipitate geoeconomic balancing as states seek to reduce their vulnerabilities to offensive geoeconomic statecraft (i.e. coercion, binding, and wedging) by reducing economic dependencies on public and private foreign actors (i.e. hedging). This balancing can be assumed to put pressure on the interdependent fabric of the global economy. Similar to "balancing power", "balancing dependence" may create an economic security dilemma as states seek to adjust their levels of dependence related to similar efforts by others.[46]

Understanding how the balance of dependence shapes economic security and sets the direction for reducing vulnerabilities and increasing capabilities in a concrete case requires an analysis of states' economic power relations from a network perspective. From the perspective of a foreign investor as a target, balancing dependence serves to explain host state treatment that seeks to reduce economic vulnerabilities, such as inbound investment screening.[47]

2.3 Implications of Geoeconomic Risk in the Context of Inbound FDI Screening

Screening inbound FDI serves as a case in point for illustrating the geoeconomic risks faced by a foreign investor. Typical features of investment screening mechanisms are that they apply to FDI (broadly defined), which the host state determines to have an adverse effect on its security or other significant public interests. Investors are obliged to notify the host state's screening authority about a contemplated investment and submit to the subsequent screening procedure. The screening authority then investigates the FDI transaction, the investor, and the investor's ultimate beneficial owners, among other factors, and collects data to assess how the FDI may affect the host state's security or other relevant interests.

Concerning investment screening on security grounds, security threat analysis must almost necessarily be confidential because the mere disclosure of relevant security concerns can undermine the security of the host state. This confidentiality makes it difficult for the foreign investor to obtain full transparency concerning the procedure. As a result, the investor's ability to question, challenge, or seek legal remedies against a screening decision is severely hampered. A further consequence

[44] Choer Moraes and Wigell (2022).

[45] Drezner et al. (2021); Leonard (2021).

[46] Choer Moraes and Wigell (2022).

[47] Lenihan (2018).

is that foreign investors are left without meaningful legal guarantees against host state abuse of its screening legislation. Hence, any allegation of abuse is very difficult to substantiate; without scrutiny of the investment screening process, the investor is without evidence. The investor may take some comfort in the hypothesis that such abuse is contrary to the host state's interests to maintain a reputation for a sound investment climate. However, with neoliberal ideals on the wane and increased geoeconomic competition, this comfort may more appropriately be labelled as unfounded hope.

How exactly host states assess the security risk that an FDI transaction poses is naturally not well understood. Each state's threat assessment methodology is itself a closely guarded state secret, which, if commonly known, would constitute a security vulnerability. Nevertheless, some contours have been envisioned in the literature. Theodore H. Moran, writing in 2009, identified three categories of threats that investment screening served to address.[48]

First, the screening investigates the threat that a foreign-controlled owner of a domestic enterprise in a critical situation may cease operations or otherwise deny, delay, or place conditions on the supply of critical goods or services in the host state (Threat I). In other words, the threat is one of potential coercion or "binding" (i.e. a strategy of making the host state dependent on the investor or, ultimately, its home state). Such dependency then serves as the basis for economic coercion.

Second, the host state screens FDI transactions to assess the threat that important technologies or expertise may be leaked or otherwise appropriated by a foreign government that (directly or indirectly) owns or controls the foreign investor (Threat II). In a narrow sense, this threat concerns the transfer of military or dual-use technologies and expertise. However, broadly, it is about transferring technologies and expertise that can increase the home state's technological capabilities and expertise at the expense of the host state. The ultimate end use of such technologies or expertise need not be military. Even purely civilian uses, including personal data or trade secrets, can be used to shift economic capabilities from the host state to the home state.

Third, host state screening examines the likelihood that FDI can serve as a channel for infiltration, surveillance, or sabotage (Threat III). The idea here is that FDI can be a "Trojan horse" through which a foreign government may facilitate espionage operations, gain crucial insights into the operation of the host state's critical infrastructure and supply lines, and use such intelligence to hamper the host state's mobilization of capabilities in a conflict.

Moran further developed this three-tiered threat analysis to construct a threat-assessment decision tree based on two tests.[49] First, screening authorities are faced with evaluating the impact of each threat (i.e. the criticality test). With respect to Threat I, the authority examines the goods or services supplied by the enterprise in which the foreign investor is investing. The goal is to quantify the impact of costs

[48] Moran (2009).

[49] Moran and Oldenski (2013).

in the event that the supply of these goods or services is denied, delayed, or subjected to certain conditions. With respect to Threat II, the authority assesses the national security-related advantage that the foreign investor or its home state may gain through FDI. Finally, with respect to Threat III, the authority investigates the damage foreseen to result from surveillance or disruption through foreign ownership.

Second, in the event that the overall analysis of Threats I, II, and III yields a conclusion of "high criticality" (i.e. a high-cost impact of denied, delayed, or conditioned access to goods or services, a high national security advantage gained by the foreign investor or home state, and/or a high expected damage from surveillance or disruption), the next test seeks to assess plausible mitigating factors (i.e. the plausibility test). Specifically, the screening authority explores whether the foreign investor can control substitute goods and services, how widely available those substitutes are on global markets, how competitive alternative suppliers are, and what the cost would be of switching to new suppliers.

In the event of satisfactory substitute goods and services, the competitive suppliers of these substitutes, and acceptable switching costs, the plausibility test yields a negative result, which implies that the contemplated FDI does not pose an economic security threat and can proceed. However, if a plausible threat exists because of a lack of substitutes, poor competitiveness in substitute markets, or high switching costs, the authority must decide how to deal with FDI transactions. According to Moran, it should block the transaction only if the blocking would leave the target enterprise capable of being internationally competitive. In other words, blocking should not be used if it would harm the enterprise's international competitiveness. Conversely, FDI transactions should be allowed if they are the only way for domestic enterprises to remain internationally competitive.

The position advocated by Moran that international competitiveness should ultimately prevail over national security concerns can readily be disputed. However, the preceding analytical steps—the criticality test and the plausibility test—remain useful as a simplified structure of national security threat assessment in the context of FDI. Although the literature on investment screening has proliferated in recent years, Moran's investment security risk blueprint remains relevant.

Scholarship has yet to undertake a systematic treatment of geoeconomic strategy in the area of FDI, including a typology of geoeconomic instruments applied to FDI. Such attempt could examine the full spectrum of instruments and coercer-target roles. As sketched at the outset of this subchapter, FDI can be an instrument of the home state against the host state, including various kinds of sovereign-driven investments, such as investments by state-controlled or state-affiliated investors (notably, SOEs and SWFs), as well as state-financed, state-subsidized, state-contracted, and otherwise (directly or indirectly) state-incentivized privately owned investors. The latter categories are challenging to detect. Even the most thorough analysis of ultimate beneficial ownership proves useless since no foreign state ownership is involved. Indirect lines of loyalty, including clientelism, are typically clandestine and unlikely to be properly documented or easily discoverable.

This typology should also consider FDI as an instrument of the host state against the home state, a kind of "reverse influence" whereby the host state uses lawful or perhaps unlawful means (e.g. strategic corruption) to access the investor's upstream ownership structure. Thus, the host state can deny or manipulate access to goods or services in the home state. Alternatively, the host state can gain a national security advantage vis-à-vis the home state (e.g. by seizing control of the investor's assets and operations). Alternatively, the host state may gain access to technology and expertise higher up in the corporate structure of the foreign investor. Recent policy debates and scholarly discussions about outward FDI screening have partly considered these scenarios.

2.4 Investment Screening as a Mitigant Against Geoeconomic Risks Posed by Weaponized Investments

Investment screening allows governments to selectively restrict foreign investments by means of a case-by-case review conducted by a specialized public authority tasked with determining whether an investment is in accordance with state policy.[50] As such investment screening is a technique for controlling FDI.[51] The subject matter of foreign investment controls, including investment screening, is investment in the state concerned by nationals of another state.[52] In the case of foreign investment, the admission or entry of the investment made by a national of a state (the investor's home state) in another state (the investor's host state) is controlled by the host state. Thus, for investment screening purposes, the state concerned is the host state.

The present subchapter introduces the subject matter of investment screening by outlining the phenomenon of investment screening, specifically national security screening (Sect. 2.4.1) and the recent increase in its use (Sect. 2.4.2).

---

[50] Normally referring to a special administrative procedure laid down in national legislation, investment screening differs from ad hoc government interventions targeting investments by specific foreign investors, as exemplified by recent efforts to restrict the procurement and use of 5G wireless telecommunications equipment sourced from Chinese vendors Huawei and ZTE. See Segal (2021). The U.K. National Security and Investment Act 2021 (NSIA) is an example of the latest generation of investment screening laws. The law requires that certain investments in key sectors be notified to the U.K. government prior to being completed so that it can screen those investments and decide whether to allow them to be completed or to impose conditions that mitigate identified national-security risks.

[51] Other techniques for restricting foreign investment include total or sectoral exclusion of foreign investment, foreign-ownership restrictions, mandated foreign-local joint ventures, and foreign exchange and capital controls, all of which are non-selective control mechanisms insofar as they single out foreign investments or capital transfers generally instead of following a detailed case-by-case investigation.

[52] Another type of investment screening relates to outward investments (i.e. the control by the investor's home state of investments by a national of the home state in a host state).

2.4.1 Anatomy of an Investment Screening Mechanism: The Case of the EU Screening Regime

By way of illustration, Regulation (EU) 2019/452 of the European Parliament and of the Council of 19 March 2019 establishing a framework for the screening of foreign direct investments into the Union ("EU FDI Screening Regulation") provides an example of a definition of a "screening mechanism":

> [A]n instrument of general application, such as a law or regulation, and accompanying administrative requirements, implementing rules or guidelines, setting out the terms, conditions and procedures to assess, investigate, authorize, condition, prohibit or unwind foreign direct investments on the grounds of security or public order.

The reason for screening foreign investments is typically a vital societal interest. Investment screening may concern the economic benefit of the investment to the host state's national economy, including concerns about "economic sovereignty", economic planning, or the development of economic sectors.[53] However, investment screening has become most widely used as a technique for controlling investments that are deemed to adversely affect the national security of the host state.[54]

---

[53] See further at n. 90 below. An example of this type of investment screening is the "net benefits test" under the Investment Canada Act (R.S.C., 1985, c. 28 [1st Supp.]), pursuant to which the Canadian government may prohibit a foreign investor from implementing an investment or force an investor to divest if the investment is not deemed to provide "net benefit" to Canada. In determining whether an investment is of "net benefit", the Minister will consider the following factors (section 20 of the Act):

(a) the effect of the investment on the level and nature of economic activity in Canada, including, without limiting the generality of the foregoing, the effect on employment, on resource processing, on the utilization of parts, components and services produced in Canada and on exports from Canada;
(b) the degree and significance of participation by Canadians in the Canadian business or new Canadian business and in any industry or industries in Canada of which the Canadian business or new Canadian business forms or would form a part;
(c) the effect of the investment on productivity, industrial efficiency, technological development, product innovation and product variety in Canada;
(d) the effect of the investment on competition within any industry or industries in Canada;
(e) the compatibility of the investment with national industrial, economic and cultural policies, taking into consideration industrial, economic and cultural policy objectives enunciated by the government or legislature of any province likely to be significantly affected by the investment; and
(f) the contribution of the investment to Canada's ability to compete in world markets.

[54] UNCTAD Investment Policy Hub maintains an updated list of FDI screening laws, currently listing such laws of 52 States (https://investmentpolicy.unctad.org/investment-laws); the OECD tracks investment screening laws in its member countries (https://www.oecd.org/investment/investment-policy/investment-policy-national-security.htm); see also the PRISM dataset maintained by Princeton University and Hamilton Lugar School of Global and International Studies, Indiana University (https://investmentscreening.princeton.edu/dataset); the European Commission maintains an updated list of EU Member States' investment screening laws (https://policy.trade.ec.europa.eu/enforcement-and-protection/investment-screening_en).

The EU FDI Screening Regulation establishes a system for EU Member States to review foreign investments based on considerations of "security or public order".[55] This system reflects influences from similar mechanisms employed globally, particularly the Committee on Foreign Investment in the United States (CFIUS) and its reforms under the Foreign Investment Risk Review Modernization Act (FIRRMA) of 2018.[56]

The CFIUS, established in 1975, plays a critical role in evaluating the national security implications of foreign investments in the United States. FIRRMA, enacted in 2018, significantly expanded CFIUS's authority, introducing new categories of covered transactions, including certain real estate transactions and non-controlling investments in critical technology, infrastructure, and businesses handling sensitive personal data. FIRRMA also enhanced CFIUS's review process by extending timelines and increasing the resources allocated for its operations.

The EU FDI Screening Regulation, while distinct in its structure, incorporates several principles that reflect the CFIUS/FIRRMA approach. Both frameworks emphasize the protection of critical infrastructure and technology, scrutinize investments for potential threats to national security, and ensure governmental authority to intervene in transactions that may pose such threats. Specifically:

- **Scope of Review:** Similar to FIRRMA's broadening of CFIUS's scope, the EU regulation includes a comprehensive list of factors that Member States and the European Commission may consider, such as the impact on critical infrastructure, technologies, and sensitive information.
- **Information Sharing:** Both frameworks enhance mechanisms for information sharing among relevant authorities. FIRRMA introduced mandatory declarations for certain transactions, akin to the EU's requirement for Member States to notify and share information on FDI with the Commission and other Member States.
- **Cooperation Mechanisms:** FIRRMA's emphasis on interagency cooperation within the US government parallels the cooperative nature of the EU framework, which mandates coordination between the Commission and Member States, ensuring a unified approach to FDI screening.

These similarities suggest a cross-influence where the EU framework has adopted key elements of the robust CFIUS model, adapting them to the EU's legal and institutional context. This convergence highlights the global trend towards tightening control over foreign investments to safeguard national security, influenced significantly by the CFIUS/FIRRMA reforms.

[55] See further Wagner (2023). The European Commission's initial annual report on the EU FDI Screening Regulation noted that 24 EU Member States either implemented a new screening mechanism, modified an existing one, or began a consultative or legislative process. Only three Member States reported no initiatives. Further details can be found in the European Commission (2021) report, page 9, accessible at https://ec.europa.eu/commission/presscorner/detail/en/ip_21_6226.

[56] U.S. Congress. (2018). *Foreign Investment Risk Review Modernization Act of 2018*. Pub. L. No. 115–232, § 1701–1771, 132 Stat. 2173–2186.

In the following paragraphs, the EU FDI Screening Regulation serves as the principal basis for illustrative and comparative references of the functioning of investment screening mechanisms to draw generalized inferences about national laws on investment screening, complemented as appropriate by references to other states having well-established investment screening mechanisms.[57] This choice is motivated by the fact that the EU FDI Screening Regulation sets the framework for EU Member States' screening laws and is thus indicative of their common legislative features. Although this screening framework is not directly applicable to investors, it determines the basic characteristics of Member State screening laws, should a Member State decide to adopt them. Indeed, Member States conduct the screening, even though the European Commission has the right to issue opinions. Nevertheless, neither the EU FDI Screening Regulation nor any other EU legislation mandates such adoption. Since the EU represents a high proportion of the total number of advanced economies with screening laws, most of the EU screening laws have recently been adopted or modified. Since the EU is an important capital exporter, the EU FDI Screening Regulation serves as a source of illustration of screening mechanism features in the following discussion.[58]

National screening laws exhibit considerable diversity in their scope of application, procedural characteristics, screening objectives, and review standards.[59] Despite these variations, which stem from differing administrative law traditions, common procedural elements can be identified and categorized for analytical purposes. A specific government authority (i.e. the screening authority) is typically given powers to operationalize investment screening by assessing and investigating foreign investment transactions and requesting information and documents from the prospective investor, as well as, in the case of an acquisition of an existing enterprise, from the enterprise in question. At the closure of the procedure, the authority may decide to authorize the investment, conditionally or unconditionally, or to prohibit it. If the investment has already occurred, the authority can often order its unwinding. Conditional authorization may involve a negotiated arrangement that satisfies the authority so that any identified potential negative effects of the investment can be managed.

The following paragraphs provide a brief comparative overview of other pertinent points of similarity with respect to national investment screening procedures. First, investment screening laws share similarities with respect to the types of investments that may be subject to the screening (scope of application ratione

[57] See further Wagner (2023). Article 3(8) mandates that the EU Commission must publicly disclose a list of screening mechanisms reported by Member States. This list, which includes non-authoritative English translations of several screening laws, is accessible at: https://policy.trade.ec.europa.eu/enforcement-and-protection/investment-screening_en. Additionally, numerous other EU FDI Screening laws can be found on the UNCTAD Investment Policy Hub at: https://investmentpolicy.unctad.org/investment-laws. For scholarly discussions on various screening laws, refer to the contributions in Hindelang and Moberg (2021).

[58] For a comparative review of U.S., EU and Chinese FDI screening legislation, see Bian (2020).

[59] For an overview of different types of investment screening systems, see Esplugues Mota (2018) 254–256. See further Wagner (2023).

materiae). Second, there are similarities in determining the timing of the economic operation at which the screening takes place (scope of application ratione temporis).[60] Third, investment screening laws exhibit commonalities in the scope of review, such as the assessment of a threat to "security or public order" and the criteria used to apply this standard.

Unlike investment agreements, the EU FDI Screening Regulation, along with many national investment screening laws, does not provide detailed definitions or list specific types of investment activities that fall under investment screening.[61] The Regulation adopts a broad understanding of FDI as "an investment of any kind by a foreign investor aiming to establish or to maintain lasting and direct links [...] in order to carry out an economic activity in a Member State".[62] This understanding highlights two general features of the material scope of screening: the covered activity in question must be one of investment, and the investment in question must be foreign.

First, regarding the investment nature of the covered activities, the quintessential FDI may be the establishment of entirely new productive assets (e.g. greenfield investment) in the host state. Generally, however, screening mechanisms are not strictly limited to FDI but also cover investments through the acquisition of control, or even non-controlling stakes, of an existing enterprise, such as mergers and acquisitions (M&As).[63]

Some screening mechanisms also cover the acquisition of certain assets or business lines of an existing company or the establishment of new companies and subsidiaries.[64]

Screening laws typically only apply to more significant investments. Thus, the scope of application may be limited to investment transactions of a certain minimum value or, frequently in the context of share acquisitions, to investment transactions where the investor acquires a certain minimum level of influence over the enterprise in question. Such minimum levels are known as "screening thresholds", which may typically be set at 20%, 30%, or 50% of the shares or voting rights, with any acquisition above such threshold triggering

[60] See further Wagner (2023).

[61] Ibid.

[62] Article 2(1) EU FDI Screening Regulation. See further Wagner (2023).

[63] See e.g. Section 2(5) Act on the Screening of Foreign Corporate Acquisitions 172/2012 (Finland), on Finnish mechanism; see also Hallberg (2021) 212 f; Section 2(1)(a) Investment Control Act (Austria); Section 55(a) Foreign Trade and Payments Ordinance (Germany); On the German mechanism, see also Stompfe (2021) 82 ff.; Article L.151–2 Monetary and Financial Act Legislative Section (France); On the French mechanism see also Stompfe (2021) 99 ff; Section 4 (4) Investment Control Act (Denmark). See further Wagner (2023).

[64] Section 2(1) of Act LVII of 2018 on Controlling Foreign Investments Violating Hungary's Security Interests available at: https://trade.ec.europa.eu/doclib/docs/2019/june/tradoc_157938.pdf; Article L. 151–2 (c) Monetary and Financial Act (France); for the acquisition of an establishment from a 'protected company' as a transaction subject to screening in the Polish Law on Control of Certain Investments, see Jaśkowski and Pawłowski (2021) 145. See further Wagner (2023).

screening.[65] To the extent thresholds apply below the level assumed to result in control, the screening may also encompass portfolio investments.[66] Screening may then be repeated if the investor expands its control over the enterprise by acquiring additional shares, and the total percentage of shares or voting rights controlled by the investor thereby exceeds a higher threshold.

The EU FDI Screening Regulation provides a broad understanding of control in the context of its investment definition by the words "including investments which enable effective participation in the management or control of a company carrying out an economic activity".[67] The acquisition of control extends beyond the simple purchase of shares and may also encompass shareholder agreements related to decision-making or the right to appoint members to governing bodies.[68] Similarly, operating, supplier, or service agreements may be included "if a foreign investor thereby gains control of or significant influence over the company or entity".[69]

Second, investment screening concerns foreign investments. The EU FDI Screening Regulation limits its application to investments by a "foreign investor", defined as "a natural person of a third country or an undertaking of a third country, intending to make or having made a foreign direct investment", where "undertaking of a third country" means "an undertaking constituted or otherwise organised under the laws of a third country".[70] Hence, an undertaking organized under the laws of an EU Member State falls outside the definition of a foreign investor. Neither the definition of FDI nor a foreign investor applies to investments by EU undertakings, even if they are controlled by non-EU investors. Nevertheless, the Screening Regulation also provides that Member States are obliged to ensure that their screening mechanisms and screening decisions are not circumvented.[71] It is also clear that this definition covers both prospective and actual investors.[72]

---

[65] Section 10 Act on Screening of Certain Foreign Direct Investments, etc. in Denmark (the Investment Screening Act) 842/2021; Article R. 151–2 (c) Monetary and Financial Code Regulatory Section (France); Section 2(1)(a) Act LVII of 2018 on Controlling Foreign Investments Violating Hungary's Security Interests; Section 4 (2) Investment Control Act (Austria). See further Wagner (2023).

[66] Section 58(1)(1) German Foreign Trade Ordinance; Section 4(1) Investment Control Act (Austria). See further Wagner (2023).

[67] Cf. Article 2(1) EU FDI Screening Regulation.

[68] See further Wagner (2023); cf. Section 2(1)(3)(b) of the Investment Control Act (Austria): "A controlling interest [...] is attained irrespective of specific shares of voting rights"; Article R-151-2 (a) France Monetary and Financial Code Legislative Section; Section 4(1) Act No. LX of 2020 (Malta).

[69] See further Wagner (2023); cf. Section 4(5) Investment Screening Act (Denmark).

[70] Article 2(2) and (7) of the EU FDI Screening Regulation.

[71] Cf. Article 3(6). According to Recital 10, "[T]his should cover investments from within the Union by means of artificial arrangements that do not reflect economic reality and circumvent the screening mechanisms and screening decisions, where the investor is ultimately owned or controlled by a natural person or an undertaking of a third country". An investment of an EU undertaking controlled by non-EU investors could in these situations be covered by national screening mechanisms, even though it would not be "foreign direct investment" under the Screening Regulation.

[72] Note specifically the words "intending to make or having made an investment".

Investment screening can take place before an investment is executed (i.e. ex-ante screening) or afterwards (i.e. ex-post screening).[73] If a screening mechanism sets a threshold for ownership or voting rights, exceeding this limit triggers the application of the screening process. In this scenario, the screening procedure can be activated by expanding an existing investment beyond the set threshold. Therefore, any additional investment that increases an existing stake, such as the acquisition of additional shares, typically falls under the scope of the screening mechanism.[74] If a foreign investor acquires further shares in a company after an initial investment, and if this subsequent transaction exceeds an applicable screening threshold, the additional investment is subject to screening.

In contrast, certain FDI screening mechanisms scrutinize planned investments and review those that have already been implemented (i.e. ex-post screening). Some legal frameworks also allow for the retrospective examination of investments upon receipt of a notification from the investor.[75] While the EU FDI Screening Regulation does not specifically require ex-post screening, the inclusion of terms like "to unwind" in its definitions suggests that it is contemplated.[76] In the EU, ex-post screening commonly addresses instances where an investor has failed to comply with notification duties, submitted erroneous data, left out essential details during the screening process, or violated approval conditions.[77] Ex-post screening can also be triggered by changes in circumstances that call for a reassessment of the potential threats to security or public order from an existing investment.[78] Additionally, screen-

[73] In the United States, the Committee on Foreign Investment in the United States (CFIUS) may unilaterally initiate a review of an investment in certain cases, including where the investment has not previously been screened and the President of the United States has not previously announced a decision not to undertake such a review. Similarly, the UK NSIA provides a "call-in" power to the Secretary of State with respect to actual or anticipated "trigger events", which may be given within six months of the Secretary of State becoming aware of the event, and within five years of its occurrence. In the European Union, by contrast, Regulation (EU) 2019/452 does not provide for ex-post screening per se, it provides a "cooperation mechanism" whereby a Member State may provide comments, or the European Commission may issue an opinion up to 15 months after completion of an investment that has not undergone screening. The host Member State of that investment must "give due consideration" to such comments or opinion. The Regulation does not prevent Member States from conducting ex post screening, which the legislation of several Member States foresees.

[74] See further Wagner (2023).

[75] See further Wagner (2023) citing Article 4(1) and (5) Decree-Law 138/2004 (Portugal); Vargiu (2021) 129–130; See also Article 10(1) Royal Decree 664/1999; Vargiu (2021) 125.

[76] Article 2(3) f (4) EU FDI Screening Regulation.

[77] See further Wagner (2023) citing Section 4(2) of the Finnish Act on the Screening of Foreign Corporate Acquisitions 172/2012 as an example of a screening mechanism enabling the Minister of Economic Affairs to set a deadline for submitting the application if the investor has failed to apply; Section 8(2), (5) Investment Control Act (Austria).

[78] See further Wagner (2023) citing Section 13 Subsection 7 Investment Screening Act (Denmark).

ing authorities may have the authority to independently initiate a screening within a certain period following an investment's completion.[79] Outcomes from such screenings can lead to the reversal of transactions that profoundly impact economic activities and the broader investment law regime.

Screening frameworks typically use broad criteria such as "public order"[80] and "security",[81] but these terms are rarely defined explicitly. Due to the ambiguous nature of these concepts, the screening process relies on supplementary criteria to determine which investments need to be examined. Legislation often points to investments in particular asset classes, economic sectors, or activities deemed more likely to influence security or public order. Although the EU FDI Screening Regulation does not provide clear definitions for "security or public order", it lists both objective and subjective considerations that the Member States or the Commission may evaluate.[82] These considerations include the possible impact on critical infrastructure, critical technologies, sensitive information, and the influence on media freedom and pluralism.[83]

1. In determining whether a foreign direct investment is likely to affect security or public order, Member States and the Commission may consider its potential effects on, inter alia:
    a. critical infrastructure, whether physical or virtual, including energy, transport, water, health, communications, media, data processing or storage, aerospace, defence, electoral or financial infrastructure, and sensitive facilities, as well as land and real estate crucial for the use of such infrastructure;
    b. critical technologies and dual use items as defined in point 1 of Article 2 of Council Regulation (EC) No 428/2009 (15), including artificial intelligence, robotics, semiconductors, cybersecurity, aerospace, defence, energy storage, quantum and nuclear technologies as well as nanotechnologies and biotechnologies;
    c. supply of critical inputs, including energy or raw materials, as well as food security;
    d. access to sensitive information, including personal data, or the ability to control such information; or
    e. the freedom and pluralism of the media.

[79] See further Wagner (2023) citing Section 2 (2) (b) and Section 2 (4) (b) (ii) National Security and Investment Act 2021 (United Kingdom) available at https://www.legislation.gov.uk/ukpga/2021/25/contents/enacted accessed 2 August 2022; Section 8(1)b and (4)(b) Act no. 34/2021 Coll. on the screening of foreign investments and amendments of related laws (Foreign Investments Screening Act Czech Republic) available at: https://www.mpo.cz/assets/cz/zahranicni-obchod/proverovani-zahranicnich-investic/2021/4/sb0017-2021-_1_.pdf accessed 2 August 2022.

[80] See further Wagner (2023) citing Article L. 151–3 French Monetary and Financial Code (France).

[81] See further Wagner (2023) citing Section 6(3) Act LVII of 2018 on Controlling Foreign Investments Violating Hungary's Security Interests "[...] Hungary's security interests".

[82] Article 4 EU FDI Screening Regulation.

[83] Article 4(1) EU FDI Screening Regulation.

States maintain similar but widely varying non-exhaustive lists of sectors and asset classes.[84] The categories of critical infrastructure and technologies have been recently updated and expanded to include new technologies and sectors deemed strategic. In recent years, personal data, including financial data, health data, private communications, internet connection data, and biometric data, have become critical resources subject to national security screening. Similarly, investments in media and electoral infrastructures reflect a contemporary understanding of national security threats. Moreover, since the COVID-19 pandemic, many states have created or expanded lists of sensitive or strategic sectors critical to safeguarding "health security".[85]

Besides the nature of the investment that may pose national security risks, the characteristics of the investor also play a crucial role in investment screening. The review process often considers subjective aspects related to the foreign investor, such as connections to foreign governments that may exert influence or offer financial backing or previous involvement in activities that undermine security and public order. The EU FDI Screening Regulation highlights a series of pertinent criteria in this context:

> 2. In determining whether a foreign direct investment is likely to affect security or public order, Member States and the Commission may also take into account, in particular:
>   a. whether the foreign investor is directly or indirectly controlled by the government, including state bodies or armed forces, of a third country, including through ownership structure or significant funding;
>   b. whether the foreign investor has already been involved in activities affecting security or public order in a Member State; or
>   c. whether there is a serious risk that the foreign investor engages in illegal or criminal activities.[86]

The investor-specific assessment naturally involves sensitive investigative information concerning the investor's potential links to a foreign government (or a non-state actor), normally conducted in close collaboration between the screening authority and the state's intelligence community.

While some legal frameworks adopt the language and screening criteria from the EU FDI Screening Regulation or incorporate its factors,[87] others reference EU

[84] Investment screening mechanisms may be sector-specific and apply only to certain sectors, such as utilities, energy, telecommunication, transportation, media, and financial sectors, that are considered critical for national security purposes. By contrast, cross-sectoral screening mechanisms allow for screening in all sectors. The CFIUS process in the United States is the most characteristic example of such a legislative framework. In addition, some mechanisms apply screening only to a predefined set of listed entities, usually state-owned and operating in sectors that are perceived as sensitive from a national security perspective.

[85] Gertz (2021).

[86] Article 4(2) EU FDI Screening Regulation.

[87] Cf. Section 55 Foreign Trade and Payments Ordinance (Germany) available at https://www.gesetze-im-internet.de/englisch_awv/ accessed 2 August 2022; Article 72(3) and (4) Act Determining the Intervention Measures to Mitigate and Remedy the Consequences of the COVID-19 Epidemic (Slovenia) available at https://trade.ec.europa.eu/doclib/docs/2020/october/tradoc_158966.6.2020.pdf accessed 2 August 2022; Schedule (Articles 11 and 12) of the Act No. LX of 2020 (Malta).

primary legislation that restricts the freedom of establishment and the free movement of capital based on comparable grounds.[88] The relationship between the definitions of "security or public order" in the EU FDI Screening Regulation and "public policy or public security" in Article 65(1)(b) of the TFEU remains ambiguous. Despite the necessity for a "real, specific and serious risk" and the stringent requirement for proportionality in related measures, the Court of Justice of the European Union (CJEU) has recognized the validity of preventive strategies aimed at ensuring the availability of essential goods or services under Article 65(1)(b).[89]

Looking beyond the EU, the objectives for FDI screening in other countries often surpass those of mere security and public order. For example, Australia employs a loosely defined criterion of "national interest", while the Investment Canada Act evaluates the net benefit and the security implications of foreign investments.[90] More explicitly, Japan's Foreign Exchange and Trade Act allows for considerations of significant negative impacts on economic stability in addition to national security concerns.[91] Globally, many jurisdictions utilise a factor-based approach to assess the compatibility of investments with screening objectives, such as CFIUS and the Investment Canada Act, which include traditional security-sensitive areas like the defence industry and broader elements like effects on critical infrastructure or emerging technologies.[92] These factors provide a framework for governmental discretion in identifying which industries, goods, or technologies are deemed critical or sensitive while potentially masking economic motives and protectionist agendas under broadly defined or vague screening criteria.

Despite the challenges in clearly defining terms such as "security or public order", some nations have attempted to clarify these concepts in their screening regulations or foundational laws.

---

[88] See further Wagner (2023) citing Article 52(1) and Article 65(1)(b) of the Treaty on the Functioning of the European Union, OJ C 326, 26 October 2012. See e.g. Section 2 (Definitions) (2) Act on the Screening of Foreign Corporate Acquisitions (Finland); Article 2 of the Act of 24 July 2015 on the Control of Certain Investments (Poland); Section 3(1) Investment Control Act (Austria).

[89] See further Wagner (2023) citing Judgment of the Court of 4 June 2002, *Commission v Belgium*, C-503/99, ECLI:EU:C:2002:328, para. 46; Judgment of the Court of 4 June 2002; *Commission v France*, C-483/99, ECLI:EU:C:2002:327, para. 47; for the qualification of a FDI review mechanism under Article 65(1)(b) cf. Judgment of the Court of 14 March 2000, *Association Eglise de scientology de Paris and Scientology International Reserves Trust v The Prime Minister*, C-54/99, ECLI:EU:C:2000:124, paras. 20–22; For the justification of confinements of the free movement of goods under Article 36 TFEU cf. Judgment of the Court of 10 July 1984, *Campus Oil v The Minister for Industry and Energy*, C-72/83, ECLI:EU:C:1984:256, para. 34.

[90] Esplugues Mota (2018) 327 ff, 355 ff; Ackhurst et al. (2016) 73–74.

[91] Fujii et al. (2021) 379, 380, 386.

[92] For the CFIUS cf. U.S.C. § 4565 (f); Lichtenbaum and Ribner (2021) 369; For the ICA cf. Guidelines on the National Security Review of Investments available at https://www.ic.gc.ca/eic/site/ica-lic.nsf/eng/lk81190.html accessed 2 August 2022.

For instance, Denmark's Investment Screening Act provides a specific definition of "national security":

> National Security: Matters relating to Denmark's territorial integrity and survival of the population. Threats to national security include actions that constitute or may constitute the risk of disruption of international relations, the peaceful coexistence of nations or threats to military interests, as well as actions intended to cause damage to Denmark, including crimes against the state's independence or crimes against the constitution and the supreme state authorities.[93]

This interpretation of national security connects it to the constitutional underpinnings of the state and encompasses threats to territorial integrity and the effective operation of state institutions. This perspective undeniably provides the state with considerable leeway in defining what constitutes security interests. Although such broad definitions can lead to arbitrary or discriminatory practices, the fundamental legal principles of a liberal constitutional regime, such as the rule of law, are upheld by authorities and courts and set boundaries at the state's discretion. Furthermore, the concept of security is also constrained by higher legal standards derived from EU law and international law.

"Security", "national security", and similar terms as may appear in investment screening legislation do not refer to any precisely defined legal concept.[94] Indeed, if considered a legal concept at all, "security" may be best understood as vague, fuzzy, or essentially contested.[95] Even in political science, notably in international relations, international security studies, and strategic studies, a range of competing approaches have evolved over the years to give meaning to "security".[96] For present purposes, it is sufficient to note that the notion of national security is central to the interpretation and application of national security screening. At the same time, the quest for giving substantive content to the notion of national security is overshadowed by the practically more pressing question of who should decide that content and subject to what level of scrutiny. Therefore, any enquiry into the legal aspect of national security cannot proceed without a discussion about the level of discretion granted to screening authorities and the scope of judicial review granted to courts or tribunals. Before revisiting that question, it is necessary to assess the relative importance of investment screening practically and legally. Is

[93] Section 4(1) Investment Screening Act (Denmark); Cf. also Section 1(1) (National Security) National Security Law (Latvia) available at https://likumi.lv/ta/en/en/id/14011-national-security-law); Article 2(7) Definitions of the Law on Protection of Objects of Importance to Ensuring National Security 2002 (Lithuania) available via https://investmentpolicy.unctad.org/investment-laws; Preamble of the Decree-Law no. 138/2014, of the 15th September (Portugal) available via https://investmentpolicy.unctad.org/investment-laws.

[94] The indeterminacy debate (the inability to derive knowable answers to concrete problems) concerning the interpretation of legal concepts provides one avenue for understanding the role of "security" in legal discourse. See Dworkin (1977); Solum (1987); Kress (1989); Tushnet (2005); du Plessis (2021).

[95] See Baldwin (1997); Gallie (1956).

[96] See, e.g. Hollnagel (2021). One rendition of the 'security' concept mentioned is that it represents a process of prevention of and resilience against harmful behaviour, id.

investment screening a phenomenon of very limited prevalence in practice? Is it a fringe legal topic, or does it raise legal matters of principle? The answers require putting investment screening into a recent political context.

2.4.2 The Increased Use of Investment Screening

Investment screening laws were first introduced in the 1970s in the United States, Canada, and Australia, prompted by fears of takeovers by mainly Japanese and Middle Eastern investors of technology companies, such as the semiconductor industry.[97] Investment screening allowed for selective case-by-case control of foreign investment while maintaining a generally open investment climate, succeeding an earlier generation of foreign investment exclusion laws.[98] For most of the ensuing decades, investment screening remained in obscurity and existed as a narrow exception to free capital mobility.

In recent years, many countries worldwide have increased the screening of foreign investment, particularly in the context of M&A. According to UNCTAD, 52 countries currently have investment screening laws.[99] In the EU alone, 18 Member States have investment screening mechanisms.[100] This shift has gathered pace following the outbreak of the COVID-19 pandemic, frequently grounded in national security concerns.

Increased screening has taken different forms, from the introduction of a screening regime where none previously existed and the identification of additional sensitive or strategic sectors or technologies to the creation of new powers to screen already established investments.

Several reasons have been proposed to explain the proliferation of investment screening. The following stand out: (1) the changing course of foreign investments, specifically the rise of "sovereign-driven" investment,[101] and (2) changes in attitude to sovereign-driven investment and the intertwining of politics and economics, notably the increasingly acknowledged role of politics in determining the distribution of economic opportunity (sometimes referred to as the "geoeconomic turn" in trade and investment policy).[102]

---

[97] The Canadian investment screening regime was introduced by the Foreign Investment Review Act of 1973 (Ch. 46, 1973–74 Statutes of Canada 620 amended by ch 52, 1976–77 Statutes of Canada 1274). The Committee on Foreign Investment in the United States (CFIUS) was established by Executive Order No. 11858 of 7 May 1975, Foreign Investment in the United States, 40 FR 20263, 3C.F.R., 1971–1975 Comp., p. 990.

[98] For a comprehensive historical overview, see Muchlinski (2007) 181–214.

[99] UNCTAD (2022).

[100] European Commission (2021) 9.

[101] This term, which will be defined in the next paragraph, is borrowed from Esplugues Mota (2018) 178–218.

[102] Roberts et al. (2019) 655–676.

In the decades since 1990, global investment flows have changed dramatically. Rapidly developing countries, most notably China, have developed into important net exporting economies and transformed from being destinations for foreign investment from the developed countries into becoming capital exporters.[103] In emerging economies, such as China, Russia, Turkey, and Indonesia, the government usually has a managerial role in promoting economic development, including economic planning and outward investment promotion, to a far greater extent than in developed countries.[104] Moreover, the export surpluses of China and other emerging economies have resulted in the accumulation of significant foreign exchange reserves. To maintain stable foreign exchange rates vis-à-vis the currencies of trading partners and to stave off an appreciation of the exchange rates of their domestic currencies, emerging economies have encouraged offsetting outward foreign investment to those trading partners, mostly developed countries.[105] As a result, outward foreign investment activity originating in emerging markets has increasingly been undertaken by SWFs, SOEs, and other sovereign investors.[106] A major concern has been the fear that such sovereign-driven investment activity distorts the competition for investment opportunities and does not occur according to commercial principles or for purposes of maximizing profit.[107]

Concerns about sovereign-driven investment are expressed as a lack of reciprocity due to the fact that sovereign investors receive support and benefit from investment-related subsidies by their home state governments in ways that are unavailable to domestic investors in the host states from their governments.[108] Hence, a situation of asymmetric openness results, where foreign investment from advanced economies into emerging economies is more restricted (more costly) than foreign investment from emerging economies into advanced economies.[109]

The fact that plentiful inbound flows of foreign investment exert downward pressure on the financing costs of domestic enterprises while promoting economic progress is a fundamental tenet of international economic theory and is reflected in the investment policies of most nations.[110] Until recently, however, international economics largely overlooked the situation where a home state government is

---

[103] Roberts et al. (2019); Farrell and Newman (2019); Gertz and Evers (2020).

[104] Alami et al. (2022); Gertz and Evers (2020); Musacchio et al. (2015); Musacchio and Lazzarini (2014).

[105] Jepson (2020); Griffith-Jones and Ocampo (2011).

[106] Balding (2012); Dixon (2017); Dixon et al. (2022).

[107] Kurlantzick (2016).

[108] At the EU level, the same concern is expressed as a lack of reciprocity with a view to the fact that foreign SOEs receive support and are subsidized by their governments in ways that are prohibited under EU single market rules.

[109] According to the OECD FDI Regulatory Restrictiveness Index, the majority of the countries that are the most restrictive are countries in the Asia-Pacific region and larger countries. EU Member States are the least restrictive according to the same index.

[110] Moran et al. (2005); Rytter Sunesen and Juul Henriksen (2021).

confronted with the effects of economic statecraft (i.e. the economic policies of another state with a non-economic rationale).[111]

Emerging interest in states' geoeconomic policy and economic statecraft is unsurprising against this background and has resulted in an important strand in scholarly assessments of global economic policy.[112] A central idea of geoeconomic reasoning is that the increase in economic interdependence among states does not necessarily facilitate cooperation, as liberal internationalists posit,[113] but may result in security externalities that make states more vulnerable to potentially hostile or otherwise harmful behaviour of other states (i.e. security threats).[114]

Geoeconomics acknowledges the role of politics in determining the distribution of competitive opportunity[115]; political power influences the chances of wealth creation among states as well as businesses and individuals in a globalized capitalist society.[116] Foreign investments may constitute instruments of economic statecraft, or indeed economic warfare, such as when the home state directs sovereign-driven investments to certain strategic (or critical) sectors of the economy that may serve to deny the host state access to such sectors. Such investments may enable the investor's home state to exert political influence, distort competition in its favour, or restrict the host state's policy autonomy.

2.5 Investment Treaties as Mitigants Against Geoeconomic Risks Posed by Host States' Overreach

Applying the prism of risk indicates an aspiration to rein in the uncertainty generated by geoeconomic competition and strategies. By forging a common understanding of the mechanisms animating such competition and the aims and means of such strategies, a risk approach can reduce the complexity of geoeconomic power plays and

[111] Blackwill and Harris (2016).

[112] For a comprehensive overview, see Wigell et al. (2018).

[113] See, e.g. Keohane (1984); Keohane and Nye (2017) 81–110.

[114] Aggarwal and Reddie (2021) 139. Economic theory acknowledges the possibility of market failure, so recognized negative externalities (e.g. environmental pollution, overuse of antibiotics, and overfishing) may justify government intervention to ensure that economic costs resulting from the externality are efficiently priced, allocated, and internalized.

[115] Mandelbaum (2014) xvi. As Michael Mandelbaum stated: "The heart of politics is power; the aim of economics is wealth". The wealth of one can be increased without another becoming poorer (Pareto efficiency), but no one can become more powerful without another becoming less powerful. Thus, while wealth is thus limitless and a positive-sum game, power is limited and zero-sum.

[116] In acknowledging the intervening role of (political) power in international economics and the inherent, functional tension between power and wealth, geoeconomics provides a framework for reconciling international economic theory with the reality of (geo)political practice.

render at least some aspects susceptible to analysis and remedies. Nevertheless, important conceptual limitations exist.

First, geoeconomic risk focuses on economic vulnerabilities and capabilities, which have, in theory, observable or tangible manifestations, such as infrastructure, technologies, supplies of economic inputs, and otherwise intersubjectively (objectively) ascertainable manifestations, such as data and knowledge. Geoeconomic risk does not capture subjective elements, such as geoeconomic competitors' interests (intent) or their willingness to sacrifice other interests in pursuit thereof (resolve). The same limitation often applies to risks. The risk perspective does not promise certainty; rather, it is an analytical approach to dealing with a particular kind of uncertainty.

Second, meaningful geoeconomic risk requires accurate data, which can be particularly difficult to come by when the subject matter of the risk relates to state secrets or otherwise confidential matters. Considering the data required to conduct the three-step threat-assessment analysis discussed in the previous subsection, it should be obvious just how difficult data gathering may be. The criticality test for Threat I and the plausibility test both require extensive market data, whereas the other aspects of the criticality test require foreign policy and intelligence data. Data on ultimate beneficial owners are essential but insufficient, as discussed above. Therefore, meaningful geoeconomic risk analysis requires privileged access to the required information as well as superior data processing capabilities.

Third, geoeconomic risk does not address the effect of risk mitigants. Tools that may contribute to mitigating geoeconomic risk posed by a foreign investor and its home state are (third-party) political risk insurance and (bilateral) investment guarantees contained in investment treaties (e.g. BITs), the host state's national legislation, or contracts specifically concluded between the host state and the foreign investor (investor-state contracts).

The highly standardized terms of BITs illustrate how such mitigants operate. When applied to a host state's screening of inward FDI, BITs principally offer two kinds of protection. The first protection is guaranteed against discriminatory treatment of a foreign investor or its investment, based on two types: discrimination compared to the treatment of national (non-foreign) investors or investments (i.e. the national treatment [NT] standard) and discrimination compared to the treatment afforded to other more favourably treated foreign investors or investments (i.e. most-favoured-nation treatment or the MFN standard). In theory, both standards can be invoked to support a case against the host state for compensation. In practice, however, these discrimination standards have been interpreted to incorporate general, public interest exceptions.[117]

According to the second kind of guarantee, the host state must live up to specific absolute standards of treatment. The most typical standard is "fair and equitable treatment" (FET). Expropriation can also be considered an absolute standard of

[117] Pohl (2020b).

treatment. However, these standards leave some room for arbitral deference to executive decisions, with the emphasis being on procedural justice.[118] While it is arguable that procedural justice is in jeopardy in the event of limitations on transparency, optimism should be tempered. As the well-known *Ralls* case demonstrated, judicial transparency (i.e. rights to due process) may be interpreted to apply only to publicly available information, not secret intelligence and other confidential evidence, which may determine the outcome of screening decisions.[119]

Moreover, it is uncertain whether relevant treatment standards would apply to an investment subject to screening where the BIT in question applies only to completed investments while screening only applies to non-consummated investments.[120] Indeed, some treaties expressly state that the standards of treatment do not apply to the pre-establishment phase or matters of market access.[121] It is also possible that the investor cannot invoke rights derived under the BIT because of its links to a foreign government.[122] Moreover, the BIT may include exceptions for conduct that the host state deems necessary for its national security.[123] Finally, even if none of the above restrictions apply, an investment tribunal may simply defer to the host state's investment screening authority on matters concerning the host state's national security concerns.[124]

2.6 Conclusion

This chapter outlined the role of FDI as a tool in global power strategies and underlined the shift from economic transactions to instruments of geopolitical leverage. The increasing use of FDI by states highlights the transformation of economic interdependencies—once seen as mutual benefits—into potential sources of vulnerability. This shift is intensified by a growing great power rivalry, which has transformed these economic ties into arenas for geopolitical contestation.

The emergence of geoeconomic risks, particularly highlighted by the COVID-19 pandemic, has prompted host states to reconsider the role of FDI. Recognizing FDI's potential for foreign influence, states have implemented more stringent inbound FDI screening processes. These measures aim to protect national security and preserve economic independence from the potentially domineering effects of foreign investments, especially in essential sectors.

---

[118] Ibid.

[119] *Ralls Corp. v CFIUS*, 758 F.3d 296, 305–06 (D.C. Cir. 2014); see further Eichensehr and Hwang (2023).

[120] Pohl (2020b).

[121] Ibid.

[122] Ibid.

[123] Ibid.

[124] Ibid.; see also Verellen (2021); see generally, Shirlow (2021).

Despite these defensive strategies, the absence of a coherent theoretical framework on the weaponization of FDI and its broader implications marks a significant shortfall in current geoeconomic analysis. The fragmented global policy landscape further complicates the development of effective strategies to mitigate these risks.

Concurrently, investment arbitration serves as a counterbalance by mitigating risks posed by host states to foreign investors. This form of arbitration ensures that investors have recourse to address unfair treatment or expropriation by host states to maintain the trust and viability of cross-border investment flows. However, the protective function of investment arbitration often comes into tension with the objectives of investment screening.

This tension is most evident in the differing priorities concerning a host state's national security interests. While investment screening is governed by the host state's prerogative to defend its national security, which can lead to restrictive measures against foreign investments, investment arbitration seeks to uphold international legal standards that protect investors. These standards often challenge the host state's actions, particularly when national security is cited as the reason for economically detrimental measures against foreign investments.

The intersection of investment screening and investment arbitration highlights a significant conflict in international investment law—balancing the host state's right to protect its national security with the need to adhere to established international norms that protect investors. This balance is precarious, as the invocation of national security by host states can override international safeguards and lead to a potential erosion of investor confidence and international norms.

Ergo, there is a critical need for a detailed examination of geoeconomic strategies involving FDI. Future research must aim to develop a thorough classification of these strategies and evaluate their impacts on global security and economic stability. This work requires collaboration across disciplines, including international law, economic policy, and geopolitical studies, to build a robust understanding of how nations can effectively respond to and manage geoeconomic threats.

Furthermore, enhancing an understanding of the balance of economic power in the global arena requires advanced analytical tools and theoretical frameworks. Hence, scholars and policymakers must work together to create models that accurately reflect and predict the outcomes of geoeconomic interactions. As economic and political realms become increasingly intertwined, developing strategic and predictive frameworks is crucial to ensuring economic resilience and security in a rapidly evolving global context. Future research must address these challenges by refining the theoretical frameworks surrounding geoeconomic risks in FDI. It is crucial to develop a comprehensive understanding of how investment screening and investment arbitration can coexist and complement each other to ensure that the economic sovereignty of host states and the legal protections for investors are maintained. This course requires a multidisciplinary approach that encompasses international law, economic policy, and geopolitical analysis and aims to forge strategies that enhance global economic stability and security while respecting the delicate balance of power in international relations.

References

Aaltola M, Ketola J, Vaakanainen K, Peltonen A (2021) Solidarity during COVID-19 at national, regional and global levels: an enabler for improved global pandemic security and governance. Finnish Institute of International Affairs

Ackhurst K, Nattrass S, Brown E (2016) CETA, the Investment Canada Act and SOEs: a brave new world for free trade. ICSID Rev Foreign Invest Law J 31(1):58–76

Aggarwal V, Reddie A (2021) Economic statecraft in the twenty-first century: implications for the future of the global trade regime. World Trade Rev 20(2):137–151

Alami I, Babic M, Dixon AD, Liu IT (2022) Special issue introduction: what is the new state capitalism? Contemp Polit 28(3):245–263

Alter KJ (2021) Contracting v. multilateralism in global economic governance: before, during and after the WTO. In: Elsig M, Polanco R, van den Bossche P (eds) International economic dispute settlement: demise or transformation? World Trade Forum Series. Cambridge University Press

Ascari R (2010) Political risk insurance: an industry in search of a business? SACE Work Pap No 10:3. https://www.sace.it/docs/default-source/documenti-importati-(pubblicazioni)/wp12_political_risk_xcx-pdf.pdf?Status=Master&sfvrsn=0

Balding C (2012) Sovereign wealth funds: the new intersection of money and politics. Oxford University Press

Babić M, Dixon AD, Liu IT (eds) (2022) The political economy of geoeconomics: Europe in a changing world. Palgrave Macmillan

Baldwin D (1997) The concept of security. Rev Int Stud 23(1):5–26

Bauerle DS, Meunier S (2021) The big screen: Mapping the diffusion of foreign investment screening mechanisms. https://papers.ssrn.com/sol3/papers.cfm?abstract_id=3913248

Bian C (2020) National security review of foreign investment: a comparative legal analysis of China, the United States and the European Union. Routledge

Blackwill RD, Harris JM (2016) War by other means: geoeconomics and statecraft. Harvard University Press

Blomström M, Kokko A (1997) How foreign investment affects host countries. Policy Research Working Paper No 1745

Bonnitcha J (2019) Investment wars: contestation and confusion in debate about investment liberalization. J Int Econ Law 22(4):629–654

Brennan L, Vecchi A (2021) The European response to Chinese outbound foreign direct investment: introducing a dynamic analytical framework. Dev Change 52(5):1066–1089

Bruff I (2014) The rise of authoritarian neoliberalism. Rethink Marxism 26(1):113–129

Busse M, Hefeker C (2007) Political risk, institutions and foreign direct investment. Eur J Polit Econ 23(2):397–415

Carroll T (2023) Constrained, competing and eking – the limits of economic statecraft in East Asia after national development. Pac Rev 36(5):949–977

Casey CA (2020) Nationals abroad: globalization, individual rights, and the making of modern international law. Cambridge University Press

Choer MH, Wigell M (2020) The emergence of strategic capitalism: geoeconomics, corporate statecraft and the repurposing of the global economy (FIIA Working Paper 117). Finnish Institute of International Affairs

Choer MH, Wigell M (2022) Balancing dependence: the quest for autonomy and the rise of corporate geoeconomics. In: Babić M, Dixon AD, Liu IT (eds) The political economy of geoeconomics: Europe in a changing world. Springer, pp 29–55

Cutler C (2000) Globalization, law and transnational corporations: a deepening of market discipline. In: Cohn T, McBride S, Wiseman J (eds) Power in the global era: grounding globalization. Springer, pp 53–66

Dixon AD (2017) The state as institutional investor: unpacking the geographical political economy of sovereign wealth funds. In: Martin R, Pollard J (eds) Handbook of the geographies of money and finance. Edward Elgar, pp 279–297
Dixon AD, Schena PJ, Capapé J (2022) Sovereign wealth funds: between the state and markets. Agenda
Drezner DW, Farrell H, Newman AL (eds) (2021) The uses and abuses of weaponized interdependence. Brookings Institution Press
Dworkin R (1977) No right answer? In: Hacker PMS, Raz J (eds) Law, morality, and society. Clarendon Press
du Plessis Q (2021) Sources of legal indeterminacy. South Afr Law J 138:115
Eichensehr KE, Hwang C (2023) National security creep in corporate transactions. Colum Law Rev 123(2):549–614
Esplugues MC (2018) Foreign investment, strategic assets and national security. Intersentia
European Commission (2021) First annual report on the screening of foreign direct investments into the Union and report on the implementation of Regulation (EU) 2021/821 setting up a Union regime for the control of exports, brokering, technical assistance, transit and transfer of dual-use items, Publications Office of the European Union. https://data.europa.eu/doi/10.2781/90680
European Commission (2023) Joint Communication to the European Parliament, the European Council and the Council on "European Economic Security Strategy". JOIN/2023/20 final
Farrell H, Newman AL (2019) Weaponized interdependence: how global economic networks shape state coercion. Int Secur 44(1):42–79
Farrell H, Newman A (2020). Will the coronavirus end globalization as we know it? Foreign Affairs. https://www.foreignaffairs.com/world/will-coronavirus-end-globalization-we-know-it
Fjäder C, Helwig N, Wigell M (2021) Recognizing 'geoeconomic risk': rethinking corporate risk management for the era of great-power competition. FIIA Briefing Paper
Fujii K, Yodogawa N, Wako M (2021) Foreign investment screening in Japan. In: Hindelang S, Moberg A (eds) YSEC yearbook of socio-economic constitutions 2020: a common European law on investment screening (CELIS). Springer, pp 379–401
Gallie WB (1956) Essentially contested concepts. Pro Aristo Soc, 56, 167–198
Gehrke T (2021 Apr) Threading the trade needle on open strategic autonomy? In: Helwig N (ed) Strategic autonomy and the transformation of the EU (FIIA Report 67). Finnish Institute of International Affairs, pp 89–105
Gertz G, Evers MM (2020) Geoeconomic competition: will state capitalism win? Wash Q 43(2):117–136
Gertz G (2021) Investment screening before, during, and after COVID-19. Glob Perspect 2(1):24538
Gourinchas PO, Jeanne O (2002) On the benefits of capital account liberalization for emerging economies. Unpublished manuscript presented at the World Bank conference "Financial Globalization: A Blessing or a Curse."
Greenhill KM, Krause P, Art R (2018) Coercion: an analytical overview. In: Greenhill KM, Krause P (eds) Coercion: the power to hurt in international politics. Oxford University Press, pp 3–32
Griffith-Jones S, Ocampo JA (2011) The rationale for sovereign wealth funds: a developing country perspective. In: Bolton P, Samama F, Stiglitz J (eds) Sovereign wealth funds and long-term investing. Columbia University Press, pp 60–66
Grimson A, Kessler G (2006) On Argentina and the Southern Cone: neoliberalism and national imaginations. Routledge
Grünberg N, Brussee V (2021 Apr 9). China's 14th Five-Year Plan—strengthening the domestic base to become a superpower. Merics. https://merics.org/en/short-analysis/chinas-14th-five-year-plan-strengthening-domestic-base-become-superpower

Hallberg J (2021) Foreign investment screening in Finland, Norway, Sweden and Denmark. In: Hindelang S, Moberg A (eds) YSEC yearbook of socio-economic constitutions 2020: a common European law on investment screening (CELIS). Springer, pp 209–226
Hanemann T, Witzke M, Vest C, Dudley L, Featherston R (2022) An outbound investment screening regime for the United States? Rhodium Group and National Committee on US-China Relations
Helwig N, Wigell M (2022 Mar) The EU's quest for geoeconomic power: FIIA Briefing Paper 334. Finnish Institute of International Affairs
Hindelang S, Moberg A (eds) (2021) YSEC yearbook of socio-economic constitutions 2020: a common European law on Investment screening (CELIS). Springer Nature
Hobér K, Fellenbaum J (2015) Political risk insurance and investment treaty protection. In: Bungenberg M, Griebel J, Hobe S, Reinisch A, Kim YI (eds) International investment law: a handbook. C. H. Beck, pp 1517,1519
Hollnagel E (2021) Managing for security. In: Jacobs G, Suojanen I, Horton K, Bayerl P (eds) International security management. Springer, pp 43–53
Hymer SH (1960) The international operations of national firms, A study of direct foreign investment [Doctoral dissertation, Massachusetts Institute of Technology]. ProQuest Theses and Dissertations Global
Jaśkowski M, Pawłowski S (2021) Foreign investment screening in Poland, Lithuania, and Latvia. In: Hindelang S, Moberg A (eds) YSEC yearbook of socio-economic constitutions 2020: a common European law on investment screening (CELIS). Springer, pp 139–186
Jepson N (2020) In China's wake: how the commodity boom transformed development strategies in the Global South. Columbia University Press
Kaczmarczyk P (2023) Foreign direct investment in neoclassical theory of international trade: a conceptual weak spot. Int J Polit Econ 52(1):70–87
Kaushal A (2009) Revisiting history: how the past matters for the present backlash against the foreign investment regime. Harv Int Law J 50:491
Knight FH (1921) Risk, uncertainty and profit. Houghton Mifflin
Keohane RO (1984) After hegemony: cooperation and discord in the world political economy. Princeton University Press
Keohane RO, Nye JS (1987) Power and interdependence revisited. International Organization 41 (4):725–753
Kress KJ (1989) Legal indeterminacy. Calif Law Rev 77:283
Kurlantzick J (2016) State capitalism: how the return of statism is transforming the world. Oxford University Press
Lall S, Streeten P (1977) Foreign investment, transnationals and developing countries. Springer
Lavery S, McDaniel S, Schmid D (2022) European strategic autonomy: new agenda, old constraints. In: Babić MA, Dixon D, Liu IT (eds) The political economy of geoeconomics: Europe in a changing world. Springer, pp 57–80
Polanco RL (2019) The return of the home state to investor-state disputes: bringing back diplomatic protection? Cambridge University Press
Lenihan AT (2018) Balancing power without weapons: state intervention into cross-border mergers and acquisitions. Cambridge University Press
Leonard M (2021) The age of unpeace: how connectivity causes conflict. Penguin Books
Lichtenbaum G, Ribner DJ (2021) Foreign investment screening in the USA. In: Hindelang S, Moberg A (eds) YSEC yearbook of socio-economic constitutions 2020: a common European law on Investment screening (CELIS). Springer, pp 363–378
Liu Z (2008) Foreign direct investment and technology spillovers: theory and evidence. J Dev Econ 85(1–2):176–193
London B, Ross RJ (1995) The political sociology of foreign direct investment: global capitalism and capital mobility, 1965–1980. Int J Comp Sociol 36(3–4):198–219

McDonagh N, Pohl JH (2023). Reconceptualizing the legal-economic nexus in the era of great power rivalry: the case of foreign direct investment screening [Conference paper]. Princeton University
McMillan SM (1999) Foreign direct investment in three regions of the South at the end of the twentieth century. Springer
Mandelbaum M (2014) The road to global prosperity. Simon & Schuster
Moon PW (2022) When the target fights back: Economic coercion and interstate conflict in the era of global value chains [Doctoral dissertation, UC Irvine]. ProQuest Theses and Dissertations Global
Moran TH (2004) International political risk management: the brave new world. World Bank and Multilateral Investment Guarantee Agency
Moran TH (2009) Three threats: an analytical framework for the CFIUS process, vol 89. Peterson Institute for International Economics
Moran TH, Graham EM, Blomström M (2005) Introduction and overview. In: Moran TH, Graham EM, Blomström M (eds) Does foreign direct investment promote development? Institute for International Economics, pp 1–19
Moran TH, Oldenski L (2013) Foreign direct investment in the United States: benefits, suspicions, and risks with special attention to FDI from China, vol 100. Peterson Institute for International Economics
Muchlinski P (2007) Multinational enterprises and the law. Oxford University Press
Musacchio A, Lazzarini S (2014) Reinventing state capitalism: leviathan in business, Brazil and beyond. Harvard University Press
Musacchio A, Lazzarini SG, Aguilera RV (2015) New varieties of state capitalism: strategic and governance implications. Acad Manage Perspect 29(1):115–131
Newcombe AP, Paradell L (2009) Law and practice of investment treaties: standards of treatment. Kluwer Law Int BV 488–500
OECD (2020) Investment screening in times of COVID-19 and beyond
OECD (2021) Investment policy developments in 62 economies between 16 October 2020 and 15 March 2021
OECD (2022) Framework for screening Foreign direct investment into the EU: Assessing effectiveness and efficiency
Pohl JH (2020a) Emergency, security and strategic autonomy in EU economic regulation. ERA Forum 21:143–154
Pohl JH (2020b) The impact of investment treaty commitments on the design and operation of EU investment screening mechanisms. In: Hindelang S, Moberg A (eds) YSEC yearbook of socio-economic constitutions 2020. Springer, pp 725–768
Pohl JH 2023 Open strategic autonomy and the new geoeconomics: consequences for EU trade policy Institute of International Trade Policy Brief, vol 18. University of Adelaide
Protopsaltis PP (2019) Investment guarantees and political risk insurance. In: Krajewski M, Hoffmann RT (eds) Research handbook on foreign direct investment. Edward Elgar Publishing, p 299
Raik K, Blockmans S, Dandashly A, Noutcheva G, Osypchuk A, Suslov A (2023) Tackling the constraints on EU foreign policy towards Ukraine: from strategic denial to geopolitical awakening. JOINT Res Pap 20
Rietveld M, Toledano P (2017) The new frontiers of sovereign investment. Columbia University Press
Roberts A, Choer MH, Ferguson V (2019) Toward a geoeconomic order in international trade and investment. J Int Econ Law 22(4):655–676
Rytter Sunesen E, Juul Henriksen J (2021) The economics of FDI screening. In: Bourgeois JH (ed) EU framework for foreign direct investment control. Kluwer Law International BV, pp 3–21
Saari S (2021b). Russia's corona diplomacy and geoeconomic competition: a Sputnik moment? FIIA Briefing Paper, 315. Finnish Institute of International Affairs

Schott JJ (2023) Economic sanctions against Russia: how effective? How durable? Peterson Inst Int Econ Policy Brief 23:3

Segal A (2021) Huawei, 5G, and weaponized interdependence. In: Drezner DW, Farrell H, Newman AL (eds) The uses and abuses of weaponized interdependence. The Brookings Institution

Shirlow E (2021) Judging at the interface: deference to state decision-making authority in International Adjudication. Cambridge University Press

Sinkkonen V, Ruokamo A (2022) Vaccines as contentious connectivity in the Indo-Pacific: the case of US-China competition during the COVID-19 pandemic. Finnish Institute of International Affairs

Solum L (1987) On the indeterminacy crisis: critiquing critical dogma. Univ Chicago Law Rev 54:462

Stompfe P (2021) Foreign investment screening in Germany and France. In: Hindelang S, Moberg A (eds) YSEC yearbook of socio-economic constitutions 2020: a common European law on investment screening (CELIS). Springer, pp 79–115

Tushnet M (2005) Critical legal theory (without modifiers) in the United States. J Polit Philos 13(1):99

Vargiu P (2021) Foreign investment screening in Italy, Spain, Portugal, and Greece. In: Hindelang S, Moberg A (eds) YSEC yearbook of socio-economic constitutions 2020: a common European law on investment screening (CELIS). Springer, pp 117–137

Vaughan EJ, Vaughan, TM (1996) Fundamentals of risk and insurance. Wiley

Verellen T (2021) When integration by stealth meets public security: the EU Foreign Direct Investment Screening Regulation. Leg Issues Econ Integr 48(1):19–41

von Krogh G, Rossi-Lamastra C, Haefliger S (2012) Phenomenon-based research in management and organization science: when is it rigorous, and does it matter? Long Range Plann 45(4):277–298

Wagner K (2023) Determining the role of FDI screening in international investment law. In: Pohl JH, Papadopoulos T, Wiesenthal J, Warchol J (eds) Weaponising investments, vol 2. Springer

Wigell M, Borchert H, Christie EH, Fjäder C, Hartwig LH (2022a) Navigating geoeconomic risks: toward an international business risk and resilience monitor FIIA Report, vol 71. The Finnish Institute of International Affairs

Wigell M, Deschryvere M, Fjäder C, Helwig N, Kaitila V, Koski H, Seilonen J, Suominen A (2022b) Europe facing geoeconomics: assessing Finland's and the EU's risks and options in the technological rivalry. Prime Minister's Office, Republic of Finland

Wigell M, Scholvin S, Aaltola M (2018) Geo-economics and power politics in the twenty-first century: the revival of economic statecraft. Routledge

Yackee JW (2014) Political risk and international investment law. Duke J Comp Int Law 24(3):477–479

Chapter 3
National Security as Subject Matter of Investment Arbitration

Abstract This chapter examines the intersection of national security and international arbitration by exploring how disputes related to investment screening are arbitrated under international law. It critically examines the absence of a mandatory rule that precludes arbitration for disputes involving national security considerations and demonstrates that public policy does not inherently restrict such arbitration. The analysis reveals that unless explicitly excluded, disputes affecting national security are presumed to fall within the scope of an arbitral tribunal's jurisdiction. This chapter underscores the capacity of international tribunals to handle sensitive matters by balancing respect for state sovereignty with the obligations of international investment law. It concludes that national security can be justiciable in arbitration, provided that clear consent is given, to maintain the transparency and predictability essential to the arbitration process.

3.1 Introduction

It is widely recognized that not all disputes may, in a legally valid sense, be settled by arbitration, even with the agreement or consent of the parties to the dispute.[1] Hence, the law applicable to the arbitral proceedings in question may impose certain limitations of a mandatory nature to the availability of arbitration as a legal remedy, which may override the parties' mutual consent to have a dispute settled by arbitration.[2]

As a point of departure, it has also long been held that a state is free to decide to submit any kind of dispute to settlement by arbitration.[3] The basis for the jurisdiction

[1] Born (2021a) §§6.01–6.03; Blackaby et al. (2009) 80; Mistelis (2007) 217–229; Fouchard and Goldman (1999).

[2] Lew et al. (2003) 187–188; Kirry (1996) 373–390.

[3] States are unlikely to be willing to consent to have all possible disputes settled by arbitration, as will be further examined in this chapter.

J. H. Pohl, *Arbitration of Disputes related to National Security Screening of Foreign Investments*, EYIEL Monographs - Studies in European and International Economic Law 50,
https://doi.org/10.1007/978-3-032-26342-1_3

of international arbitral tribunals is state consent.[4] Nevertheless, it is the practice of states to rely on the concept of public policy to limit the availability of arbitration as a legal remedy for the purpose of ensuring that the activity of arbitrators does not undermine the rule of law or the fundamental values of society (which would be self-defeating from the point of view of the state).[5] By virtue of public policy, states limit the scope of arbitration ex ante (non-arbitrability) and reserve the right to restrict the effects of arbitral awards ex post (non-enforceability). These two aspects correlate: the more restriction ex ante, the less need for restriction ex post.[6]

In the relationship between a state and an investor, the consent to arbitration is commonly expressed in a treaty containing an arbitration clause. It may also result from an investment contract between the state and an individual investor or from the national legislation of a state, which provides for such a right in favour of the investor, as well as from ad hoc consent. The clauses contained in a treaty, as well as other legal provisions providing for this possibility, are analysed as offers of arbitration made by the state and accepted by an investor when it brings a case before the arbitral tribunal.[7]

If no (overriding) mandatory rules of public policy[8] precluded a state from consenting to have disputes relating to national security matters settled by arbitration, then how would such consent be interpreted? Is there a presumption against interpreting the consent to encompass disputes that are not of a legal nature or that concern matters affecting the state's vital interests, including its national security interests?

Answering these questions first requires examining whether mandatory limitations apply to the consent of a host state to submit to arbitration in the case of an investment dispute relating to its national security (3.2) and, second, the existence of an implied presumption that the consent to arbitrate must be interpreted restrictively (3.3). The chapter ends with concluding remarks (3.4).

3.2 National Security and Public Policy Challenges to Arbitrability and Enforceability

This subchapter examines devices used by arbitral tribunals that achieve complete deference (i.e. submission) to the host state's decision-making authority on matters of national security, with specific reference to investment screening. As discussed

[4] In the *Corfu Channel* case, the ICJ affirmed the fundamental rule that consent provides the jurisdictional basis for international courts and tribunals.

[5] Lalive (1987), 258, 262; Mistelis (2000) 248; Hanotiau (1996) 391–404; Paulsson (2005), 601–18; Lehmann (2004) 753–75; Fazilatfar (2012) 289–314; Seelig (2009) 116.

[6] Hanotiau et al. (2008); Wolff (2019) paras. 158–163, 492; Barcelo (2014) 14–24.

[7] See Schreuer (2009) 196–205; Delaume (1998) 161–164; Paulsson (1995) 234.

[8] On this term, see further Subchapter 3.2 below.

in Chap. 2, devices of deference include any method used in legal reasoning to justify adjudicatory deference (i.e. the yielding by adjudicatory authority to executive authority). In this subchapter, special attention is focused on submission on the basis of overriding or mandatory considerations. The word "mandatory" is used here in the sense of overriding the wishes of the parties to a dispute—the investor and the host state.[9]

The following paragraphs outline the structure of such devices, which are centred on the concept of public policy. As discussed below, an arbitrator must consider what may happen to an arbitral award after it has been rendered (the post-award phase), such as whether national courts may refuse to recognize or enforce the award or even set aside the award. Therefore, pre-award and post-award considerations are analysed in the present context.

This pre-versus post-award perspective reflects the nature of international arbitration. Investment arbitration proceedings are often conducted under the supervision of a national court, which must recognize the arbitration agreement and may intervene during the arbitration proceedings by granting injunctive relief. After the proceedings are over, the national court may be asked to set aside the award, recognize or refuse its recognition, enforce it, or refuse its enforcement. Moreover, the winning party may seek for the award to be recognized or enforced in third countries. These pre-versus post-award phases look noticeably different in the event that states commit to not allowing post-award challenges to arbitral awards, which is the case under the Washington Convention, as further discussed in this chapter.

This subchapter is structured as follows. After first examining the general public policy-related limitations applicable to the availability of arbitration as a means of dispute settlement (3.2.1), the question of whether an investment dispute relating to the host state's national security may be settled by arbitration is addressed by (a) first examining how public policy challenges may be brought under the New York Convention (3.2.2), before (b) analysing which restrictions to such challenges may derive from the Washington Convention (3.2.3). The conclusion of the subchapter is summarized at the end (3.2.4).

3.2.1 General

A flexible notion, public policy defies attempts at precise definition.[10] Its content is not unlimited, however, but is informed by its sources and applications to the dispute in question.[11] Despite the difficulty in giving precision to the concept of

---

[9] Kleinheisterkamp (2018).

[10] Lew et al. (2003) 721–724; Lalive (1987) 258; Fazilatfar (2012) 291–292. See also Blackaby et al. (2015) ¶11.61 ("the 'public policy' exception, discussed below, enables some States to play the game less fairly than others"); Gaillard and Savage (1999) 997; Born (2021a) §19.04[B][1]; §25.04[H][1]; §26.05[C][9][g].

[11] Sheppard (2004); Kessedjian (2007) 857; Fazilatfar (2012) 292.

public policy, a differentiation of such a concept in terms of its scope and content is commonly made. When approaching this subject, one must distinguish between national public policy,[12] international public policy,[13] and transnational public policy.[14]

First, the application of the concept of national public policy in arbitration proceedings is, given the territorial nature, subject to the determination of the applicable law.[15] If the parties have agreed on a specific substantive law for the dispute, the national concept of public policy, lex contractus, applies.[16]

Second, because arbitrators are under a duty to render an award, which must be binding and enforceable,[17] arbitrators must also consider the public policy deriving from the applicable lex arbitri or the law of the place of performance,[18] as well as the public policy of the country or countries in which recognition or enforcement of the award is or is likely to be sought.[19] This rationale supports the notion of international public policy, which comprises the most basic norms of national public policy.[20] For example, if applying the national public policy according to the lex contractus would violate the international public policy in force at the seat of the arbitral tribunal or the place of enforcement, the arbitrators should also consider or apply the latter or risk that the award will be set aside or that its recognition or enforcement will be refused.

---

[12] Catherine Kessedjian defined this term as "those fundamental rules, developed by each State, which are of utmost importance for that State's society and from which the citizens (and very often residents) of that State cannot derogate. It is territorial in nature." See Kessedjian (2007) 859. See also Lalive (1987) 260; Fry (2009); Seelig (2009) 119–120.

[13] Buchanan (1988); Lalive (1987) 266–269; Kessedjian (2007) 859–860; Seelig (2009) 120–122.

[14] Kessedjian (2007) 860–862; Lalive (1987) 272–275; Fazilatfar (2012) 291–294.

[15] Kreindler (2003) 241; Seelig (2009) 119–120; Wolff (2019) 493–498.

[16] However, in certain circumstances, the arbitrator should also consider the norms of other national laws (e.g. the lex arbitri, the lex societatis or the law of the place of performance). The extent to which the arbitrator is obliged to do so depends on whether the violation of public policy constitutes a violation of a mandatory provision, for example, the law applicable at the place of arbitration or the law of the place of performance.

[17] See Subsection 3.2.2.2 below. Generally, see Lew (1999).

[18] Wolff (2019) para. 492.

[19] Gaillard and Savage (1999) para 559; see also ICC Rules Article 35; for a detailed discussion of whether an arbitration tribunal having its seat in Geneva should take into account the provisions of the lex causae, see Partial Award ICC case no 8420, XXV YBCA 328 (2000) 330 et seq.; Kreindler (2003) 241.

[20] For example, Art. V 2 (b) of the New York Convention provides that the recognition or enforcement of the arbitral award may be refused if such recognition or enforcement would be contrary to the public policy of the country in which recognition or enforcement is sought. See Lalive (1987) p. 264: "The notion of the international public order of a given community, here a state, consists of a set of rules or principles relating to a wide range of areas and of varying intensity, forming a kind of 'hard core' of legal or moral values or to express it, be it in its negative or be in its positive function".

Third, given the transnational nature of enforcing international arbitral awards and the uncertainty as to where recognition or enforcement will be sought, arbitrators also consider the application of transnational (or truly international) public policy.[21] Unlike international public policy, which is country-specific, transnational public policy is commonly understood as being detached from a specific legal system, comprising a set of overarching fundamental norms, principles, and values common to the legal orders of most, if not all, states.[22]

As follows, the notion of public policy is multifaceted and requires careful consideration of which of the public policy concepts to apply in the specific context of the arbitration.[23] In terms of content, the concepts of national, international, and transnational public policy overlap, as explained above, insofar as international public policy is generally narrower than national public policy and encompasses the essential and fundamental rules and values of a state's national public policy. Likewise, transnational public policy encompasses the most fundamental norms of public policy, which each state should ideally have enshrined in its legal order and which, therefore, overlaps with a state's international public policy. Given these significant overlaps and the international nature of international arbitration, which is not bound by any national legal system, the following analysis focuses on the content of transnational public policy before discussing in detail its implications for arbitration.

As to the content of public policy in general and transnational public policy in particular, a distinction is often made between procedural and substantive public policy. Procedural public policy concerns the procedural aspects of arbitration and comprises certain basic procedural rules, principles and values, which have accrued and evolved and found expression in treaty practice and arbitral jurisprudence.[24] They include requirements that arbitral tribunals be impartial,[25] that the making of the award not be brought about or influenced by fraud or corruption,[26] that equal treatment be observed in the appointment of the arbitral tribunal,[27] and that the

[21] Lalive (1987) 272–275; Kessedjian (2007) 860–862.

[22] Sheppard (2003) 217–248 ("[Transnational public policy] constitute[s] an international consensus on universal standards and accepted norms of behavior that must always apply. The concept of transnational public policy encompasses the basic rules of natural law, the principles of universal justice, the jus cogens of international law, and the general principles of morality accepted by so-called 'civilized nations'".); Kessedjian (2007) 861–862 ("Transnational public policy is composed of mandatory norms which may be imposed on actors in the market either because they have been created by those actors themselves or by civil society at large, or because they have been widely accepted by different societies around the world. These norms aim at being universal. They are the sign of the maturity of the international communities (that of the merchants and that of the civil societies) who know very well that there are limits to their activities".)

[23] Sheppard (2004) 34.

[24] Gebauer and Berner (2019); Tosun (2019, pp. 48–51).

[25] Mayer and Sheppard (2003) 255; Rubino-Sammartano (2014, p. 516).

[26] Brunet et al. (2006, p. 291); Fouchard and Goldman (1999, p. 948).

[27] Rubino-Sammartano (2014, p. 521).

rules of procedural justice be observed,[28] including the right to a fair or reasonable opportunity to present one's case.[29]

Substantive public policy governs the rights and obligations of a disputing party in relation to the subject matter of the dispute. It thus has a bearing on the merits of the claim and the question of the jurisdiction of the arbitral tribunal, the arbitrability of the subject matter in dispute, and the admissibility of the claims.[30] Like transnational procedural public policy, the content of transnational substantive public policy is subject to evolution, as evidenced in arbitral case law.[31] Rules and principles that, over the years, have taken on a universal character and are generally considered part of the transnational public order include the principle of good faith,[32] the prohibition of abuse of rights,[33] pacta sunt servanda,[34] the prohibition of expropriation without compensation,[35] and the prohibition of unjustified discrimination.[36] In addition, fundamental principles such as the prohibition of corruption,[37] genocide,[38] piracy,[39] terrorism,[40] slavery,[41] drug trafficking,[42] and paedophilia[43] are also part of the transnational public order, as they are contrary to good morals.[44]

When raised during arbitral proceedings, the impact of public policy is to deny the existence of a dispute that may be settled by arbitration and result in a legally valid arbitral award (non-arbitrability).[45] When raised after arbitral proceedings, the impact is to challenge the recognition of an arbitral award as legally valid or the enforceability of an award in the jurisdiction where such recognition or enforceability is sought. In investment arbitration, public policy challenges, if sustained, have the effect of justifying complete deference (i.e. submission) to the decision-making authority of the respondent host state as to the settlement of the dispute.[46]

[28] Zeller et al. (2021, pp. 110–113).

[29] Sheppard (2004, p. 8).

[30] Gebauer and Berner (2019); Yang (2015).

[31] See further Reisman (2007).

[32] Kunz (2016); Lalive (1987, p. 295); Sheppard (2004, p. 8).

[33] Lalive (1987, p. 295); Mayer and Sheppard (2003, p. 255); Sheppard (2004, p. 8).

[34] Kunz (2016); Sheppard (2004, p. 4); Wolff (2019, para. 560).

[35] Sheppard (2004, p. 9); Wolff ibid.

[36] Fouchard and Goldman (1999, p. 962); Mayer and Sheppard (2003, p. 255); Wolff (2019, para. 560).

[37] Wolff (2019, para. 576).

[38] Sheppard (2004, p. 5).

[39] Sheppard (2004, p. 10); Wolff (2019, para. 575).

[40] Lalive (1987, p. 306); Wolff (2019, para. 575).

[41] Lalive (1987, p. 289); Wolff ibid.

[42] Sheppard (2004, p. 10); Wolff (2019, para. 575).

[43] Sheppard (2004, p. 10); Wolff (2019, para. 575).

[44] Lalive (1987, p. 292); Wolff (2019, para. 560).

[45] Lew et al. (2003, pp. 707–708).

[46] Born (2021a, §17.05[H][1]); Wolff (2019, para. 489–492).

Therefore, public policy in international arbitration constitutes an interface between the national and international planes.

In the context of international arbitration, respondent states may invoke public policy at any stage of the proceedings before the merits of the case have been heard to exclude the dispute from the scope of arbitration[47] by objecting to such effect before either the arbitral tribunal[48] or a competent domestic court (anti-arbitration injunction).[49] Conversely, a respondent state may invoke public policy after an arbitral award has been rendered against it to deny the effects of such an award,[50] either by requesting the setting aside (sometimes referred to as "annulment") of the award[51] or by requesting the denial of recognition or enforcement of the award.[52]

These two aspects are closely related: the more effectively a state defines the public policy issues it reserves for ex-post control (through restrictions on recognition and enforceability), the less its need to restrict ex ante the powers of arbitrators (through arbitrability) and vice versa.[53]

The arbitrability of the dispute is a precondition for the jurisdiction of an arbitral tribunal and involves the question of what issues or classes of disputes may legally be resolved by arbitration.[54] As such, non-arbitrability precludes the arbitral tribunal's jurisdiction to hear the dispute and the subsequent question of admissibility.[55]

Arbitrability is a jurisdictional precondition, so tribunals have the duty and authority, pursuant to the doctrine of competence-competence,[56] to determine the scope of their jurisdiction, including the question of whether the dispute submitted to it is arbitrable.[57] If sustained at the pre-merits phase, a challenge of non-arbitrability concludes the proceedings.[58] Nevertheless, the arbitral tribunal's competence may be challenged after the rendering of the arbitral award as a ground for denial of recognition or enforcement of the award.[59] If successfully invoked

[47] Born (2021b, pp. 1045–1059, 1133–1137); Blackaby et al. (2015, pp. 110–112, 415–420); Lew et al. (2003, pp. 149–151).

[48] See, e.g. *Plama Consortium Ltd. v Republic of Bulgaria*, ICSID Case No. ARB/03/24, Award of 27 August 2008, at para 146; *Inceysa Vallisoletana S.L. v Republic of El Salvador*, ICSID Case. No. ARB/03/26, Award of 2 August 2006, at para 249.

[49] Article II (3) of the New York Convention. See further Subsection 3.2.2.1 below. See also Lew et al. (2003, p. 362); Nollkaemper (2006, pp. 301–303, 312–321).

[50] Blackaby et al. (2015, pp. 438–439).

[51] Blackaby et al. (2015, pp. 583–586); Markert and Bubrowski (2015).

[52] Bungenberg and Reinisch (2020).

[53] Barcelo (2014); Hanotiau et al. (2008); Wolff (2019, paras. 158–163, 492).

[54] See Lew et al. (2003, p. 187): "Arbitrability involves the simple question of what type of issues can and cannot be submitted to arbitration".

[55] Brekoulakis (2009).

[56] Waibel (2015, §§ 75–79).

[57] Lew et al. (2003, pp. 219–221); Waibel (2015).

[58] Lew et al. ibid.

[59] Kröll (2015) 1495.

after an arbitral award has been rendered, the lack of arbitrability may also justify the setting aside of the award.[60]

As a conception of sovereignty,[61] arbitrability encapsulates the extent to which states may legally subject themselves to the jurisdiction of a dispute resolution system (beyond its control)[62] and, conversely, the extent to which they retain an inalienable freedom to unilaterally deny such jurisdiction with respect to non-arbitrable disputes despite any previously given consent to arbitration.[63] Hence, whether a dispute is arbitrable is independent of the disputing parties' consent to arbitrate.[64] As such, arbitrability delimits the freedom of the parties of an arbitration agreement to submit disputes to arbitration involving sensitive policy issues concerning the public interest.

A distinction is generally made between objective and subjective arbitrability. Objective arbitrability (also referred to as arbitrability ratione materiae) refers to disputes which have a subject matter that neither of the disputants is allowed to bind themselves to have settled by arbitration.[65] As such, objective arbitrability derives directly from the nature of the subject matter in dispute, irrespective of the identity or volition of the parties to the dispute.[66]

By contrast, the notion of subjective arbitrability (also referred to as arbitrability ratione personae) denotes restrictions that may apply to the capacity of either of the parties to an arbitration agreement to consent to arbitrate disputes of a certain subject matter.[67] In other words, even if a dispute is objectively arbitrable (i.e. in principle, the dispute could be settled by arbitration), a disputing party may nevertheless be incapable of validly submitting the dispute to arbitration due to lack of internal competence (i.e. insufficient delegated power). National law frequently provides that consent to arbitration may not be validly given by certain persons or entities in respect of certain types of disputes.[68] Thus, subjective arbitrability delimits the legal capacity of a disputant to enter into a valid arbitration agreement and to validly give consent to arbitrate.[69]

---

[60] Blackaby et al. (2015) 586.

[61] Carbonneau and Janson (1994) 193; Schwab (1995) 814; Wallace (2002) 944.

[62] Sever (1991) 1661, 1664.

[63] See generally Mistelis (2009) 5–9.

[64] Jones (1997) 121–149.

[65] See Lew et al. (2003) para 9–1; Poudret and Besson (2007) para 326; Fouchard and Goldman (1999) para 532.

[66] Wolff (2019) para. 430.

[67] See generally Quinke (2012).

[68] See Schreuer (2009).

[69] A lack of subjective arbitrability implies the absence of a procedural condition precedent for the tribunal to assume jurisdiction over the dispute in question and is more precisely a substantive defect that renders the arbitration agreement a nullity. Consequently, while objective non-arbitrability precludes jurisdiction over the relevant dispute, a lack of subjective arbitrability may be raised as a bar against the exercise of jurisdiction over the dispute in a particular case

Importantly, even in the case of a dispute deemed to be (objectively and subjectively) arbitrable, public policy may still be raised as a bar against the recognition or enforcement of an arbitral award in a legal order.[70] This issue comprises cases where the subject matter of the dispute may, in principle, be settled by arbitration—or at least not uniformly excluded from arbitration—but where the effects of recognition or enforcement of the award nevertheless would be contrary to public policy because of its content or the manner in which it came about.[71]

In the context of investment arbitration, the ability to raise public policy challenges, and thus the availability of arbitration as a legal remedy, depends crucially on the application of international arbitration conventions, as discussed next. Most states are parties to the 1958 Convention on the Recognition and Enforcement of Foreign Arbitral Awards (i.e. the New York Convention), which generally governs the refusal of recognition and enforcement of arbitral awards by the domestic courts of the contracting states.[72] Moreover, investment arbitration cases may be brought under the Convention on the Settlement of Investment Disputes between States and Nationals of Other States (i.e. the Washington Convention),[73] which then overrides the provisions of the New York Convention.[74] To date, the vast majority of concluded investment arbitration proceedings have been brought under the Washington Convention.[75] It is important, however, to understand the situation that applies in the absence of this Convention before examining how the Convention modifies the situation.

3.2.2 Public Policy Challenges Under the New York Convention

The general situation, which applies to cases not subject to the Washington Convention, is that when an investor has won an arbitration case against a host

---

and thus renders the disputed claims inadmissible. On admissibility, see generally Waibel (2015) 1218, 1274.

[70] Böckstiegel (1986) 183.

[71] This distinction is captured by the different wordings of Article V(2)(a) and (b) of the New York Convention. Whereas Article V(2)(a) refers to the "subject matter of the difference" not being capable of settlement by arbitration, Article V(2)(b) emphasizes the acts of recognition or enforcement of the award. Even if the award concerns an arbitrable subject matter, recognizing or enforcing that award may nevertheless be contrary to public policy. In other words, the two paragraphs are not entirely overlapping in scope.

[72] Convention on the Recognition and Enforcement of Foreign Arbitral Awards, signed in New York on 10 June 1958, 330 UNTS 38 (New York Convention).

[73] Convention on the Settlement of Investment Disputes between States and Nationals of Other States, signed in Washington on 18 March 1965, 575 UNTS 159 (Washington Convention).

[74] Born (2021a) §1.09; Kröll (2015) 1483–1484.

[75] UNCTAD Investment Policy Hub.

state in a non-arbitrable dispute and then seeks to enforce the award in another state, the other state may refuse to recognize or enforce the award in certain situations. Article V(2)(a) of the New York Convention codifies the principle that states may refuse to recognize and enforce arbitral awards in respect of disputes arising out of subject matters that are incapable of settlement by arbitration (i.e. are not arbitrable).[76] Importantly, under this article, the issue of arbitrability is determined under the law applicable in the state where recognition and enforcement are sought.[77]

Another, more far-reaching consequence of a lack of arbitrability is that the losing party may apply to have the award set aside by a competent court in the state whose laws apply in the seat of arbitration (*lex loci arbitri*).[78] In line with the UNCITRAL Model Law on International Commercial Arbitration,[79] the domestic law of many states provides that an award may be set aside if a competent court in the state of the place of arbitration finds that the subject matter of the dispute is incapable of settlement by arbitration under the law of such state.[80] In cases where the award has been set aside, all other states where the successful claimant seeks enforcement may, in turn, pursuant to the New York Convention, refuse recognition and enforcement of that award upon request by the losing respondent.[81]

The New York Convention is addressed to the contracting states and their courts and gives such courts a supervisory role ex ante and ex post over the activities of arbitral tribunals.[82] This power leaves the question of what means the host state has in the recognition and enforcement of an arbitral award rendered against it (3.2.2.1). Considering the dual role of host states as disputants and potential supervisors of an arbitral process, are arbitral tribunals obliged to ensure that their awards are binding and enforceable in the host state, not only internationally (3.2.2.2)? To the extent that the host state does not have a supervisory role in the arbitration or enforcement proceedings (with no conflict of interest as to the outcome of the proceedings), what can be derived from arbitral jurisprudence about national security as an arbitrable subject matter (3.2.2.3)? Interim conclusions to these questions are summarized in Subsection 3.2.2.4.

---

[76] Article V(2)(a) of the New York Convention.

[77] Blackaby et al. (2009) 640.

[78] Markert and Bubrowski (2015) paras. 16–20; Wolff (2019) paras. 378–379.

[79] UNCITRAL Model Law on International Commercial Arbitration (1985), with amendments as adopted in 2006. The Model Law is designed to assist states in reforming and modernizing their laws on arbitral procedure to consider the particular features and needs of international commercial arbitration. https://uncitral.un.org/en/texts/arbitration/modellaw/commercial_arbitration Accessed 23 July 2022.

[80] Article 34(2)(b)(i) of the UNCITRAL Model Law on International Commercial Arbitration.

[81] Article V(1)(e) of the New York Convention.

[82] Articles II and V, respectively, of the New York Convention.

3.2.2.1 Challenges at the National Level

National courts can influence investment arbitration proceedings because of the role of national law in governing certain aspects of the proceedings.[83] The rulings of national courts are determinative in matters of domestic law, so an arbitral tribunal considers these decisions when interpreting and applying the relevant domestic law. The Canada-EU Comprehensive Economic and Trade Agreement (CETA) is illustrative of this point and recognizes the relevance of national court decisions as follows:

> For greater certainty, in determining the consistency of a measure with this Agreement, the Tribunal may consider, as appropriate, the domestic law of the disputing Party as a matter of fact. In doing so, the Tribunal shall follow the prevailing interpretation given to the domestic law by the courts or authorities of that Party and any meaning given to domestic law by the Tribunal shall not be binding upon the courts or the authorities of that Party.[84]

The provision treats national law as a question of fact. However, in other cases where the parties do not adopt that interpretation, domestic law continues to be "applicable law", not merely a factual consideration. In any event, this provision requires an arbitral tribunal to follow the national courts' interpretation of national law. For treaties without a provision such as the aforementioned one in CETA, national court decisions are considered authoritative pronouncements alongside international law as applicable law in investor-state disputes.[85]

Nevertheless, whenever a national measure is internationally adjudicated and examined for consistency with an international standard (e.g. presented before the Appellate Body of the WTO, the International Tribunal for the Law of the Sea or the European Court of Human Rights), the meaning of the measure must be ascertained by adopting a national court's interpretation of the relevant national law that governs the measure.

Nevertheless, it does not mean that such adoption of an interpretation of national law by an international adjudicator is binding as a matter of that national law. In this respect, it is pertinent to recall the famous 1925 ruling of the Permanent Court of International Justice in *Certain German Interests in Polish Upper Silesia*:

> It might be asked whether a difficulty does not arise from the fact that the Court would have to deal with the Polish law of July 14th, 1920. This, however, does not appear to be the case. From the standpoint of International Law and of the Court which is its organ, municipal laws are merely facts which express the will and constitute the activities of

---

[83] See generally Rajput (2021).

[84] Article 8.31(2) CETA. A similar provision was included in other free trade agreements that have not yet been finalised, including Art. 3.23, footnote 7, to the EU-Singapore investment protection agreement (available at <trade.ec.europa.eu/doclib/docs/2018/april/ tradoc_156731.pdf>, visited 27 October 2023) and Art. 15(3) and (4) of the provisional chapter on the resolution of investment disputes of the EU-Mexico free trade agreement (agreement in principle announced on 21 April 2018, available at trade.ec.europa.eu/ doclib/docs/2018/april/tradoc_156814.pdf, visited 6 November 2023).

[85] See in general Nollkaemper (2011); Sasson (2017); Kjos (2013).

> States, in the same manner as do legal decisions or administrative measures. The Court is certainly not called upon to interpret the Polish law as such; but there is nothing to prevent the Court's giving judgment on the question whether or not, in applying that law, Poland is acting in conformity with its obligations towards Germany under the Geneva Convention.[86]

Thus, the factual character of national law for purposes of its interpretation by an international tribunal remains regardless of whether the national law or international law is explicitly designated as the law applicable to the settlement of the dispute.

National courts can impact the arbitral process before or after an arbitral tribunal has issued its award, even when an investment treaty's compulsory dispute settlement clause precludes the jurisdiction of national courts.[87] National courts may intervene in ongoing or forthcoming investment arbitration proceedings by issuing anti-arbitration injunctions.[88] An anti-arbitration injunction is a judicial order compelling an arbitral tribunal to halt proceedings or mandating that parties refrain from continuing with arbitration.[89] Such injunctions stem from a court's inherent authority to safeguard its jurisdiction and aim to prevent conflicting outcomes in concurrent or redundant proceedings in other forums.[90] The influence of national courts' anti-arbitration injunctions on arbitration proceedings hinges significantly on the depth and persuasiveness of their legal reasoning.[91]

In some instances, arbitral tribunals have disregarded anti-arbitration injunctions or have issued counteracting "anti-suit injunctions".[92] For example, in *Chevron v Ecuador*, the tribunal granted a preliminary injunction that directed

---

[86] *Certain German Interests in Polish Upper Silesia* (*Germany v Poland*) [1926] PCIJ Rep Series A No 7, 19 (para. 52).

[87] Some treaties may maintain the involvement of national courts through the rule requiring the exhaustion of local remedies. This rule can be absolute so that an investor cannot start investment arbitration until national courts have issued a final decision. Alternatively, the rule may be time-limited or conditional. Furthermore, certain treaties do not preclude simultaneous proceedings in national courts and arbitral tribunals. The presence of "fork-in-the-road" clauses in some treaties means that if an investor chooses to challenge a measure in national courts, the jurisdiction of an arbitral tribunal is excluded and compels the investor to decide between pursuing litigation in the host state's national courts or initiating investment arbitration. See further Rajput (2021).

[88] Lew et al. (2003) 363–367; Born (2021a) §2.07[C]; Born (2021b) 1410–1416.

[89] Blackaby et al. (2009) 433–438.

[90] *Paul Donin de Rosiere v Iran*, Award No. ITM 64–498-1, (1986) 13 Iran-US Claims Tribunal 193, 194.

[91] Rajput (2021) 45. In the ICSID cases *RWE v Netherlands* and *Uniper SE et al. v Netherlands,* the Netherlands took advantage of a provision in German civil procedure (§1032(2) German Code of Civil Procedure), which allows German courts, when seized before the arbitration tribunal is formed, to declare an arbitration inadmissible. The court declared the two cases inadmissible (at least with respect to the German claimants in the ICSID proceedings), due to the intra-EU nature of the underlying disputes.

[92] *SGS Société Générale de Surveillance SA v Pakistan*, Procedural Order No. 2, 16 October 2002, 8 ICSID Reports 293, p. 305; see generally Kaufmann-Kohler et al. (2018) 633–678. See also Rajput (2021).

Ecuador to prevent its national court from advancing the case.[93] Despite this injunction, the Ecuadorian court proceeded and concluded the case. The tribunal deemed this action a breach of its directive and subsequently ordered Ecuador to compensate the investor.[94]

The main opportunity for national courts to review decisions of arbitral tribunals is at the post-award stage. National courts can then question the jurisdictional basis for the arbitration.[95] The main measures available to a national court at the post-award stage are setting aside (i.e. annulment) the award,[96] refusal to recognize the award,[97] and refusal to enforce the award.[98] Recognition proceedings involve a national court being requested by the claimant seeking recognition of the award in the domestic legal order, which is preliminary to the making of a domestic legal claim on the basis of such an award, the voluntary compliance with such claim, or the enforcement of such award.[99] Enforcement proceedings involve the claimant taking effective steps to have the host state comply with the award.[100] By contrast, setting aside proceedings are initiated by the losing party (whether the investor or the host state) to have the national court set aside the award.[101]

Typically, the national court responsible for recognizing or enforcing an investment award is not the court of the investor's home state.[102] The New York Convention does not explicitly designate which state's court has the authority to recognize, enforce, or annul an arbitral award. It is generally assumed that this responsibility falls to the courts of the state where the arbitration is seated.[103] The New York Convention acknowledges that an award may be annulled if the underlying arbitration agreement is invalid under the laws of the seat of arbitration.[104] Similarly, an award will not be enforced if the arbitration agreement is invalid under the law agreed upon by the parties.[105] Additionally, in cases where the law of the host state is the governing law, its courts can challenge the recognition or enforcement of an arbitral award. Furthermore, any jurisdiction where the losing party possesses assets becomes relevant for enforcement purposes, which

---

93 *Chevron Corporation and Texaco Petroleum Corporation v Republic of Ecuador*, UNCITRAL, PCA Case No. 2009–23, Order on Interim Measures (May 14, 2010).

94 *Chevron Corporation and Texaco Petroleum Corporation v Ecuador*, UNCITRAL, Second Partial Award on Track II, 30 August 2018, para. 9.17.

95 Blackaby et al. (2009) 581. See further Rajput (2021).

96 See generally Markert and Bubrowski (2015).

97 Blackaby et al. (2009) 611.

98 Blackaby et al. (2009) 611–612.

99 Kröll (2015) 1492.

100 Kröll (2015) 1486.

101 Markert and Bubrowski (2015).

102 Lew et al. (2003) 664.

103 Rajput (2021) 48.

104 Article V(1)(a) of the New York Convention.

105 Ibid.

expands the number of potential jurisdictions involved in recognition and enforcement proceedings.

The primary reasons for a court to annul an arbitral award or refuse its recognition or enforcement include the invalidity of the arbitration agreement,[106] exceeding jurisdictional bounds,[107] arbitrability issues,[108] and conflicts with public policy.[109] Courts can scrutinize the rationale and foundations of an award, even when it involves international law. For instance, in *Mexico v Metalclad*, the Supreme Court of British Columbia partially annulled an award on the grounds that the tribunal exceeded its jurisdiction by incorporating "transparency" not recognized in customary international law.[110]

Awards that cover non-arbitrable subject matter are neither recognized nor enforced due to their ineligibility for arbitration.[111] Determinations of arbitrability are made by the courts in the jurisdiction where enforcement or recognition is sought or in the jurisdiction of the arbitration seat based on local laws and judicial precedents.[112] Investment arbitration often touches on both private and public interests, which increases the likelihood of invoking non-arbitrability and enhances the role of national courts.[113]

National courts possess considerable discretion when enforcing awards based on public policy considerations. An award can be contested if it contravenes the public policy of the enforcing state.[114] Even if an award has been enforced in one jurisdiction, it may still be subject to scrutiny under the laws of another jurisdiction.[115] While national courts typically respect the findings of arbitral tribunals and refrain from contesting their merits, they extensively evaluate these decisions based on public policy during the enforcement stage.[116] Though not equivalent to an appellate review, their examination standards are relatively lenient.[117] Courts may

---

[106] Ibid. See further Rajput (2021).

[107] Article V(1)(c) of the New York Convention.

[108] Article V(2)(a) of the New York Convention.

[109] Article V(2)(b) of the New York Convention.

[110] See further Pohl (2017). The Supreme Court of British Columbia set aside the arbitral award in *Mexico v Metalclad,* noting that "[n]o authority was cited or evidence introduced to establish that transparency has become part of customary international law"; see Mexico v Metalclad Corporation, [2001] B.C.S.C. 664, Supreme Court of British Columbia, Reasons for Judgment, ¶68 (May 2, 2001). *Metalclad Corporation v United Mexican States*, ICSID Case No. ARB(AF)/97/1, Award, ¶¶76, 88, 99 (Aug. 30, 2000).

[111] Article V(2)(a) of the New York Convention. See further Rajput (2021).

[112] Wolff (2019) paras. 446–447.

[113] Mistelis (2009) 5–9; Lew et al. (2003) 187.

[114] Wolff (2019) para. 493. See further Rajput (2021).

[115] Sheppard (2003) 243.

[116] *Anatolie Stati, Gabriel Stati, Ascom Group SA and Terra Raf Trans Trading Ltd v Kazakhstan*, SCC Case No. V 116/2010, Judgment of the UK Commercial Court on the Enforcement of the Award, 6 June 2017, para. 87.

[117] Rajput (2021) 50.

also assess whether an arbitral tribunal's interpretations align with international law or the relevant national laws.[118]

In the *Yukos* case, the District Court of The Hague identified errors in the arbitral tribunal's interpretation of the provisional application of the Energy Charter Treaty (ECT),[119] particularly regarding its context, purpose, and the nature of international law.[120] As the Russian Federation had not ratified the ECT, and Russian laws and constitution require ratification for a treaty's binding effect, the court ruled that the treaty's dispute resolution provisions were inapplicable,[121] which led to a lack of jurisdiction for the tribunal.[122] The Court determined that provisional application of Article 45 of the ECT was permissible as long as it did not conflict with national law.[123] However, Russian legislation prohibited arbitration of investment disputes, which rendered the dispute resolution clauses of the ECT inapplicable.[124] As a result, the arbitral tribunal was deemed to lack jurisdiction.[125] This case illustrates that national courts can diverge from arbitral findings and annul awards if they determine that the dispute falls outside the tribunal's jurisdiction.

In *Achmea*, the CJEU ruled that disputes under bilateral investment treaties between EU Member States (intra-EU BITs) cannot be resolved through investment arbitration, as this would involve interpreting EU law—a prerogative exclusive to the EU judicial system, with the CJEU as final interpreter.[126]

3.2.2.2 Challenges at the International Level

It is clear that when an investor accepts an offer to settle an investment dispute by arbitration, the investor expects that the arbitral tribunal will render an award that the investor can enforce.[127] In fact, an award delivered by an arbitrator is

---

[118] *Russian Federation v Veteran Petroleum Ltd*, The Hague District Court, Judgment, 20 April 2016, paras 5.12–5.13, 5.19–5.20.

[119] *Russian Federation v Veteran Petroleum Ltd*, The Hague District Court, Judgment, 20 April 2016, paras 5.12–5.13. See further Rajput (2021).

[120] *Russian Federation v Veteran Petroleum Ltd*, The Hague District Court, Judgment, 20 April 2016, paras 5.19–5.20.

[121] *Russian Federation v Veteran Petroleum Ltd*, The Hague District Court, Judgment, 20 April 2016, paras. 5.33–5.34, 5.96.

[122] *Russian Federation v Veteran Petroleum Ltd*, The Hague District Court, Judgment, 20 April 2016, para. 5.19.

[123] *Russian Federation v Veteran Petroleum Ltd*, The Hague District Court, Judgment, 20 April 2016, para. 5.20.

[124] *Russian Federation v Veteran Petroleum Ltd*, The Hague District Court, Judgment, 20 April 2016, paras. 5.33–5.34.

[125] *Russian Federation v Veteran Petroleum Ltd*, The Hague District Court, Judgment, 20 April 2016, para. 5.96.

[126] Pohl (2018). See also Rajput (2021).

[127] Barraclough and Waincymer (2005).

characterized by its bindingness, in contrast with, for instance, good offices or the recommendations of a mediator or a conciliator. However, whether such expectation amounts to a duty incumbent on arbitrators to make an award also enforceable is debatable, as is the potential legal basis for such a duty.[128] It may be an express or implied term of the arbitration agreement.[129] In any event, the consequences of such a duty (whether "hard" or "soft") oblige arbitrators to consider the enforceability of the award under the laws of the relevant states, which includes the state of the law governing the arbitration proceedings and the law of the state (or states) in which recognition or enforcement is likely to be sought.[130] Several states' laws may be considered in this process. Nevertheless, the argument that an award would not be enforceable in a particular state where enforcement could be sought does not prevent an arbitral tribunal from holding that it has jurisdiction. A tribunal cannot consider all national laws or hypothesize which national laws may be relevant and only consider those.

The practical effect of the (at least, de facto) "duty" to render enforceable awards is to invite deference of arbitral tribunals to state decision-making authority on matters of public policy.[131] The duty does not mean that the tribunal must guarantee that the award it renders is effectively enforceable in all relevant jurisdictions.[132] The arbitrator's obligation is better characterized as a "best-efforts" duty to produce a legally enforceable award.[133] If the parties point the tribunal to a particular state as a likely place of performance or enforcement, the tribunal should also consider the law of that state.

3.2.2.3 National Security as Public Policy in Arbitral Jurisprudence

Whether disputes related to national security screening are arbitrable seems not to have featured in the context of a challenge against an investment arbitration award.[134] However, disputes involving questions concerning a state's national

---

[128] See generally Horvath (2001). For the view that such duty exists, see Lalive (1987) 258, 273; Kreindler (2003) 241; Lew (1999) 114–145. For the opposite view, see Boog and Moss (2013).

[129] See e.g. ICC Rules of Arbitration (1 March 2017) art 42 ("The arbitral tribunal shall act in the spirit of the Rules and shall make every effort to make sure that the award is enforceable at law"); Blackaby et al. (2009) 608; Lew et al. (2003) 689; Horvath (2001) 135–158.

[130] Barraclough and Waincymer (2005); Lalive (1987) 273.

[131] The reasoning being that absent arbitral deference to the courts of the state where the recognition or enforcement of the award is likely to be sought, such courts may otherwise refuse recognition or enforcement pursuant to Article V(2)(a) or (b) of the New York Convention; for similar arguments see Derains (1986); Kryvoi (2018).

[132] Barraclough and Waincymer (2005) 216.

[133] Ibid.; Lalive (1987) 273; Blackaby et al. (2009) 608; Lew et al. (2003) 689.

[134] The question of arbitrability of national security screening matters has not been raised in investment arbitration. From the heavily redacted public version of the *Global Telecom v Canada* award, it seems that the question of arbitrability was not raised. However, an Indian Supreme Court case from 2019, *Vidya Drolia v Durga Transport Corporation* (2021) 2 SCC 1, affirmed

security interests have occurred in the context of economic sanctions and trade sanctions, including embargoes.[135]

Case law from national courts largely supports the arbitrability of disputes concerning economic sanctions.[136] U.S. courts, in particular, strongly support this proposition, even in the context of the most stringent sanction regimes such as those in place vis-à-vis Cuba.[137] Similarly, Swiss courts have consistently taken the same view over the years.[138] Likewise, in the context of disputes related to export control regulations, the mandatory nature of such regulations does not negate arbitrability.[139] In the context of investor-state arbitration, it should be recalled that the state cannot invoke its internal law as an excuse for not complying with an international obligation.[140] As such, the fact that internal law would prevent the state from agreeing on a subject matter with the investors is not a valid argument on the international plane.

Thus, the mere fact that questions concerning mandatory law are involved is insufficient to affect the validity of the arbitration agreement.[141] This effect is in line with the doctrine of separability (severability), according to which the validity of the arbitration agreement is unaffected by the invalidity of the underlying agreement to which the arbitration agreement applies.[142] Just because a matter

---

that "sovereign functions of the State being inalienable and non-delegable are non-arbitrable as the State alone has the exclusive right and duty to perform such functions". This statement was understood as rendering non-arbitrable "[m]atters concerning citizenship, grant of patents, [and] national security, unless the contrary has been specified in the statutory provisions". See Kumar and Rawat (2022). The prevailing view elsewhere, however, appears still to be that a presumption of non-arbitrability does not exist. See Wolff (2019) paras. 451–454. As regards the United States, Brian J. Farrar has argued for international arbitration of investment disputes involving national security, see Farrar (2008) 167. See further Voon and Merriman (2022).

[135] On the arbitrability of matters concerning economic sanctions, see Szabados (2018); Kotelnikov (2020). The question of the arbitrability of matters concerning trade embargoes was considered in *Fincantieri-Cantieri Navali Italiani S.p.A. & Oto Melara S.p.A. v Ministry of Defence, Armament & Supply Directorate of Iraq et al., Italy No. 138*, Corte di Appello, Genoa, Judgment of 7 May 1994. The conclusion of the court was that such matters were not arbitrable. Generally, see Wolff (2019) para. 466.

[136] Born (2021a) §§6.04[E], 26.05[C][9][i][iii]. See generally, Szabados (2018); Kotelnikov (2020).

[137] See e.g. *Belship Navigation Inc v Sealift Inc*, 1995 U.S. DIST LEXIS 10541, 1996 AMC 209 (US District Court for the Southern District of New York, 1995); *Mitsubishi Motors Corp. v Soler Chrysler-Plymouth, Inc.*, 473 U.S. 614 (1985).

[138] See, e.g. *G. SA v V. SpA et Tribunal Arbitral*, 28 April 1992, DFT 118 II 193, c. 5 c.a.a, English translation in Yearbook Commercial Arbitration 1993 at 143; *X SA & Y SA v Z SA*, 4 P.119/1998, ASA Bull. 1999 at 529.

[139] Born (2021a) §§6.04[E], 26.05[C][9][i][iii].

[140] See 1969 Vienna Convention on the Law of Treaties (VCLT), 115 UNTS 331, Article 27.

[141] Kronke et al. (2010) 354–355; Born (2021a) §6.02[G].

[142] See *Mitsubishi Motors Co. v Soler Chrysler-Plymouth*, 473 U.S. 614 (1985); *Société Labinal v Société Mors et Société Westland Aerospace Ltd.*, Cour d'appel de Paris (1ère chambre, s. A), Judgment of 19 May 1993, *Journal du Droit International*, vol. 120, 957; see also Idot; CA Paris,

annulled if the tribunal has manifestly exceeded its powers (Subsection 3.2.3.2). The final subsection (Subsection 3.2.3.3) provides an interim summary.

3.2.3.1 Pre-Award Phase Challenges

Under Article 25 of the Washington Convention, only legal disputes may be subject to arbitration under the Convention. Whether a legal dispute exists is determined by the nature of the claim and the nature of the arguments supporting the claim.[147] If the claim is based on contracts, statutes, and other sources of law and seeks remedies such as restitution for damages, the claim is legal.[148] A dispute must relate to clearly identified facts and have specific consequences to serve as a basis for jurisdiction.[149] Thus, all a claimant needs to do is to present the claims in legal terms. As such, attempts by the defendant to characterize a dispute as political rather than legal cannot be expected to be successful.[150]

Article 25(4) of the Washington Convention allows contracting states to exclude certain types of disputes from settlement by arbitration under the Convention, essentially designating them as non-arbitrable:

> Any Contracting State may, at the time of ratification, acceptance or approval of this Convention or at any time thereafter, notify the Centre of the class or classes of disputes which it would or would not consider submitting to the jurisdiction of the Centre. The Secretary-General shall forthwith transmit such notification to all Contracting States. Such notification shall not constitute the consent required by paragraph (1).[151]

In the event of a conflict between the instrument of consent and an Article 25 (4) notification purporting to exclude a class of dispute covered by the consent, the consent prevails.[152] Article 25(4) notifications are meant for informational purposes and do not have independent legal effect.[153] The content of a notification must be included in the instrument of consent to be legally effective.[154] A consent clause that is not entirely clear may be interpreted by reference to prior notification.

The notification also does not operate to modify the jurisdictional conditions.[155] In *PSEG v Turkey*, the respondent unsuccessfully raised a jurisdictional objection

---

[147] Schreuer 978; Schreuer (2009) paras. 57–67.

[148] Ibid.

[149] Ibid.

[150] Ibid.

[151] Article 25(4) of the Washington Convention.

[152] *PSEG v Turkey*, Decision on Jurisdiction, 4 June 2004, paras. 125–130; Schreuer (2009) paras. 931–932.

[153] *PSEG v Turkey*, Decision on Jurisdiction, 4 June 2004, paras. 135–147; Schreuer (2009) para. 933.

[154] Ibid.

[155] Ibid.

by reference to its notification under Article 25(4), which included the condition that investment activities must have "actually commenced" so as to exclude prospective investments.[156] The applicable US-Turkey BIT did not reflect this requirement.[157] According to the tribunal, notifications under Article 25(4) have no independent legal effect but are merely declarations for informational purposes. As such, they cannot modify the instrument of consent, such as the investment treaty.

3.2.3.2 Post-Award Phase Challenges

An arbitral award rendered under the Washington Convention is self-executing because it is treated as a final decision of the highest court of each State party to the Convention. Article 54(1) of the Convention provides the following:

> Each Contracting State shall recognize an award rendered pursuant to this Convention as binding and enforce the pecuniary obligations imposed by that award within its territories as if it were a final judgment of a court in that State. [...][158]

Together with Article 53 of the Convention, which provides for the binding force of an ICSID award, this provision excludes the possibility of challenging an arbitral award rendered under the Washington Convention by setting it aside or by refusing to recognize or enforce it.[159, 160]

An arbitral award rendered under the Washington Convention may not be set aside by a national court, as affirmed by Article 53(1):

> The award shall be binding on the parties and shall not be subject to any appeal or to any other remedy except those provided for in this Convention. Each party shall abide by and comply with the terms of the award except to the extent that enforcement shall have been stayed pursuant to the relevant provisions of this Convention.[161]

Instead, the Convention foresees a process by which an award may be reviewed and annulled at the international level by an annulment committee constituted under the Convention. Article 52(1) lists the grounds for annulment:

---

[156] *PSEG v Turkey*, Decision on Jurisdiction, 4 June 2004, paras. 125–147.

[157] *PSEG v Turkey*, Decision on Jurisdiction, 4 June 2004, paras. 144–145.

[158] Article 54(1) of the Washington Convention.

[159] Articles 53–57 of the Washington Convention.

[160] It has been argued that, where national law provides for a possibility to exceptionally refuse to enforce final judgments of the highest national court, the same refusal to enforce should also apply to an award rendered under the Washington Convention. This refusal would open the possibility of a challenge to such an award in a national court, albeit on limited grounds. See Baldwin et al. (2006) 9 et seq.

[161] Article 53(1) of the Washington Convention.

> Either party may request annulment of the award by an application in writing addressed to the Secretary-General on one or more of the following grounds:
>
> (a) that the Tribunal was not properly constituted;
> (b) that the Tribunal has manifestly exceeded its powers;
> (c) that there was corruption on the part of a member of the Tribunal;
> (d) that there has been a serious departure from a fundamental rule of procedure; or
> (e) that the award has failed to state the reasons on which it is based.[162]

Of interest for present purposes is that an unsuccessful respondent may argue at the post-award stage, pursuant to Article 52(1)(b), that a tribunal that ignored a mandatory rule of transnational public policy manifestly exceeded its powers.[163] However, an argument based on the public policy of the host state is unlikely to succeed.[164] As codified in Article 27 of the Vienna Convention on the Law of Treaties (VCLT), "[A state] may not invoke the provisions of its internal law as justification for its failure to perform a treaty".[165] This mandate is without prejudice to Article 46 of that Convention, which provides:

> 1. A State may not invoke the fact that its consent to be bound by a treaty has been expressed in violation of a provision of its internal law regarding competence to conclude treaties as invalidating its consent unless that violation was manifest and concerned a rule of its internal law of fundamental importance.
> 2. A violation is manifest if it would be objectively evident to any State conducting itself in the matter in accordance with normal practice and in good faith.[166]

For a respondent to successfully argue that a tribunal manifestly exceeded its powers by not dismissing a claim related to the host state's national security matters by referencing a mandatory rule of the host state's public policy, it would have to show that the rule was "objectively evident".[167] However, even a prima facie manifest violation of an internal law may not be invoked by the relevant state unless the law in question is of "fundamental importance", which also would be for the state to show.[168] With respect to the host state's essential security interests, it may well be possible to argue that such matters are of fundamental importance.

3.2.3.3 Interim Summary

Under the Washington Convention, the arbitrability of disputes is protected by Article 54, which compels contracting states to recognize and enforce arbitral

[162] Article 52(1) of the Washington Convention.
[163] Article 52(1)(b) of the Washington Convention.
[164] Schreuer (2009) paras. 48–52.
[165] Article 27 of the VCLT.
[166] Article 46 of the VCLT.
[167] Schreuer (2009) para. 630.
[168] Ibid.

awards without exception, including arbitrability concerns. In practice, there is essentially no scope for challenging the arbitrability of a dispute at the pre-award stage, as national courts do not exercise supervisory jurisdiction. However, Article 25(1) retains the concept of arbitrability at the pre-award stage by requiring that disputes qualify as "legal disputes". While a dispute may be challenged as being not "legal", in reality, the scope for such an argument is negligible. Additionally, Article 25(4) allows states to specify classes of disputes they would not consider for ICSID arbitration at the time of the Convention's ratification or at any time thereafter. However, such notifications do not modify the instrument of consent and are primarily informational. While states may declare their unwillingness to submit certain disputes to arbitration, such declarations are not in themselves sufficient to modify the instrument of consent.

At the post-award phase, while national courts are precluded from setting aside or refusing recognition or enforcement of ICSID awards, an annulment committee established under the Convention may do so on limited grounds, including manifest excess of powers (Article 52). To prevail on this ground in the context of national security is possible in theory but would require the host state to successfully invoke the public policy provisions of its national law as a justification for failing to perform its treaty obligations. This provision supports the robust framework of the Convention by emphasizing the finality and binding nature of ICSID awards, with a very limited scope for challenge based on national law or public policy concerns. This provision reinforces the separation between national legal systems and the international arbitral process and ensures minimal interference from domestic jurisdictions in the enforcement of ICSID awards.

3.2.4 Summary

Under the New York Convention, host state national courts have extensive power to influence the outcome of an international investment dispute before, during, and after the conclusion of international arbitration proceedings. International arbitral tribunals are inclined to give due consideration to the enforceability of their awards, not just in the host state but anywhere else the investor is likely to seek their enforcement. This inclination creates a link between the international and national planes that may result in the arbitral tribunal's consideration of and deference to host state national public policy and international public policy.

Under the Washington Convention, there is practically no scope for challenging the arbitrability of a dispute at the pre-award stage. While ICSID awards may also not be challenged before national courts at the post-award stage, they may be annulled by a committee convened pursuant to the Washington Convention.

Arbitral jurisprudence confirms that, in principle, national security is generally an internationally arbitrable subject matter. Thus, transnational public policy does not prevent states from submitting disputes relating to matters concerning their national security interests to international arbitration. Mandatory rules of public policy may prevent arbitration of matters provided that the matters are clearly reserved exclusively for national courts. Relevant case law suggests that mandatory rules of public policy only exceptionally reserve exclusive jurisdiction in matters where national security interests play an important part.

The burden is on host states to clearly communicate what matters cannot be subject to arbitration in their instrument of consent. Thus, host states should communicate to investors in the instrument of consent the classes of disputes the subject matter of which the host state reserves for the exclusive jurisdiction of their national courts to ensure that the host state complies with Articles 27 and 46 of the VCLT and the specific requirements under the Washington Convention. Therefore, the risk of legal uncertainty is carried by the host state.

3.3 Arbitrating Vital National Interests: Interpreting the Consent to Arbitration

Except for objectively non-arbitrable disputes which concern subject matter incapable of settlement by arbitration, as discussed in Subchapter 3.2, states generally enjoy the freedom to agree to settle any dispute by recourse to arbitration. However, in practice, disputes rarely confine themselves to non-arbitrable subject matters and at least partially concern matters that states may agree to arbitrate.[169] More commonly, there may be disagreement as to the scope of the consent to arbitration.

Even if not constituting a class of non-arbitrable disputes, is it reasonable for an arbitrator to interpret a host state's consent to arbitrate to encompass any and all types of subject matter? Can it be presumed that the host state has submitted subject matters of a political nature that affect its vital interests? It is not difficult to imagine arguments for and against such a proposition.

On the one hand, if no state ever accepted arbitration concerning its national security interests, the presumption would be justified. If arbitrating a matter of national security depended on disclosing sensitive information that could harm a state's national security interests, it seems that no state would make such disclosure.

On the other hand, not all aspects of a dispute related to national security review necessarily concern the national security interests or information of the host state. Hence, it could arguably be meaningful to arbitrate. Moreover, absent a legal remedy, the host state could abuse the "vital interest" argument to shield itself from disputes that do not have any significant link to the host state's true national security interests. Indeed, the notion of "national security" is dynamic, as is the notion that a case may "relate" to a national security interest.

The question of the validity of the consent to international arbitration is a matter to be addressed by the law pursuant to the modality with which the consent was

[169] See 3.2 above.

given, which may be international law in the case of consent given by treaty, national law where consent is provided by national law, or the law governing an investment contract containing such consent, or, in the case of an ad hoc consent, any law to which the parties agree to submit a dispute.[170] Notably, as follows from the previous subchapter, the assessment of whether the consent to arbitration is invalid to the extent it encompasses non-arbitrable disputes is practically indistinguishable from the issue of interpreting the substantive scope of the consent. Whether the consent is invalid because it extends to non-arbitrable subject matter or the consent is interpreted to exclude that matter, the practical implications are the same: a case concerning such matter is not entertained, or, in the case of a post-award challenge, should not be entertained. This conclusion is reinforced by the annulment provision of the Washington Convention, which provides for the annulment of awards in the event of a tribunal's manifest excess of powers.[171] If indeed the host state's consent were not validly given, the excess of powers would be manifest.[172] Likewise, the New York Convention provides that a state may refuse recognition and enforcement of an arbitral award that deals with a dispute not contemplated by or not falling within the terms of the submission to arbitration (i.e. excess of jurisdiction).[173] The burden is on the unsuccessful respondent to request such refusal and to prove the excess of jurisdiction.[174] Moreover, pursuant to the UNCITRAL Model Law,[175] an excess of jurisdiction may also result in a setting aside of the award by a competent court in the state of the place of arbitration,

---

[170] Born (2021a) §2.06.

[171] Article 52(1)(b) of the Washington Convention.

[172] As discussed above, the issue of arbitrability in the context of ICSID cases is principally an aspect of the substantive scope of the consent to arbitration. Article 25(1) of the ICSID Convention provides that ICSID jurisdiction "shall extend to any legal dispute arising directly out of an investment [. . .] which the parties to the dispute consent in writing to submit [to arbitration]". In ICSID cases, the requirement that the dispute arises "directly" out of an investment is an objective criterion, which means that the dispute must retain a sufficiently close connection with the relevant investment. A respondent may argue that national security screening applies only to ancillary transactions that are peripheral to the investment and thus that any dispute relating to such restrictions do not arise "directly". However, ICSID practice indicates that ancillary transactions deemed vital to the investment are nonetheless sufficiently closely related to satisfy the directness requirement. This outcome could arguably be the case with payment transactions needed to maintain an investment or repatriate proceeds generated by an investment.

[173] Article V(1)(c) of the New York Convention. The same provision also provides for refusal of recognition and enforcement in the event that the award contains decisions on matters beyond the scope of the submission to arbitration (i.e. excess of competence). While excess of jurisdiction takes aim at the factual scope of the consent to arbitration, excess of competence concerns the application of correct law and the correct application of the law to the dispute at hand. These aspects are subsumed under the annulment ground in Article 52(1)(b) of the Washington Convention, which note that the tribunal has manifestly exceeded its powers.

[174] Blackaby et al. (2009) 622.

[175] See 3.2 above.

which in turn may result in a refusal to recognize and enforce the award in other states under the New York Convention.[176]

The first question in interpreting the scope of arbitral competence is to ascertain the law governing the instrument of consent (3.3.1). The subsequent question is how the consent ought to be interpreted (3.3.2). The conclusions of this subchapter are summarized in the final section (3.3.3).

3.3.1 Applicable Law for Interpreting the Instrument of Consent

The law applicable to the consent to arbitration delimits the extent to which the parties to the arbitration agreement may agree to submit certain disputes to arbitration, as discussed in the previous subchapter.[177] The applicable law furthermore informs the interpretation of the parties' consent to arbitration by indicating the parties' mutual intention that their consent be construed in accordance with the interpretive principles prevailing in the relevant jurisdiction.[178] In addition, the applicable law may provide default rules and facultative principles to be applied in the event that the specific intent of the parties cannot be ascertained.[179]

Three modalities of consent exist.[180] An arbitration clause may be agreed directly with an investor in an investment contract between the host state and the investor. Alternatively, the consent may consist of an offer of arbitration that may be contained in domestic legislation, such as a national investment code. Finally, an investment treaty may contain an offer of arbitration. With respect to each of these three types (and ad hoc consent, which may be subjected to either of the three types of law), the law governing the consent, and thus the interpretation of the scope of jurisdiction, may differ. In the case of the former two modalities, national law is normally implicated, if not determinative (3.3.1.1), whereas in the latter case, international law alone may govern (3.3.1.2). The final subsection summarizes the interim conclusions (3.3.1.3).

3.3.1.1 Consent Governed by National Law

A host state and an investor may agree directly to settle investment disputes through arbitration. Such an agreement may be concluded as a separate instrument

[176] Article 34(2)(a)(iii) of the UNCITRAL Model Law; cf. Article V(1)(e) of the New York Convention.

[177] See 3.2.3 above.

[178] Schreuer (2008b) 864.

[179] Schreuer (2009) paras. 578–585.

[180] See 3.2.3 above.

or as a compromissory clause in an investment contract between them.[181] This instrument of consent may refer to the national law of the host state to govern its scope. Alternatively, the parties may choose the national law of a third state (e.g. the laws of England and Wales or the State of New York) to govern the investment contract. In each of these cases, the parties' autonomy and freedom of choice are generally respected.[182] However, the situation becomes more complicated when such a choice is not clearly evident.[183]

Concerning cases to which the New York Convention applies, the Convention does not expressly provide for the law governing the scope of the arbitration agreement, failing any indication of the parties' intention.[184] Nevertheless, the predominant view is that the law governing the validity of the agreement also governs its scope,[185] which refers to the lex loci arbitri, failing an express choice of law by the parties.[186]

Cases to which the Washington Convention applies differ in that where the parties have not specifically agreed on the law governing the scope of the arbitration agreement, the tribunal determines the law according to the Washington Convention.[187] As expressed by the arbitral tribunal in *CMS v Argentina*, jurisdiction is in such cases governed "solely by Article 25 of the Convention and those other provisions of the consent instrument which might be applicable".[188] In practice, it has meant that tribunals have referred to international law as set out in Article 25 and the relevant investment treaty.[189]

The situation where the investor and host state have concluded an arbitration agreement directly is to be distinguished from the oft-occurring case of a host state making an offer to arbitrate, which is accepted by the investor by means of submission of a dispute.[190] Such a "standing offer" is made by means of an offer to arbitrate contained in the host state's national investment laws.[191] This pattern is complicated by the fact that the consummated mutual consent to arbitrate involves an additional international element, which is partly so by default because the relevant national legislation often does not specifically indicate the law governing

181 Schreuer (2008b) 832–833.

182 Notable exceptions include *SPP v Egypt*, Decision on Jurisdiction II, 14 April 1988, 3 ICSID Reports 131; and *CSOB v Slovakia*, Decision on Jurisdiction, 24 May 1999, 5 ICSID Reports 335.

183 See, e.g. *Amco v Indonesia*, Decision on Jurisdiction, 25 September 1983, paras. 18–23; *Zhinvali v Georgia*, Award, 24 January 2003, para. 229.

184 Article V(1)(a) of the New York Convention.

185 Borris and Hennecke (2019).

186 Article V(1)(a) of the New York Convention in fine ("the law of the country where the award was made").

187 Schreuer (2009) paras. 578–585.

188 *CMS v Argentina*, Decision on Jurisdiction, 17 July 2003, 7 ICSID Reports 494, 42 ILM 788, at para. 88.

189 Schreuer (2009) para. 552.

190 See generally Waibel (2015) §§47–51.

191 Schreuer (2019).

the scope of the instrument of consent.[192] It is also in part because the resulting mutual consent is not purely a contractual arrangement but an acceptance of an offer, which, although in the form of national law, nonetheless constitutes a unilateral declaration under international law.[193] As expressed by the tribunal in *SPP v Egypt*, the decision on jurisdiction is governed by "general principles of statutory interpretation taking into consideration, where appropriate, relevant rules of treaty interpretation and principles of international law applicable to unilateral declarations".[194]

In summary, the interpretation of the consent to arbitrate, which sets the scope of arbitral competence concerning disputes relating to national security screening, depends on the modalities of the instrument of consent, which in turn indicates the method for determining the law governing that scope. Regarding instruments of consent that are based on national law, the choice of law of the parties is generally respected, except with respect to consent expressed in national legislation, which is also governed by relevant principles of international law.

3.3.1.2 Consent Governed by International Law

In the event that an investment treaty contains an ISDS clause, the clause is understood to constitute a standing offer to arbitrate, which the investor accepts by bringing arbitration proceedings, as detailed below. The question of how to interpret such an offer or (unaccepted) consent to arbitrate is not exhaustively addressed by the Washington Convention or any other applicable source of international law.[195] In general, an offer or (unaccepted) consent to arbitration given by a state to investors through an investment treaty is a unilateral declaration, the interpretation of which is not subject to generally accepted international principles of a binding nature.[196]

The interpretation of the scope of the instrument of consent—and thus the issue of whether disputes relating to national security screening may be covered by it—is

---

[192] Ascertaining the law applicable to the consent thus becomes an exercise of private international law. See Fernández Arroyo and Mbengue (2018) 825–826.

[193] Schreuer (2019) 449–457.

[194] *SPP v Egypt*, Decision on Jurisdiction II, 14 April 1988, para. 61. See also *CEMEX Caracas Investments B.V. and CEMEX Caracas II Investments B.V. v Bolivarian Republic of Venezuela*, ICSID Case No. ARB/08/15, Decision on Jurisdiction of 30 December 2010, paras. 81–85.

[195] The rules of treaty interpretation, notably Articles 31 and 32 of the VCLT, do not apply to unilateral declarations. The International Law Commission (ILC) of the United Nations adopted in 2006 Guiding Principles applicable to unilateral declarations of States, see International Law Commission, Unilateral Acts of States: Report of the Working Group, UN Doc A/CN.4/L.703, 20 July 2006. These are, as the title implies, guidelines and not binding rules.

[196] Ibid.

comparatively straightforward where the instrument is entirely contained in an investment treaty. It appears that such a consent would be governed by international law on treaty interpretation.[197] This situation is the most common based on investment treaty case law.[198] However, an instrument of consent contained in a treaty is just an arbitration offer. Once accepted by the investor, the resulting arbitration agreement is not a treaty but an agreement between the host state and the investor based on a treaty.[199]

The scope of consent, and hence the resulting arbitration agreement, is often determined pursuant to one of three types of clauses: (1) the arbitration clause may provide for arbitration in respect of "any dispute relating to investments" or similar wording,[200] (2) the clause may be limited to "any alleged breach of an obligation under this Treaty" or similar,[201] or (3) an enumeration of treaty obligations may be provided and possibly supplemented by non-treaty obligations, such as obligations under investment contracts and investment authorizations.[202]

With respect to each of these types of arbitration clauses mentioned in the previous paragraph, it remains to be construed whether a relevant dispute relating to national security screening may be covered. The first and second types may offer less trouble (except if qualifying language is used, such as claims arising "directly" from an investment), as the plain meaning of these wordings does not offer a ground for arguing that any type of dispute or alleged breach should be excluded.[203] The third type, namely the enumeration of treaty obligations covered by the consent, may constitute a bar against arbitration, which depends on the substantive basis of the claim because the host state may argue that the listed obligations within the scope of arbitration do not apply to national security screening, which again depends on the substance of the claim and the obligation in question. Hence, by narrowing the scope, the arbitration clauses narrow the range of legal arguments that the investor may invoke in support of its claims in an ISDS action. Occasionally, a treaty clause on which a dispute relating to national security screening would potentially rely will be excluded from the scope of the arbitration clause.[204] In such cases, it may instead be possible to invoke another standard, notably the non-discrimination or FET standards.

Finally, when international law applies to the instrument of consent, tribunals have applied the rules on interpretation enshrined in Articles 31 and 32 of the

[197] *Fedax v Venezuela*, Decision on Jurisdiction, 11 July 1997, para. 20.

[198] Schreuer (2009) para. 579.

[199] Ibid.

[200] Dolzer et al. (2022) 372–373.

[201] Ibid. 374–375.

[202] Ibid. 375–376.

[203] See 3.2.

[204] See, e.g., Article 8.18 of CETA, which excludes the treaty's market access provisions from ISDS.

VCLT analogously, even though, as noted above, the perfected arbitration agreement (i.e. the accepted consent) is not a treaty.[205]

Therefore, in the event that it is not evident from the instrument of consent that disputes relating to national security screening fall outside the scope of the consent, the availability of invoking external means of interpretation is circumscribed to the situations set forth in Article 32 of the VCLT. In the absence of concurrent or subsequent agreements or instruments, which may be taken into consideration as context or together with the context, pursuant to Article 31(2) and (3), it would only be permissible to resort to supplementary means of interpretation under the narrow conditions of Article 32.[206]

3.3.1.3 Interim Summary

The law applicable to the consent to arbitration defines the scope and interpretation of disputes eligible for arbitration. This law is crucial for delineating the extent of arbitration agreed upon by the parties and providing interpretive guidelines and default principles. Consent to arbitration can be manifested through various modalities, each governed by distinct legal frameworks.

Where the instrument of consent is set out in an investor-state contract, the law that applies to the interpretation of the instrument will be the law chosen by the parties. By contrast, consent contained in host state national legislation will be interpreted in accordance with host state national law in addition to relevant principles of international law.

In cases where consent is embedded within domestic legislation or unspecified by the parties, the scope is typically governed by the law of the host state unless dictated otherwise by international principles or treaty rules. The New York and Washington Conventions guide the interpretation of these agreements, with the New York Convention relying on the law governing the validity of the agreement to determine its scope and the Washington Convention directing tribunals to derive applicable law from the treaty provisions themselves.

When the instrument of consent is set out in an investment treaty, the law that governs the interpretation of the instrument is international law on treaty interpretation, notably as codified in Articles 31 and 32 of the VCLT. The interpretation of such consent, if not explicitly governed by the treaty, is generally handled under these international law principles. For purposes of interpreting the scope of consent, particular attention is afforded to the formulation of the relevant arbitration clause, whether it covers a dispute, treaty breach, or specifically mentioned type of dispute.

---

[205] See, e.g., *Mondev v United States* (AF), Award, 11 October 2002, para. 42.

[206] Recourse to supplementary means of interpretation is limited to cases where application of the general rule of interpretation in Article 31 would leave the meaning of the treaty ambiguous or obscure or would lead to "a result which is manifestly absurd or unreasonable". Article 32 of the VCLT.

The arbitration agreement resulting from an accepted treaty-based offer is interpreted using principles of treaty interpretation and focuses on the plain meaning of the text and the intentions of the parties. The specificity of these clauses affects the arbitrability of disputes related to national security screenings, with broader clauses providing less ground for excluding such disputes from arbitration.

This comprehensive view is essential for understanding how different legal frameworks influence the interpretation and scope of consent in arbitration agreements. It highlights the importance of precise drafting and clarity in consent provisions to ensure predictability and enforceability in arbitration outcomes.

3.3.2 Interpreting the Instrument of Consent

Modern investment treaties often contain explicit consent provisions that cover all types of disputes arising under the relevant treaty, which have not been explicitly excluded.[207] In relation to investment treaty obligations contained in those treaties, specific exclusions do not normally apply.[208] In those cases, disputes arising in relation to investment screening are covered. However, some treaties, such as CETA, exclude national security screening from arbitration,[209] viz., disputes relating to investment screening under the Investment Canada Act. Specifically, the exclusion covers "[a] decision by Canada following [investment screening under the Investment Canada Act] regarding whether or not to permit an investment that is subject to [screening measure]".[210] Notably, CETA does not contain any similar exclusion applicable to investment screening by the EU or its Member States, which may reflect that when CETA was signed, the EU FDI Screening Regulation did not exist.

Treaties that provide for investor-state arbitration sometimes limit the application of such arbitration to certain types of disputes and explicitly exclude other types.[211] Concerning investment screening, treaties such as CETA limit the scope of investor-state arbitration to exclude national security-related disputes. Similarly, the Comprehensive and Progressive Agreement for Trans-Pacific Partnership (CPTPP) and the United States-Mexico-Canada Agreement (USMCA) incorporate provisions to protect national security, while the Regional Comprehensive

[207] See above 3.2.

[208] Dolzer et al. (2022) 362, 372.

[209] Article 8.45 CETA. The same is true for many Canadian investment treaties, including the Agreement between Canada and Egypt for the Promotion and Protection of Investments, signed 13 November 1996 (entered into force 3 November 1997) (Canada-Egypt BIT), which was applicable to the dispute in *Global Telecom v Canada*. See further Voon and Merriman (2022).

[210] Annex 8-C CETA. Another example is Annex 9-H of the Comprehensive and Progressive Agreement for Trans-Pacific Partnership (2018), which however remains affected by the suspension of Article 9.19 (on the submission of a claim to arbitration) pursuant to Article 2.

[211] See 3.2 above.

Economic Partnership (RCEP) focuses on state-to-state dispute resolution with flexibility for national security concerns.

Article 8.18(1)(a) CETA limits the scope of investor-state arbitration to allegations of breach of the non-discrimination standards "with respect to the expansion, conduct, operation, management, maintenance, use, enjoyment and sale or disposal of its covered investment".[212] By not mentioning "establishment" and "acquisition", the scope of arbitral jurisdiction is limited to the post-investment phase. However, the arbitral jurisdiction covers the "expansion" of investments, which seems to imply that a dispute arising out of ex-ante screening related to a prospective expansion of an existing investment can be arbitrated.[213] This issue is not called into question by Article 8.18(2) of CETA, which provides:

> [C]laims under [Article 8.18(1)(a)] with respect to the expansion of a covered investment may be submitted only to the extent the measure relates to the existing business operations of a covered investment and the investor has, as a result, incurred loss or damage with respect to the covered investment.

Rather, it appears that Article 8.18(2) of CETA serves to exclude expansions of investments into future business operations, presumably to avoid circumvention of the exclusion of establishment or acquisition of new investments. Pursuant to Article 8.18(1)(b) of CETA, the scope of arbitral jurisdiction also covers alleged breaches of the FET standard without limitation.

Unless national security screening is excluded, whether such matters are covered should be ascertained, including which of the parties carries the burden to demonstrate it. Next, we examine to what extent arbitral practice exists to place the burden on the claimant to demonstrate that the consent to arbitrate includes matters that contradict the host state's public policy, notably matters that are justiciable in the host state's national courts (Subsection 3.3.2.1) and those that concern the host state's vital interests (Subsection 3.3.2.2). A summary of interim conclusions is found at the end (Subsection 3.3.2.3).

3.3.2.1 Presumption Against Consent to Arbitrate Nationally Non-Justiciable or Non-Arbitrable Matters

The argument that a dispute that is non-justiciable or non-arbitrable in the host state can be presumed to fall outside the scope of the host state's consent to arbitrate has not prevailed in investment arbitration case law.[214] Similarly, in *Global Telecom v Canada*, which was a case under the Washington Convention, the host state's

---

[212] Similarly, see Article 2(1) of the chapter on the resolution of investment disputes of the draft modernised EU-Mexico Global Agreement, published 25 April 2018, available via: http://trade.ec.europa.eu/doclib/cfm/doclib_section.cfm?sec=132. Accessed 23 July 2022.

[213] Pohl (2020).

[214] *Achmea B.V. v The Slovak Republic*, UNCITRAL, PCA Case No. 2008–13 (formerly Eureko B.V. v The Slovak Republic), para. 227; *Republic of Ecuador v Occidental Exploration and*

consistent treaty practice of excluding certain disputes from international arbitration did not result in a presumption for exclusion. Canada, the respondent state, referred to its consistent treaty practice of excluding national security screening as a relevant circumstance for interpreting its consent to arbitrate with respect to the dispute at hand.[215] The tribunal rejected that argument.[216]

The *Global Telecom* case concerned the application of the bilateral investment treaty between Canada and Egypt, as provided in Article II(4)(b):

> Decisions by either Contracting Party not to permit establishment of a new business enterprise or acquisition of an existing business enterprise or a share of such enterprise by investors or prospective investors shall not be subject to the provisions of Article XIII of this Agreement [the investment arbitration clause].[217]

As noted above, most arbitrators in the tribunal held that this seemingly simple exclusion from the arbitral jurisdiction was inapplicable to the circumstances of the case.[218]

The claimant, GTH, a public company incorporated in Egypt and listed on the Egyptian Stock Exchange, operated mobile networks.[219] In 2008, Wind Mobile, a joint venture between GTH and two Canadian network operators, won spectrum licences in an auction organized by Canada.[220] The auction was governed by Canada's ownership control regulations (a sector-specific national security screening mechanism), which provided that GTH could not own more than 20% of Wind Mobile's voting shares.[221] After these rules were relaxed, a wholly-owned subsidiary of GTH sought approval of its plans to acquire voting control of Wind Mobile, subject to review and approval under the Investment Canada Act (Canada's cross-sectoral national security screening mechanism).[222]

The arbitral tribunal found that Canada did not refer to the pre-existing ownership control regulations in the investment treaty, which indicated that the treaty's jurisdictional exclusion did not cover these regulations.[223] The tribunal also found that GTH's acquisition of voting control was not an "acquisition" within the meaning of Article II(4)(b) but merely "enhance[ment]" of its shareholder rights.[224] The award also demonstrated that even a seemingly clear jurisdictional exclusion

Production Corporation, English Commercial Court, Case No: 2004 FOLIO 656, judgement 29 April 2005, para. 85.

215 *Global Telecom v Canada*, para. 305.

216 *Global Telecom v Canada*, para. 326.

217 Article II(4)(b) of the Canada-Egypt BIT.

218 *Global Telecom v Canada*, para. 326.

219 *Global Telecom v Canada*, paras. 31–43.

220 *Global Telecom v Canada*, para. 27.

221 *Global Telecom v Canada*, para. 67–70.

222 *Global Telecom v Canada*, para. 71.

223 *Global Telecom v Canada*, para. 326.

224 *Global Telecom v Canada*, para. 329. In contrast, the minority arbitrator found that the acquisition of control over voting rights constituted an acquisition of an existing business

clause could lead to uncertainty in its application to given circumstances. While the *Global Telecom v Canada* award was just one case that does not represent settled arbitral practice, the tribunal's interpretation of the jurisdictional exclusion clause seems correct. As the tribunal noted, Canada's reference to its treaty practice of systematically excluding foreign ownership and control legislation from international treaty dispute settlement was insufficient to bind an international arbitral tribunal. Instead, the tribunal had to determine the scope of its jurisdiction with reference to the terms of the relevant treaty, as interpreted in accordance with Articles 31 and 32 of the VCLT.

3.3.2.2 Presumption Against Consent to Arbitrate Vital National Interests Before International Tribunals

The notion of vital interest is the argument that a state is entitled to exclude from the scope of jurisdiction of an international court or tribunal certain matters that are considered very important (vital) from the perspective of state sovereignty.[225] The concept originated as a formulation of exclusion clauses in arbitration agreements, modelled on the treaty of arbitration between Great Britain and France, which was concluded in London on 14 October 1903.[226] Substantively, the notion of vital interests cannot be defined,[227] given that each state unilaterally determines what constitutes its vital interests, which allegedly renders the concept self-judging.[228] Elements often referred to include the survival, existence, and independence of the state, including national security, public order, and certain economic interests.[229]

The vital interest argument generally invites an arbitrator to defer to the legal or factual contentions of the state concerned without engaging its own scrutiny.[230] In this sense, the alleged self-judging character of vital interests is in conflict with, and potentially a derogation from, the doctrine of competence-competence, which acknowledges that an international court or tribunal can decide on its own jurisdiction.[231]

---

enterprise within the meaning of Article II(4)(b). See Dissenting opinion of arbitrator Gary Born. See further Voon and Merriman (2022).

[225] Hahn (1991) 562–563.

[226] Moore (1905); Partsch (1987); Snow (1911) 153; Fenwick (1924); Brierly (1944) 51–57.

[227] Udich (2013) para. 3.

[228] Ibid. para. 5–9.

[229] In the law of treaties, the exception of fundamental change of circumstances (rebus sic stantibus) to terminate a treaty is based on the same idea of vital interests. See Hahn (1991) 561.

[230] Schill and Briese (2009) 74–81.

[231] Ibid. Note that vital interest may also be asserted at the merits stage as an argument that certain legal issues are of a self-judging character and that a tribunal consequently must defer to the affected state's determinations.

In the *Gabcíkovo-Nagymaros* case, the International Court of Justice (ICJ) interpreted the term "essential interest" as not shielded from justiciability.[232] While essential interests are not necessarily identical to (albeit reminiscent of)[233] vital interests, the interpretation would negate the non-justiciable character if extended to the latter. However, the ICJ made a more cautious assessment of the self-judging character of an essential security clause in the *Certain Questions of Mutual Assistance in Criminal Matters* and limited its judicial review to ensure that the interpretation by the state was exercised in good faith.[234] In the latter case, the clause specifically refers to measures that the state "considers" necessary. However, both cases confirm that the concepts of essential interests and essential security are not beyond judicial scrutiny by the ICJ. This conclusion, when applied to the subject matter of the present study, implies that neither these concepts nor the reminiscent concept of vital interests are beyond arbitral scrutiny.

The recent case of *Certain Iranian Assets* confirmed the justiciability of cases involving national security concerns.[235] That case arose out of claims related to asset freezes imposed by the United States against Iran in connection with the 1979 Iranian Islamic Revolution. In 2016, Iran lodged a case against the United States before the ICJ on the basis of the 1955 US-Iran Treaty of Amity, Economic Relations, and Consular Rights. Of relevance here, the court held that the mere assertion that a measure is "necessary to protect [a state's] essential security interests" is insufficient. Citing its jurisprudence in the *Oil Platforms* and *Nicaragua* cases,[236] the court held that the essential security clause in question was not self-judging and that the court had jurisdiction to ascertain whether a measure was "necessary" to protect a state's "essential security interests". The courts distinguished the case at hand from *Certain Questions of Mutual Assistance in Criminal Matters,* where the language of the essential interest clause specifically referred to measures that the state "consider[ed]" necessary.

Given the broad, potentially indeterminate scope of the vital interest clause, earlier treaty practice confirms that states submitting to arbitration and yet relying on the vital interest argument chose to include vital interest clauses in their

[232] *Gabčikovo-Nagymaros Project (Hungary v Slovakia)* Judgment [1997] ICJ Rep 7., para. 142. The court held that while the notion of essential interest as an element of the defence of necessity is self-judging and the discretion of the state invoking the defence is very extensive, the discretion must nevertheless be exercised reasonably and not in a manner that defeats the purpose of the defence.

[233] See Hahn (1991).

[234] *Certain Questions of Mutual Assistance in Criminal Matters (Djibouti v France),* Judgment of 4 June 2008.

[235] *Certain Iranian Assets (Islamic Republic of Iran v United States of America)*, Judgment of 30 March 2023.

[236] *Oil Platforms (Islamic Republic of Iran v United States of America)*, Judgment of 12 December 1996 and Judgment of 6 November 2003; *Military and Paramilitary Activities in and against Nicaragua (Nicaragua v United States of America),* Judgment of 26 November 1984 and Judgment of 27 June 1986.

arbitration agreements.[237] Vital interest clauses became more specific over time to avoid abuse and excluded defined types of disputes from the vital interest clause.[238]

The limitations to the material scope of investment treaty obligations pursuant to general and security exceptions, discussed in Chap. 5 below, normally also limit the scope of arbitral jurisdiction.[239] However, with respect to consent clauses that apply to "any dispute relating to investments" or similar wording (see Sect. 3.3.1.2 above), the scope of jurisdiction extends beyond the treaty's subject matter. In either case, with respect to the allegedly self-judging necessity requirement of GATT/GATS-style security exceptions, the question of material scope and scope of jurisdiction can easily be conflated.[240] However, this conflation should be approached with caution because while the former may limit the latter, it is possible that the consent to arbitration further limits the latter. Nevertheless, recent investment treaties have provided additional limitations to the arbitral jurisdiction concerning the matters covered by the general and security exceptions, which is the case of non-precluded measures (NPM) clauses discussed in Chap. 5 below, to the extent that they are worded in a manner reminiscent of the essential interest clause in *Certain Questions of Mutual Assistance in Criminal Matters*. There, the operative language hinges on what the host state "considers" necessary to protect its essential interests.

3.3.2.3 Interim Summary

Modern investment treaties often include provisions for consent that define the scope of disputes that can be arbitrated and may contain specific exclusions, particularly related to national security. Generally, these provisions encompass all disputes not specifically excluded. For example, treaties like CETA have explicit provisions excluding certain disputes related to national security screenings from arbitration.[241] Similarly, the CPTPP and the USMCA have tailored provisions that address the balance between investor protection and state sovereignty, including exceptions for national security.[242] RCEP, on the other hand,

---

[237] Udich (2013) para. 12.

[238] Udich (2013) para. 14.

[239] With respect to the general exceptions in Article 28.3(2) CETA, this point was highlighted in ECJ Opinion 1/17, *CETA*, EU:C:2019:341, 30 April 2019, paras. 152–153.

[240] Ibid.

[241] CETA explicitly excludes certain disputes related to national security screenings from its investor-state dispute settlement (ISDS) provisions. Article 8.9(2) of CETA provides that nothing in the agreement shall be construed to prevent a Party from adopting or maintaining measures necessary to protect national security interests.

[242] The USMCA has modernized its ISDS provisions, narrowing the scope and requiring the exhaustion of local remedies before arbitration in certain sectors. Annex 14-E specifically addresses national security, allowing Parties to deny benefits of the agreement in cases where investment activities are related to national security.

emphasizes state-to-state dispute resolution while still providing robust protections for investors, with a flexible approach to ISDS that can address national security concerns.[243]

Some treaty exclusions are asymmetric. CETA, for example, explicitly excludes certain disputes related to national security screenings (e.g. the Investment Canada Act), but does not similarly restrict investment screenings by the EU or its Member States, which reflects differing legislative contexts at the time of signing. This asymmetry highlights the need for a balanced approach to dispute inclusion and exclusion within the framework of consent in investment treaties.

Investment treaties typically circumscribe the scope of investor-state arbitration. For instance, CETA limits arbitration to post-establishment phases of investment while explicitly excluding disputes related to the initial establishment and acquisition. Nonetheless, it allows for arbitration concerning the expansion of existing investments, which suggests a limited but significant window for arbitral jurisdiction over investment screening that impacts the expansion. This interpretation is supported by the specific language of CETA, which restricts claims to those affecting existing operations and resulting in direct loss or damage.

Arbitral practice does not support the presumption that non-justiciable or non-arbitrable matters in the host state fall outside the state's consent to arbitration. For example, in *Global Telecom v Canada*, the tribunal dismissed Canada's argument based on its consistent treaty practice of excluding national security screenings from arbitration, which emphasized the specific treaty language over broader interpretative presumptions. This case underscored that the tribunal's jurisdiction is determined by the terms of the treaty itself, as interpreted under international law principles, particularly those codified in the VCLT.

There is no support in international jurisprudence for the proposition that the consent to arbitrate should be presumed to exclude classes of disputes that are not justiciable or arbitrable under national law. In other words, public policy that restricts justiciability or arbitrability at the national plane cannot be determinative of the interpretation of the consent to arbitrate before international tribunals. Consistent state practice is insufficient to produce a different conclusion.

The concept of vital interests, which allows states to exclude certain sovereign-sensitive matters from international adjudication, is traditionally not self-judging and is subject to arbitral scrutiny. Historical and recent ICJ cases, such as the *Gabcíkovo-Nagymaros* and *Certain Iranian Assets* cases, illustrate that tribunals are empowered to scrutinize state assertions regarding vital interests under international law. These rulings suggest that claims related to vital national interests, including those impacting national security, are justiciable in principle, barring explicit treaty provisions to the contrary.

[243] RCEP focuses more on state-to-state dispute settlement and offers a more flexible approach to ISDS. While it does not explicitly exclude national security-related disputes, it allows member states significant leeway to adopt measures necessary to protect their national security.

Moreover, there is no support in international jurisprudence for the proposition that vital national interests are to be interpreted to restrict arbitral jurisdiction as set out in the consent to arbitrate. Thus, exceptions for essential interests are not self-judging in the sense of precluding review by international tribunals (i.e. complete deference [submission]). The design of the relevant exception clause may, however, result in varying degrees of arbitral deference to national determinations.

The interpretation of consent instruments in investment arbitration requires a fine balance between respecting state sovereignty in sensitive matters and maintaining the integrity and scope of arbitral jurisdiction. The treaty language, the specific exclusionary clauses, and the evolving arbitral jurisprudence collectively shape this dynamic legal landscape.

3.3.3 Summary

In the realm of international arbitration, applicable law governing the consent to arbitrate is crucial in defining the scope of disputes that can be submitted to arbitration and how the consent is interpreted. The nature of consent and the law applied are determined based on whether the consent is derived from an investor-state contract, host state legislation, or an investment treaty.

Where the instrument of consent is set out in an investor-state contract, the law chosen by the parties applies. If the consent is embedded within the host state's national legislation, it is interpreted according to the host state's national law and supplemented by relevant principles of international law. Conversely, when the instrument of consent is stipulated in an investment treaty, it is governed by international law, particularly as elucidated in Articles 31 and 32 of the VCLT. Attention is especially given to the formulation of the relevant arbitration clause—whether it covers any dispute, any breach of the treaty, or specific types of disputes.

International law wholly or partially governs the interpretation of the instrument of consent. Whether a state gives consent to arbitrate to an investor directly in an investment contract or by means of a standing offer to arbitrate contained in its national legislation or an investment treaty, the consent is at least partially interpreted by reference to international law as long as the consent concerns international arbitration.

Modern investment treaties often contain broad consent provisions that generally encompass all disputes unless specifically excluded. For example, treaties like CETA, CPTPP, and USMCA explicitly exclude certain disputes related to national security screenings. Asymmetries, such as CETA's exclusion of screenings under the Investment Canada Act, while not similarly limiting investment screenings by the EU or its Member States, reflect the different legislative contexts at the time of signing and underscore a need for a balanced approach to the inclusion and exclusion of disputes within the framework of consent in investment treaties.

The scope of investor-state arbitration, as defined in treaties like CETA, is typically limited to post-establishment phases of investment and explicitly excludes disputes concerning the initial establishment and acquisition of investments. However, it allows for arbitration regarding the expansion of existing investments, which suggests a significant, albeit limited, window for arbitral jurisdiction over investment screening that impacts such expansions. Arbitral practice has shown that presumptions against the arbitrability of matters non-justiciable or non-arbitrable under national law do not typically preclude such matters from international arbitration. For instance, the case of *Global Telecom v Canada* demonstrated that specific treaty language takes precedence over broader interpretative presumptions, which emphasizes that the tribunal's jurisdiction is determined by the terms of the treaty, as interpreted under international law principles.

No presumptions exclude disputes concerning national security matters from the scope of jurisdiction in international arbitration. A state's national law or public policy cannot operate to justify an interpretive presumption that certain matters be excluded from the scope of the state's unilateral consent to have disputes settled by arbitration. On the contrary, a state that wishes to exclude a particular subject matter is responsible for making such exclusion clear in the instrument of consent. Similarly, international jurisprudence does not recognize that exception clauses for essential interests or similar would result in complete deference (i.e. submission) but instead entail varying degrees of deference depending on the precise formulation of the clause in question.

The concept of vital interests, which permits states to exclude certain matters from international adjudication due to their sensitive nature, is traditionally subject to arbitral scrutiny. Historical and recent cases in international jurisprudence, such as *Gabcíkovo-Nagymaros* and *Certain Iranian Assets*, illustrate that tribunals have the authority to scrutinize state assertions regarding vital interests under international law. These rulings suggest that claims related to vital national interests, including those impacting national security, are justiciable in principle, barring explicit treaty provisions to the contrary.

This interpretation of the instrument of consent in investment arbitration points to a balance between respecting state sovereignty over sensitive matters and maintaining the integrity and scope of arbitral jurisdiction. The detailed analysis of specific treaty clauses and relevant arbitral decisions is essential to provide a comprehensive view of how consent to arbitration is interpreted across different contexts to ensure that the arbitration process remains transparent, predictable, and fair.

3.4 Conclusion

The exploration of national security as a subject matter in investment arbitration throughout this chapter has underscored the absence of a mandatory rule that precludes the arbitration of disputes related to investment screening. It is evident from arbitral practice and jurisprudence that no recognized rule of public policy inherently prevents a host state from consenting to submit such disputes to arbitration. Even when national laws deem certain disputes non-arbitrable, these disputes can still be subjected to international adjudication, provided there is consent from the state involved. This scenario affirms the principle that the sphere of international arbitration is not strictly limited by domestic legal constraints when a state consents to arbitration under international law frameworks.

This chapter demonstrated that no basis exists for presuming that consent to arbitration does not extend to disputes involving matters that affect a host state's national security. Such matters, unless specifically excluded by clear and express terms in the arbitration agreement or relevant legislation, are presumed to fall within the arbitral tribunal's jurisdiction. This presumption supports the broader interpretation that international arbitral tribunals have jurisdiction over disputes related to the application of national security measures, provided that these disputes are brought before them under the terms of an applicable international treaty or agreement.

Significantly, the discussions herein have revealed that overriding considerations of public policy and vital interests related to national security do not automatically preclude such matters from arbitration. Case law, such as that from the ICJ and various arbitral decisions, suggests that international tribunals are equipped to handle disputes involving national security under the scrutiny of international law. Thus, arbitral tribunals are seen as competent to adjudicate on the merits of cases involving national security considerations when applying a balanced approach that respects the sovereign rights of states and the enforcement of international legal obligations.

In conclusion, the intricacies of national security in the context of investment arbitration require careful navigation between respecting state sovereignty and upholding the enforceability of international arbitration agreements. This balance is crucial to maintaining the integrity and efficacy of the international arbitration system, particularly in disputes involving sensitive matters such as national security. The findings of this chapter suggest a continued evolution of arbitral practice and jurisprudence towards an improved understanding of how national security considerations interact with international legal principles in investment arbitration.

References

Baldwin E, Kantor M, Nolan M (2006) Limits to enforcement of ICSID awards. J Int Arbitr 23(1):1–24

Barcelo JJ (2014). Arbitrability decisions before, during, and after arbitration. Liber Amicorum: Cornell Legal Studies Research Paper, 14–24

Barraclough A, Waincymer J (2005) Mandatory rules of law in international commercial arbitration. Melb J Int Law 6:205–244

Blackaby N, Partasides C, Redfern A, Hunter M (2009) Redfern and Hunter on international arbitration, 5th edn. Oxford University Press

Blackaby N, Partasides C, Redfern A, Hunter M (2015) Redfern and Hunter on International Arbitration, 6th edn. Oxford University Press

Böckstiegel KH (1987) Public policy and arbitrability, comparative arbitration practice and public policy in arbitration. In: ICCA New York Arbitration Congress. ICCA, pp 177–204

Boog C, Moss B (2013). The lazy myth of the arbitral tribunal's duty to render an enforceable award. Kluwer Arbitration Blog. http://arbitrationblog.kluwerarbitration.com/2013/01/28/the-lazy-myth-of-the-arbitral-tribunals-duty-to-render-an-enforceable-award/

Born G (2021a) International arbitration: law and practice, 3rd edn. Kluwer Law International

Born G (2021b) International commercial arbitration, 3rd edn. Kluwer

Borris C, Hennecke R (2019) Article V(1)(c). In: Wolff R (ed) New York Convention: convention on the recognition and enforcement of foreign arbitral awards of June 10, 1958: article-by-article commentary, 2nd edn. Verlag C. H. Beck

Brekoulakis S (2009) On arbitrability: persisting misconceptions and new areas of concern. In: Mistelis LA (ed) Arbitrability: international & comparative perspectives, vol 19. Kluwer Law International BV

Brierly JJ (1944) Vital interests and the law. Br Yearb Int Law 21:51–57

Brunet E, Speidel RE, Sternlight JE, Ware SJ (2006) Arbitration law in America: a critical assessment. Cambridge University Press

Buchanan MA (1988) Public policy and international commercial arbitration. Am Bus Law J 26:511–531

Bungenberg M, Reinisch A (2020) Recognition and enforcement of decisions. In: Bungenberg M, Reinisch A (eds) From bilateral arbitral tribunals and investment courts to a multilateral investment court: options regarding the institutionalization of investor-state dispute settlement. Springer, pp 155–173

Carbonneau TE, Janson F (1994) Cartesian logic and frontier politics: French and American concepts of arbitrability. Tulane J Int Comp Law 2:193

Delaume GR (1998) Consent to ICSID arbitration. In: Simmonds KR, Norton JJ, Andenæs MT, Footer ME (eds) The changing world of international law in the twenty-first century: a tribute to the late Kenneth R. Simmonds. Kluwer, pp 155–178

Derains Y (1986) Public policy and the law applicable to the dispute in international arbitration. In: Sanders P (ed) Comparative arbitration practice and public policy in arbitration. ICCA Congress, pp 227–256

Dolzer R, Kriebaum U, Schreuer C (2022) Principles of international investment law, 3rd edn. Oxford University Press

Farrar BJ (2008) To legislate or to arbitrate: an analysis of US foreign investment policy after FINSA and the benefits of international arbitration. J Int Bus Law 7:167

Fazilatfar H (2012) Transnational public policy: does it function from arbitrability to enforcement? City University of Hong Kong Law Rev 3(2):289–314

Fenwick CG (1924) National security and international arbitration. Am J Int Law 18(4):777–781

Fernández Arroyo D, Mbengue M (2018) Public and private international law in international courts and tribunals: evidence of an inescapable interaction. Colum J Transnatl Law 56 (4):797–854

Gaillard E, Savage J (eds) (1999) Fouchard, Gaillard, Goldman on international commercial arbitration. Kluwer Law International

Fry JD (2009) Désordre public international under the New York Convention: whither truly international public policy. Chin J Int Law 8(1):81–134

Gebauer M, Berner F (2019) Ordre public (public policy). In: Wolfrum R (ed) The Max Planck encyclopedia of public international law: index and tables, vol 11. Oxford University Press

Geisinger E, Bärtsch P, Raneda J, Ebere S (2012) Les conséquences des sanctions économiques sur les obligations contractuelles et sur l'arbitrage commercial international / The impact of international trade sanctions on contractual obligations and on international commercial arbitration. Revue de droit des affaires internationales / International Business Law Journal, 4:405–437

Hahn MJ (1991) Vital interests and the law of GATT: An analysis of GATT's security exception. Mich J Int Law 12(3):558–620

Hanotiau B (1996) What law governs the issue of arbitrability? Arbitr Int 12(4):391–404
Hanotiau B, Caprasse O (2008) Arbitrability, due process, and public policy under Article V of the New York Convention: Belgian and French perspectives. J Int Arbitr 25(6):721–741
Horvath GJ (2001) The duty of the tribunal to render an enforceable award. J Int Arbitr 18(2):135–158
Idot L (1993). Note under CA Paris, 1re ch. A, 19 May 1993, Société Labinal v. Société Mors et Westland Aerospace. Journal du droit international (Clunet), 120, 957, 979–980.
Jarrosson, C. (1993). Note sous Cour d'appel de Paris, 19 mai 1993, Société Labinal c. Sociétés Mors et Westland Aerospace. Revue de l'arbitrage 653–679
Jones D (1997) Arbitration and party autonomy: how free is the choice to arbitrate? In: Beresford Hartwell GM (ed) The commercial way to justice. Kluwer, pp 121–149
Kaufmann-Kohler G, Antonietti A, Potestà M (2018) Interim relief in investment arbitration. In K. Yannaca-Small (Ed.), Arbitration under international investment agreements: A guide to the key issues pp 633–678. Oxford University Press.
Kessedjian C (2007) Transnational public policy. In: Van Den Berg AJ (ed) International arbitration 2006: back to basics? Kluwer Law International
Kirry A (1996) Arbitrability: current trends in Europe. Arbitr Int 12(4):373–390
Kjos HE (2013) Applicable law in investor-state arbitration: the interplay between national and international law. Oxford University Press
Kleinheisterkamp J (2018) Overriding mandatory laws in international arbitration. Int Compar Law Q 67(4):903–930
Kotelnikov A (2020) Economic sanctions, arbitrability, and public policy. Int Arbitr Law Rev 23(1):19–39
Kreindler RH (2003) Approaches to the application of transnational public policy by arbitrators. J World Invest 4:239–250
Kröll S (2015) Enforcement of awards. In: Bungenberg M, Griebel J, Hobe S, Reinisch A, Kim Y-I (eds) International investment law: a handbook. C. H. Beck
Kronke H, Nacimiento P, Otto D (2010) Recognition and enforcement of foreign arbitral awards: a global commentary on the New York Convention. Kluwer Law International BV
Kryvoi Y (2018) Economic crimes in international investment law. Int Compar Law Q 67(3):577–606
Kumar R, Rawat P (2022) Scope of 'arbitrability' and 'public policy' as a ground for setting aside an arbitral award under Section 34 of the Indian Arbitration and Conciliation Act, 1996. Sambodhi: Indological Research Journal of L.D.I.I, 45(1[V]).
Kunz CA (2016) Enforcement of arbitral awards under the New York Convention in Switzerland: an overview of the current practice and case law of the Supreme Court. ASA Bull 34(4):836–865
Lalive P (1987). Transnational (or truly international) public policy and international arbitration. ICCA Congr Ser 3/1986
Lehmann M (2004) A plea for a transnational approach to arbitrability in arbitral practice. Columbia J Transnatl Law 42:753–775
Lew JD (1999) The law applicable to the form and substance of the arbitration clause. In: Van Den Berg AJ (ed) Improving the efficiency of arbitration agreements and awards: 40 years of application of the New York Convention. Kluwer Law
Lew JD, Mistelis LA, Kröll SM (2003) Comparative international commercial arbitration. Kluwer Law
Markert L, Bubrowski H (2015) National setting aside proceedings. In: Bungenberg M, Griebel J, Hobe S, Reinisch A, Kim Y-I (eds) International investment law: a handbook. C. H. Beck
Mayer P (1986) Mandatory rules of law in international arbitration. Arbitr Int 2:274–280
Mayer P, Sheppard A (2003) Final ILA report on public policy as a bar to enforcement of international arbitral awards. LCIA Arbitr Int 19(2):249–263
Mistelis L (2000) Keeping the unruly horse in control or public policy as a bar to the enforcement of foreign arbitral awards. Int Law FORUM du Droit Int 2(4):248–253

Mistelis L (2007) Mandatory rules in international arbitration: too much too early or too little too late. Am Rev Int Arbitr 18(1–2):217–229

Mistelis LA (2009) Arbitrability—international and comparative perspectives: is arbitrability a national or an international law issue? In: Brekoulakis SL, Mistelis LA (eds) Arbitrability: international & comparative perspectives. Kluwer Law International, pp 1–9

Moore JB (1905) Treaties and executive agreements. Political Sci Q 20(3):385–420

Nollkaemper A (2006) The role of domestic courts in the case law of the International Court of Justice. Chin J Int Law 5(2):301–322

Nollkaemper A (2011) National courts and the international rule of law. Oxford University Press

Partsch KJ (1987) Vital interests. In Bernhardt R (ed) Encyclopedia of Public International Law: Instalment 10: States, responsibility of states, international law and municipal law pp 526–527. North-Holland

Paulsson J (1995) Arbitration without privity. ICSID Rev 10(2):232–257

Paulsson J (2005) Jurisdiction and admissibility. In: Aksen G, Briner RG (eds) Global reflections on international law, commerce and dispute resolution. ICC Publishing

Pohl JH (2017) Substantive transparency requirements in international investment law. Revista Instituto Colombiano de Derecho Tributario 54(77):179–212

Pohl JH (2018) Intra-EU investment arbitration after the Achmea case: legal autonomy bounded by mutual trust? Eur Const Law Rev 14(4):767–791

Pohl JH (2020) The impact of investment treaty commitments on the design and operation of EU investment screening mechanisms. In: Hindelang S, Moberg A (eds) YSEC yearbook of socio-economic constitutions 2020. Springer, pp 725–768

Poudret JF, Besson S (2007) Comparative law of international arbitration. Sweet & Maxwell

Quinke D (2012) Article V(2)(a). In: Wolff R (ed) New York Convention: convention on the recognition and enforcement of foreign arbitral awards of June 10, 1958: article-by-article commentary, 2nd. Verlag C. H. Beck

Rajput A (2021) National courts as actors in investment arbitration. In: Titi C (ed) Public actors in international investment law. Springer, pp 37–56

Reinisch A (2010) Enforcement of investment awards. In: Yannaca-Small K (ed) Arbitration under international investment agreements: a guide to the key issues. Oxford University Press, pp 671–697

Reisman M (2007). Law, international public policy (so-called) and arbitral choice in international commercial arbitration. In: ICCA Congress Series, 13/2007

Rubino-Sammartano M (2014) International arbitration law and practice. Juris Publishing, Inc

Sasson M (2017) Substantive law in investment treaty arbitration: the unsettled relationship between international law and municipal law, 2nd edn. Wolters Kluwer

Schill S, Briese R (2009) "If the state considers": self-judging clauses in international dispute settlement. Max Planck Yearbook of United Nations Law Online 13(1):61–140

Schreuer CH (2008a) What is a legal dispute? In: Hafner G, Buffard I (eds) International law between universalism and fragmentation: festschrift in honour of Gerhard Hafner. Martinus Nijhoff, pp 959–980

Schreuer CH (2008b) Consent to arbitration. In: Muchlinski P, Ortino F, Schreuer C (eds) The Oxford handbook of international investment law. Oxford University Press, pp 830–867

Schreuer CH (2009) The ICSID Convention: a commentary. Cambridge University Press

Schreuer CH (2019) Consent to arbitration through legislation. In: Ruiz Fabri H (ed) International law and litigation: a look into procedure. Nomos Verlagsgesellschaft mbH & Company KG, pp 447–477

Schwab KH (1995) Wandlungen der Schiedsfähigkeit. In: Gerhardt W, Diederichsen U, Rimmelspacher B, Costede J (eds), Festschrift für Wolfram Henckel zum 70. Geburtstag am 21. April 1995 (pp. 803–816). De Gruyter

Seelig ML (2009) The notion of transnational public policy and its impact on jurisdiction, arbitrability and admissibility. Annals FLB – Belgrade Law Review 57(3):116–134

Sever JR (1991) The relaxation of inarbitrability and public policy checks on U.S. and foreign arbitration: Arbitration out of control? Tulane Law Review 65(6):1661

Sheppard A (2003) Interim ILA report on public policy as a bar to enforcement of international arbitral awards. Arbitr Int 19(2):217–248

Sheppard A (2004) Public policy and the enforcement of arbitral awards: should there be a global standard? Transnatl Disput Manag 1(1):1

Snow AH (1911) Legal limitation of arbitral tribunals. University of Pennsylvania Law Review and American Law Register, 60(3): 153–180

Szabados T (2018) EU economic sanctions in arbitration. J Int Arbitr 35(4):439–462

Tosun HA (2019) Public policy concepts in international arbitration. University of California, Berkeley

Udich J (2013) Vital interests. In: Wolfrum R (ed) Max Planck Encyclopedia of Public International Law. Oxford University Press

Voon T, Merriman D (2023) Incoming: how international investment law constrains foreign investment screening. Incoming: how international investment law constrains foreign investment screening. The Journal of World Investment & Trade 24(1):75–114

Waibel M (2015) Investment arbitration: jurisdiction and admissibility. In: Bungenberg M, Griebel J, Hobe S, Reinisch A, Kim Y-I (eds) International investment law: a handbook. C. H. Beck

Wallace CD (2002) The multinational enterprise and legal control: host state sovereignty in an era of economic globalization. Brill

Wolff R (ed) (2019) New York Convention: convention on the recognition and enforcement of foreign arbitral awards of June 10, 1958: article-by-article commentary, 2nd edn. Verlag C. H. Beck

Yang I (2015) A comparative review on substantive public policy in international commercial arbitration. Disput Resolut J 70(2):49

Zeller B, Mohanty G, Garimella SR (2021) The public policy exception to enforcement—The origins in private law. In: Zeller B, Mohanty G, Garimella SR (eds) Enforcement of foreign arbitral awards and the public policy exception. Springer, pp 95–125

Chapter 4
Investment Screening and Jurisdiction Under Investment Treaties

Abstract This chapter examines the jurisdictional complexities associated with sovereign investors and investment screening mechanisms within the framework of international investment law. It explores the eligibility of sovereign entities under varying conditions by particularly focusing on investments with non-commercial objectives. The chapter outlines the challenges posed by investment screening, especially when implemented before the establishment of an investment, and its implications for the jurisdiction of arbitral tribunals. It also discusses the need for clearer treaty definitions to guide arbitral tribunals in distinguishing between the commercial and governmental activities of sovereign investors. Ultimately, the chapter highlights how disputes related to national security screening often withstand jurisdictional challenges due to explicit treaty provisions that recognize the standing of sovereign investors and confirm the existence of investments under international law.

4.1 Introduction

The typical fact patterns associated with investment screening have specific characteristics that call into question the scope of jurisdiction in investor-state arbitration: (a) an investor's links to a foreign government are a key element in national security screening, and (b) investment screening often precedes the making of the investment.

Investor-state arbitration provides a remedy for disputes only between a state and an investor of another state, not between two states.[1] Only in such disputes does the arbitral tribunal have personal jurisdiction (ratione personae).

[1] On the origins of investor-state arbitration, see Sornarajah (1997) 103; Kaufmann-Kohler and Potestà (2020); Dugan et al. (2008) 11–45.

J. H. Pohl, *Arbitration of Disputes related to National Security Screening of Foreign Investments*, EYIEL Monographs - Studies in European and International Economic Law 50,
https://doi.org/10.1007/978-3-032-26342-1_4

However, in the context of investment screening, where foreign investment is deemed to adversely affect national security, an important element is whether a foreign government directly or indirectly controls the foreign investor. In fact, as discussed in Subchapter 2.1 above, the investor may be another state, an SOE, an SWF, or a private investor owned, controlled, subsidized, contractually obliged, instructed, or influenced by, or otherwise acting mainly in the interests of another state (an investor of each such type is referred to below broadly as a "sovereign investor").[2]

An investor who has suffered harm is only entitled to seek legal redress before an investment arbitration tribunal where a dispute arises out of an investment.[3] Therefore, the existence of an investment is an indispensable requirement for subject-matter jurisdiction (ratione materiae). To the extent that national security screening precedes the making of an investment (ex-ante screening), the question arises whether an investment already exists and actionable rights have accrued under the relevant arbitration clause, whether contained in a treaty, a contract, or a law.

First, it is appropriate to examine the question of whether a sovereign investor should be considered an "investor" to determine whether the claimant has standing so that the arbitral tribunals may exercise personal jurisdiction (4.2). Second is the question of the existence of an investment for purposes of determining subject-matter jurisdiction (4.3). The chapter ends with a conclusion (4.4).

4.2 Personal Jurisdiction and Sovereign Investors

Can sovereign investors avail themselves of investor-state arbitration to settle investment-treaty claims? Indeed, this situation is implicated by investment screening on national security grounds. It is a decisive question whether the foreign investor, whose prospective investment potentially affects the national security interests of the host state, is or could be under the control of another state, including the investor's home state.[4] If so, national security screening would likely be triggered, which in turn could give rise to a screening decision that may adversely affect the sovereign investor. Hence, this situation may give rise to an investment treaty claim against the host state.

In assessing whether a sovereign investor should be considered an "investor" to determine the investor's standing and the arbitral tribunal's jurisdiction, it is useful to recall the additional layer of requirements that may follow in the event that the Washington Convention is applicable. Therefore, this chapter first deals with the general case before turning to additional requirements by addressing the following

---

[2] On the national security dimension of sovereign foreign investors, see generally McLaughlin (2020).

[3] Dolzer et al. (2022) 83–90.

[4] See Chap. 2 above.

question: Should an arbitrator apply the same analysis to sovereign and private investors when interpreting and applying the "investor" definition in investment treaties (4.2.1) and the Washington Convention (4.2.2)? The findings of the subchapter are summarized in the final section (4.2.3).

4.2.1 Standing of Sovereign Investors Under Investment Treaties

When an arbitrator determines whether a foreign investor has standing to bring arbitration proceedings under a specific investment treaty, it is important to take note of any particular elements of the "investor" definition that may exclude investors owned or controlled by another government. Most treaties make no such distinction and are consequently prima facie open to sovereign investors as claimants.[5] This situation is potentially complicated by the fact that sovereign investors may act in a governmental or a commercial capacity. As discussed in Chap. 2, states are frequently engaged in investment activity through SWFs or SOEs. Does it matter in what capacity a sovereign investor acts for the determination of whether the investor has standing (4.2.1.1), and, if so, how commercial and governmental conduct can be distinguished (4.2.1.2)?

4.2.1.1 Non-Commercial Sovereign Investment: Foreign Investment Activity as Economic Statecraft

The protection afforded by investment treaties normally applies equally to sovereign and private investors.[6] However, where the foreign investment activity of sovereign investors can be classified as governmental conduct, the question arises of whether the investment relation is, in reality, one between two states rather than between one state and a national of another state. In this situation, arbitrators must

---

[5] Notably, Article 1.5 USMCA defines "enterprise" as "an entity constituted or organized under applicable law, whether or not for profit, and whether privately-owned or governmentally-owned or controlled, including a corporation, trust, partnership, sole proprietorship, joint venture, association or similar organization" [emphasis added]. Similar language appears in both the 2004 Model U.S. Bilateral Investment Treaty and Canada's 2004 model for Foreign Investment Promotion and Protection Agreements. Similarly, Article 13(a)(iii) of the Convention establishing the Multilateral Investment Guarantee Agency includes within the definition of investor legal entities "whether or not privately owned". Some other treaties go further, specifically extending protection not only to government-controlled entities but also to the home government itself. Notably, the investment treaty between the Czech Republic and Kuwait, defines "investor" to include, "with respect to either Contracting State, the Government of that Contracting State". The provision also extends coverage to "institutions, development funds, authorities, foundations, establishments [and] agencies".

[6] Dolzer et al. (2022) 58.

determine whether that conduct prevents the claimant from qualifying as an "investor" under the relevant investment treaty.[7]

In economic literature, the term "economic statecraft" has been used to describe the use by the state of economic policy tools for non-economic policy ends.[8] FDI may be characterized as an act of economic statecraft insofar as the aim of the investment is not entirely or mainly to generate profit but to pursue a geopolitical aim, such as to gain influence in another state or secure control of a strategic resource.[9] To the extent that the investor's conduct is attributable to a state, such geoeconomic investments may rightly be classified as governmental rather than commercial in capacity.[10]

Regarding the question of whether the protection of investment treaties extends to SOEs, SWFs, or other sovereign investors acting in a governmental capacity, a detailed analysis of the definition of "investor" in these treaties can provide important insights.[11] In particular, according to such definitions, some treaties explicitly include public or state-owned enterprises. Some even include governments, while others simply include legal persons without distinguishing between public and private entities.[12] These distinctions are critical in determining whether a particular treaty covers investments made by sovereign investors.

Concerning most investment treaties that define the term "investor" broadly, such as to prima facie apply to sovereign investors, arbitrators need to determine on a case-by-case basis whether investment treaty protection extends to such investors.[13] Pursuant to Article 31(1) of the VCLT, "A treaty shall be interpreted in good faith in accordance with the ordinary meaning to be given to the terms of the treaty in their context and in the light of its object and purpose".[14] Where a treaty's "investor" definition does not address sovereign investors, the ordinary meaning of the terms supports the conclusion that such investors are included in the definition.

Nevertheless, such an interpretation may not sit well with the object and purpose of the treaty. Investment treaties are intended to depoliticize investment disputes between a state and individuals (persons and entities) of another state (investor-state disputes) by enabling such individuals to settle their disputes directly with that other state.[15] Investment treaties are not capable of, or designed to, depoliticize investment disputes between two states unless the investment is purely commercial.[16] Hence, when an "investor" definition in an investment treaty, which on its

[7] Blyschak (2010) 18–19.

[8] Aggarwal and Reddie (2021).

[9] Hagemeyer-Witzleb (2021) 148–151; Wang (2017).

[10] Hagemeyer-Witzleb ibid.

[11] Feldman (2016).

[12] Ibid.

[13] McLaughlin (2019).

[14] Article 31(1) VCLT.

[15] Muchlinski (2005); Du (2021); McLaughlin (2019); Feldman (2016).

[16] Paparinskis (2010); Kriebaum (2019).

face does not exclude sovereign investors, is interpreted in the light of the object and purpose of such treaty, an arbitrator may reasonably conclude that sovereign investors are not "investors" insofar as they act in a governmental rather than commercial capacity.[17] This line of reasoning was put to the test in the *CSOB v Slovakia* case in the context of the Washington Convention, but in general, the same argument—that investment treaties concern investor-state disputes and not interstate disputes—is also relevant for cases where the Washington Convention does not apply.

Moreover, in the light of prevailing treaty practice, definitional distinctions should not be rendered meaningless by simply allowing sovereign investors to qualify as "investors" regardless of the wording of the applicable treaty and regardless of whether the sovereign investor is acting in a commercial or governmental capacity. By contrast, the inclusion of state-owned and public enterprises in the definition of "investor" suggests that the treaty drafters were indeed cognizant of the possibility of claims of sovereign investors as "investors" under the applicable treaty.[18]

Investment treaties frequently provide for investment arbitration (investor-state arbitration) and interstate arbitration (state-state arbitration) as dispute settlement methods.[19] Although the latter provisions may be used for purposes of diplomatic protection, whereby the home state espouses the claims of a private investor, their inclusion in a treaty is also compatible with the interpretation that the contracting states indeed intended to settle disputes of sovereign investors.[20] In other words, in the absence of specific provisions that limit the scope of a state-state arbitration clause, even a dispute that is politicized, as may be the case when the sovereign investor acts in a governmental capacity, is potentially covered.[21]

This interpretative possibility draws attention to the significance of the context under Article 31(1) of the VCLT in interpreting the definition of "investor", specifically the context of the surrounding language in which the term appears in the treaty. A meaningful distinction can then be made between the interpretation of "investor" as a jurisdictional requirement and as a requirement for the extension of substantive investment protection.[22] Considering also the distinction between investment arbitration and interstate arbitration, sovereign investors may enjoy the

---

[17] Blyschak (2010) 20–21.

[18] Boute (2018) 399; Blyschak (2010) 21–25.

[19] Reinisch and Malintoppi (2008).

[20] See further Mirabbasi and Siavashpour (2019); Polanco (2019) 231–273.

[21] Ibid.; Reinish and Malintoppi (2008).

[22] Boute (2018) 398–404. Boute cited *China Heilongjiang International Economic & Technical Cooperative Corp et al. v Mongolia*, Award, PCA Case No. 2010–20, Award (30 June 2017) and *Beijing Urban Construction Group Co., Ltd. (BUCG) v Republic of Yemen*, ICSID Case No. ARB/14/3, Decision on Jurisdiction (31 May 2017) in support of the argument that a "purpose-based interpretive approach" according to which an arbitral tribunal can in principle refuse jurisdiction if there is evidence that the foreign investment was made in the pursuit of the home state's strategic interest, based on express instructions by the home state government.

same protection as private investors but may be precluded from instituting investor-state arbitration proceedings. However, instead, they may have to rely on the home state espousing its claims and, if such a clause is available, bringing it before state-state arbitration.[23]

The possibility of sovereign investors acting in a governmental capacity also raises the issue of jurisdictional immunity.[24] In particular, the issue is whether a sovereign investor can be considered an "investor" under a particular investment treaty, even if the actions of that sovereign investor do not fall within the jurisdiction of the domestic courts of the host state.[25] The Swiss Federal Department of Foreign Affairs has taken the position that Swiss treaties do not protect the latter type of actions when considering the object and purpose of investment treaties.[26] This position corresponds to the concept of acta iure imperii, which determines the scope of sovereign immunity.

Under certain conditions, sovereign investors may enjoy immunity under the United Nations Convention on Immunity from Jurisdiction of States and Their Property, which affirms the immunity of a state from the jurisdiction of foreign courts (subject to certain limits).[27] For purposes of the Convention, a "state" is defined to include "agencies or instrumentalities of the State or other entities, to the extent that they are entitled to perform and are actually performing acts in the exercise of the sovereign authority of the State".[28] In other words, following the argument in the previous paragraph, even where the definition of "investor" in an investment treaty expressly includes sovereign investors, a distinction can be made between sovereign investors investing in a commercial capacity (being subject to the jurisdiction of the host state's courts, just as any private investor) and in a governmental capacity (being immune from the jurisdiction of host state courts).[29]

Of particular interest is the Convention's definition of "commercial transaction", which includes the following rule of interpretation:

> In determining whether a contract or transaction is a "commercial transaction" under paragraph 1 (c), reference should be made primarily to the nature of the contract or transaction, but its purpose should also be taken into account if the parties to the contract or transaction have so agreed, or if, in the practice of the State of the forum, that purpose is relevant to determining the non-commercial character of the contract or transaction.[30]

---

[23] Ibid.

[24] Annacker (2011) 535–536.

[25] Ibid.

[26] Ibid. See also Feldman (2016) 24–35.

[27] UN Convention on Jurisdictional Immunities of States and Their Property, UN GA Res A/59/38 (2004), 2 Dec. 2004 (not in force).

[28] Article 2(1)(b)(iii) of the UN Convention on Jurisdictional Immunities of States and Their Property.

[29] Francioni (2009).

[30] Article 2(2) of the UN Convention on Jurisdictional Immunities of States and Their Property.

Thus, the Convention suggests a fact-specific analysis focused on the nature of the contract or transaction (i.e. the nature of the investment giving rise to the dispute). Interestingly, the purpose of the investment—which may address the question of whether the investment serves political or purely economic ends—may also be relevant for the analysis. In the likely scenario that the purpose of the investment has not been the subject of agreement between the home and host states, the Convention leaves open the possibility to take the investment purpose into account if, "in the practice of the State of the forum", the purpose is relevant to determining the non-commercial character of the investment.

Although the United Nations Convention on Immunity from Jurisdiction of States and their Property does not apply to investment arbitration, it remains relevant to the question of sovereign immunity in the host state's courts, which in turn may provide important guidance for purposes of interpreting the host state's consent to (investment) arbitration.[31] If the contracting states are obliged under a multilateral treaty of general application to grant each other's sovereign investors jurisdictional immunity in their courts with respect to their non-commercial investments, should their consent to arbitration be interpreted consistently? Did they intend that their sovereign investors would remain immune before the courts of the other contracting state (i.e. not waive their immunity) while retaining the possibility to bring investor-state arbitration proceedings?

In the absence of clarifications from states, the question of the extent to which a particular investor enjoys jurisdictional immunity remains the best guide to approaching the question of whether sovereign entities engaged in investments for non-commercial purposes fall within the arbitral tribunal's jurisdiction ratione personae.

4.2.1.2 Attribution of Foreign Investment Activity to a State

On the question of how to distinguish commercial conduct from governmental conduct by sovereign investors, arbitral tribunals are faced with the question of whether particular conduct can be attributed to a state.[32]

In accordance with the International Law Commission's 2001 Articles on Responsibility of States for Internationally Wrongful Acts (ARSIWA), which reflect customary international law, actions can be attributed to a state if organs of a state conducted them[33] or if the conduct was directed or controlled by a state.[34] However, the existing standards of attribution under the ARSIWA fail to capture scenarios where the state's support for a private actor is sporadic or without

[31] Annacker (2011) 535–536.

[32] Blyschak (2010) 35.

[33] International Law Commission, "Responsibility of States for Internationally Wrongful Acts", UN GAOR 56th Session Supp No 10 UN Doc A/56/10, art 4.

[34] Ibid art 8.

involvement in the decision-making structures.[35] This scenario would typically be the case with SWFs and SOEs or private investors that benefit from investment-related subsidies. In these situations, sovereign investors would enjoy a large degree of autonomy in their decision-making but would nevertheless pursue actions at the behest of the home state. Thus, when a claim has been submitted to investment arbitration by a sovereign investor whose conduct would be attributable to another state, the question arises whether such a claim should still be considered that of an "investor" or a "state".

For treaties that include references to the home state or SOEs in the definition of "investor", the fact that a claimant's acts are attributable to the state should not affect the claimant's ability to qualify as an investor for purposes of availing itself of the treaty's substantive protection.[36] However, when the same treaty specifically provides for interstate arbitration alongside investor-state arbitration, the attribution of a sovereign investor's investment activities to the home state may affect the investor's ability to invoke investor-state arbitration.[37]

Concerning treaties that do not expressly include states or SOEs in the "investor" definition, the question of attribution principally involves the issue of whether the sovereign investor is under the "instructions" or "control" of another state.[38]

While the term "instructions" leaves little room for uncertainty, the notion of "control" is more complex.[39] Since private conduct, as a main rule, is not attributable to a state, the notion of "control" as an exception to this principle must be interpreted restrictively. Private conduct that is merely supported or planned by the state, exercised in its interest, or otherwise on its behalf, is not attributable to the state.[40]

With respect to "control", the level of ownership is not always a reliable indicator of the degree of control, as asymmetric voting rights may allow some shareholders to exercise disproportionate influence on decision-making power.[41] This situation implies that the analysis in this respect is highly fact-based.

---

[35] Ibid.

[36] Feldman (2016).

[37] Annacker (2011) 550–562.

[38] McLaughlin (2019) 606.

[39] Blyschak (2010) 36–37.

[40] The interpretation of "instructions" and "control" was in dispute in *Short v Islamic Republic of Iran* Award No 312-11135-3, Iran–United States Claims Tribunal, Chamber Three, 14 July 1987, summarized in (1988) 82 AJIL 140, and *Rankin v Republic of Iran*, Award No 326-10913-2, Iran–United States Claims Tribunal, Chamber Two, 3 November 1987, summarized in Yeager v Islamic Republic of Iran and Rankin v Islamic Republic of Iran (1988) 82 AJIL 353, and in the ICJ judgments in the *Tehran American Diplomatic and Consular Staff* case and the *Nicaragua* case.

[41] Blyschak (2010) 41–49.

4.2.1.3 Interim Summary

This section explores the complexities surrounding the standing of sovereign investors in international investment arbitration. It examines how investment treaties define "investor" and considers the implications of these definitions for SOEs and SWFs, especially when these entities function in a governmental capacity.

Most investment treaties do not distinguish between private and sovereign investors, so they allow state-owned entities the same access to arbitration mechanisms as private entities. This inclusivity can introduce complexities when sovereign entities are involved in disputes. The challenge lies in distinguishing between commercial acts, which are typically covered by investment treaties, and governmental acts, which may not be. A pivotal issue in determining the standing of a sovereign investor is whether the entity acts in a governmental or commercial capacity. Investment treaties are generally designed to depoliticize disputes between private investors and states, not to handle disputes between states. Therefore, when a sovereign investor acts in a capacity that serves broader state functions or policy objectives (termed "economic statecraft"), the nature of the dispute changes and potentially renders the investor-state dispute resolution mechanism inappropriate.

Sovereign investments driven by geopolitical aims or other state-directed objectives might not qualify as "investments" under some treaties if these actions are deemed governmental. This distinction is crucial because if an investment is primarily aimed at influencing foreign policy or controlling strategic resources, it may not warrant protection under typical investor-state arbitration frameworks designed to resolve commercial disputes. The interpretation of "investor" within the context of the treaty's objective and purpose is critical. According to the VCLT, treaties must be interpreted in good faith and in light of their object and purpose. If a treaty's purpose is to depoliticize investment disputes, extending its protection to state entities acting in a governmental capacity could contradict this purpose.

Typically, "investor" definitions in investment treaties do not exclude sovereign investors. Arguments that, in such cases, sovereign investors should nevertheless be excluded have been made on the basis of contextual distinctions between the notion of "investor" for jurisdictional and substantive purposes in the context of state-state arbitration or on the basis of actions covered by sovereign immunity. Nevertheless, such arguments have not attracted support in arbitral jurisprudence. A sovereign investor's ability to qualify as an "investor" under an investment treaty may also be affected by whether its conduct would be attributable to the home state. This issue is particularly relevant when the treaty in question does not expressly include the home state or home SOEs in the "investor" definition. In practice, difficult issues may arise in ascertaining whether an enterprise is under the "control" of the home state for the purpose of concluding that the enterprise's conduct should be attributed to the home state.

Attribution of actions to the state is another significant factor in determining whether a sovereign investor qualifies as an "investor" under a treaty, which involves understanding whether the actions of the investor, such as those of SWFs or SOEs, are directed or controlled by the state. Hence, they are essentially an arm of the government rather than independent commercial entities. Arbitral decisions have shown variability in handling cases involving sovereign investors, particularly when these entities operate in a dual capacity. Not all arbitrations have supported the exclusion of sovereign investors from the definition of "investor", especially in the absence of explicit treaty language to that effect. However, when interpreting treaties, arbitrators have often considered the broader context and the specific roles that entities play within their respective states.

The standing of sovereign investors in investment treaty arbitration is a nuanced issue that requires careful examination of treaty language and the specific circumstances of each case. While treaties generally allow sovereign entities to participate in arbitration, the capacity in which these entities act and the nature of their investment activities can significantly affect their eligibility for protection under these treaties. This reality necessitates a fact-specific analysis and a sensitive application of legal principles to ensure that the arbitration process remains true to the objectives of the underlying investment treaties. Arbitrators and treaty negotiators must be cognizant of these complexities to effectively manage disputes involving state entities and to maintain the integrity of the investor-state dispute resolution mechanism.

4.2.2 Standing of Sovereign Investors Under the Washington Convention

Even if an arbitral tribunal concludes that an investor has standing under the relevant investment treaty, it may not be possible to fulfil the requirements for personal jurisdiction under the Washington Convention. Developed by the World Bank to promote private international investment as opposed to public international investment,[42] the Washington Convention is expressly limited to claims by nationals of states against other states, including in the context of recourse claims.[43] Article 25(1) of the Washington Convention provides the following:

> The jurisdiction of the Centre shall extend to any legal dispute arising directly out of an investment, between a Contracting State [. . .] and a national of another Contracting State.

[42] As noted in the 1965 Report of the Directors of the World Bank, the ICSID Convention was formulated "in the interests of economic development" and could "serve as an important step in fostering an atmosphere of mutual confidence and thereby stimulate a greater inflow of private international capital to countries desirous of attracting it". Reflecting this objective, the ICSID Convention begins with the following words: "Recognizing the need for international cooperation for economic development and the role of private international investment therein".

[43] The drafters of the Convention considered but rejected the possibility of extending the application of Convention's arbitration framework to states.

In deciding whether and how to distinguish investor-state disputes from state-state disputes under the Convention, the General Counsel of the World Bank and first Secretary-General of ICSID, Aron Broches, proposed a test:

> A mixed economy company or government-owned corporation should not be disqualified as a "national of another Contracting State", unless it is acting as an agent for the government or is discharging an essentially governmental function.[44]

Although enjoying no binding legal authority, the Broches test has exerted a persuasive influence on investment tribunals' reasoning since first being adopted by the tribunal in *CSOB v Slovakia,* as discussed below.[45]

In applying the Broches test, the tribunal in *CSOB v Slovakia* held that in determining whether an investment activity constituted the exercise of an "essentially governmental function", it was necessary to focus on the nature of its effects rather than its purpose.[46] In other words, the tribunal found that regardless of whether CSOB's actions were in "furtherance of the policy or governmental objectives" of the home state, the ultimate determinative question was whether the actions themselves were "essentially commercial and not governmental in nature".[47]

The tribunal focused exclusively on how to characterize the nature of the investment activity in question and concluded that it did not matter that CSOB was publicly owned and controlled.[48] The decisive question was whether CSOB's investment activities crossed the line between those carried out by private undertakings and those carried out mainly by bodies governed by public law "motivated by the policy of the State" or CSOB's activities benefited from the policies and subsidies of the Czech government. The crucial fact was that CSOB was not involved in the formulation or development of policies or legislative or administrative action.[49] Hence, the tribunal did not focus on CSOB's or the Czech government's purpose of the investment but on the nature of the investment, which included the nature of the relationship between CSOB and the Czech government in terms of policy, legislation, and administration.

The application of the Broches test in the *CSOB* case deviates from the commercial transaction test under Article 2(2) of the United Nations Convention on Immunity from Jurisdiction of States and their Property.[50] Under the latter, as mentioned previously, in determining whether a contract or transaction is a "commercial transaction", the primary test is the nature of the contract or

---

[44] Broches (1972) 354–355; Amerasinghe (1979) 196.

[45] Further cases applying the test are *Rumeli Telekom A.S. v Republic of Kazakhstan*, ICSID Case No. ARB/05/16, Award (July 29, 2008) and *Flughafen Zürich A.G. v Bolivarian Republic of Venezuela*, ICSID Case No. ARB/10/19, Award (Nov. 18, 2014).

[46] Schreuer (2009) paras. 270–276.

[47] Ibid. 272.

[48] *CSOB v Slovakia*, Decision on Jurisdiction, 24 May 1999, paras. 16–27.

[49] Ibid.

[50] Blyschak (2010) 34–41.

transaction, as well as its purpose if the parties to the contract have so agreed or if, in the practice of the forum state, this purpose is relevant in determining the non-commercial nature of the contract or transaction.[51] A test that considers both nature and purpose is also arguably more appropriate for large and complex operations of global investors, such as SWFs.[52] Concretely, a test that only considers the nature of the investment ignores the broader context, such as how the investment in question fits with the investor's strategic investment agenda. An investment may or may not be in the nature of a commercial transaction when considered in isolation but may be part of a non-commercial investment strategy, and vice versa.

In view of the Washington Convention's express limitation to claims by nationals of states against other states under Article 25(1), the totality of a sovereign investor's operations must be assessed to determine whether they constitute an extension of that state's external investment policy or strategic investment programme.[53] This approach allows arbitral tribunals to determine the true geoeconomic impact of superficial business transactions.[54] Even more so than following the *CSOB* tribunal, this approach allows arbitrators to determine whether a sovereign investor has crossed the line between conduct motivated by purely commercial objectives and conduct motivated in whole or in part by the geoeconomic agenda of the home state.

The *CSOB* case did not comprehensively address the second arm of the Broches test: whether the sovereign investor acted as an agent for the government.[55] Interpreted in the light of Article 8 of ARSIWA on State Responsibility, this part of the test could be understood as whether the investor acted under the instruction, direction, or control of the home state.[56] As mentioned in that context, establishing a "specific factual relationship"[57] between the sovereign investor and the home state is likely to be a difficult evidentiary challenge. Ultimately, the second arm of the test is therefore likely to be more difficult to prove, leaving the first arm ("discharging an essentially governmental function") as the more viable (or at least practically more relevant) route to challenge standing.

Sovereign investors' standing under the Washington Convention has focused on the nature of the investment activity in question in arbitral jurisprudence. The purpose of the investment, which opens the possibility to consider the broader context of the investor's strategic aims, has not had a significant role to play in case law, nor have cases focused on whether the investor is under instructions from the home state.

---

[51] Ibid.

[52] Feldman (2016) 27–31.

[53] Boute (2018) 402–404.

[54] Ibid.

[55] See 4.2.1 above.

[56] Blyschak (2010) 35.

[57] Ibid.

4.2.3 Summary

This subchapter on the standing of sovereign investors under investment treaties and the Washington Convention examined the complexities of how SOEs and SWFs are treated within the framework of international arbitration. The broad inclusion of "investor" definitions in many treaties does not usually distinguish between private and sovereign investors, which allows entities owned or controlled by states the same access to arbitration mechanisms as private entities. This inclusion raises significant complexities when these entities engage in activities that straddle the commercial and governmental divide, a distinction critical under the Washington Convention and other international legal frameworks.

Most investment treaties are designed to depoliticize disputes between private investors and states, not to handle disputes between states. However, when a sovereign investor acts in a capacity that aligns more closely with state functions or policy objectives—termed "economic statecraft"—the nature of the dispute may shift and potentially make typical investor-state dispute resolution mechanisms inappropriate. Sovereign investments driven by geopolitical aims or that control strategic resources may not qualify as "investments" under some treaties if these actions are deemed governmental rather than commercial. This distinction is vital as it influences whether such investments receive protection under the treaties, which are primarily intended to address commercial disputes.

The interpretation of "investor" within the context of a treaty's objective and purpose, as guided by the VCLT, is critical. If a treaty's purpose is to resolve commercial disputes, extending its protection to state entities acting in a governmental capacity may contradict this objective. Thus, the nuanced examination of whether a sovereign investor acts under the control or direction of its home state becomes essential in determining its eligibility for protection under these treaties.

Arbitral jurisprudence has variably addressed these issues, with decisions often resting on the specific contexts of the disputes. The Broches test developed by Aron Broches focuses on whether a state-owned company discharges governmental functions and has been influential in guiding tribunals. This test emphasizes looking at the nature of the entity's activities rather than their purpose. For instance, the *CSOB v Slovakia* case highlighted this issue by determining that CSOB's actions were commercial, although CSOB itself was owned and controlled by the state, because they did not involve the entity in governmental policy or legislative actions.

Nonetheless, the question of whether sovereign investors should qualify as "investors" under investment treaties when acting in a governmental capacity remains open. While sovereign entities are not categorically excluded from arbitration under these treaties, the specific nature of their investments and the roles they play can limit their access to such mechanisms. For investments that are non-commercial by nature or those undertaken by entities under the direct control of a state, determining standing becomes more complex and often depends on the specifics of the treaty and the nature of the dispute.

In conclusion, sovereign investors' standing in international investment arbitration requires careful legal interpretation and a sensitive application of treaty provisions. Arbitrators must pay attention to the dual roles of sovereign entities by assessing the broader geopolitical and economic contexts of their investments. This analysis is crucial to maintaining the integrity of the international investment arbitration system and ensuring it remains an effective venue for resolving disputes while adhering to the legal frameworks established by the treaties that govern these proceedings. Arbitrators and treaty negotiators must remain vigilant to these complexities to effectively manage disputes involving state entities and uphold the depoliticized nature of investment arbitration.

4.3 Subject-Matter Jurisdiction and Ex-Ante Screening of Investments

An investor who has suffered harm is only entitled to seek legal redress before an investment arbitration tribunal where a dispute arises out of an investment.[58] Nevertheless, investment screening often takes place before an investment is completed (ex-ante screening). Does that mean that investment screening relates to activities that are preliminary to investing and potentially not protected under investment treaties?

What constitutes an "investment" is primarily to be answered in light of the instrument of consent, which, in the case of treaty-based claims, is typically found in the relevant investment treaty.[59] In cases governed by the Washington Convention, the concept of "investment" developed under that Convention in arbitral practice should also be considered.[60]

In cases where the instrument of consent is contained in an investment treaty, the "investment" definition is a matter of treaty interpretation. Nevertheless, such treaties frequently provide that to satisfy the definition, a putative investment must have been made in accordance with the laws and regulations of the host state.[61] Such "compliance requirements" refer back to domestic law, with the implication that any investment not in compliance with domestic law would not be an investment for purposes of the investment treaty.[62]

However, the prevailing view in arbitral practice is that compliance requirements refer to the legality under national law of an investment and not to its

[58] Bischoff and Happ (2015).

[59] Ibid. 499–503.

[60] Ibid. 503–514.

[61] Dolzer et al. (2022) 106–114; Diel-Gligor and Hennecke (2015) 566–576.

[62] De Mestral (2015).

coverage.[63] The latter is to be assessed under public international law, including its principles of treaty interpretation, as well as specifically international investment law.[64] Similarly, arbitral tribunals have rejected the notion that the host state, by means of the compliance requirement, could dynamically and unilaterally modify the scope of its consent to arbitration by reference to its domestic laws.[65] Consequently, such tribunals have held that the compliance requirement is a matter of substance to be assessed at the merits stage.[66]

In the event that an investment is completed without notification for screening or in defiance of a screening decision (such as a decision prescribing conditions or prohibiting the investment), such investment may be ordered to be unwound or considered null and void.[67] The nullification of a completed investment may even take effect retroactively (ex tunc).[68]

In a situation where an investment is nullified (or, in the case of nullity ex tunc, is deemed never to have existed), the question arises whether an "investment" is still deemed to exist for the purpose of determining subject-matter jurisdiction.[69] Given that the existence of an investment for purposes of the jurisdictional requirement is a matter to be addressed under the law governing the instrument of consent, which in the case of a treaty-based claim is the relevant investment treaty, the nullification would not necessarily negate the existence of an investment for purposes of arbitral jurisdiction.

Investment screening gives rise to particular factual situations that may call into question the existence of an investment for purposes of international investment law. Specifically, investment screening laws may provide for an obligation to notify a contemplated future investment for screening before the investment has been completed (ex-ante screening),[70] in which case, the question arises whether an investment ever existed for purposes of international investment law. In other cases, that obligation instead (or in addition) applies to investments already undertaken (ex-post screening).[71]

Most screening mechanisms oblige prospective investors to notify the respective competent authority which undertakes the screening of certain types of contemplated investments and obtain authorization before making certain types of investments.[72] Whether investment treaty obligations apply to such ex-ante

[63] Diel-Gligor and Hennecke (2015) 569.

[64] Ibid.

[65] Douglas (2003)198–199.

[66] Diel-Gligor and Hennecke (2015) 570.

[67] See Chap. 2 above.

[68] Ibid.

[69] Sasson (2010) 46–49.

[70] See Chap. 2 above.

[71] Ibid.

[72] Such ex-ante screening exists (e.g. in Denmark, Germany, Spain, France, Italy, Latvia, Lithuania, Hungary, Netherlands, Austria, and Finland).

screening mechanisms depends, in part, on whether the scope of application of the relevant investment treaty extends to future investments and, in part, on what counts as a future investment under the relevant treaty, as further illustrated in the next subchapter.

Some screening mechanisms, including those of Germany, allow for the screening of certain types of investments after the investment has been made.[73] In these systems, the competent authority undertaking the screening can, normally within a certain period, decide to prohibit the investment after it has been established or acquired, to impose conditions for the investor's continued conduct, operation, management, use or enjoyment of the investment, or to order its unwinding (i.e. its sale or disposal).[74]

In the case of ex-post screening, an investment already exists for purposes of international investment law and benefits from protection pursuant to the relevant international investment agreement.[75]

In addition, as just mentioned, because of the use of quantitative or qualitative screening criteria, ex-ante screening occurs in the post-investment phase for purposes of investment treaty obligations, even though the additional investment that triggers the screening has not yet been made. It occurs when such investment is deemed to be an expansion of an already established or acquired investment that has previously not met screening criteria.

For purposes of assessing the existence of investment under an investment treaty in the context of investment screening, it is useful to distinguish between ex-ante screening that takes place in the period preceding an investment during the pre-investment phase (i.e. screening of genuinely future or prospective investment; Sect. 4.3.1), and ex-ante screening that takes place after the initial investment is made during the post-investment phase (i.e. screening of an expansion of an already existing investment; Sect. 4.3.2). A summary of the findings concludes the subchapter (Sect. 4.3.3).

4.3.1 *Exclusion of Future Investments*

Most investment treaty obligations, including core investment protection standards, do not apply to investments that have not yet been made.[76] The obligation to provide, inter alia, national treatment, most-favoured-nation treatment, fair and

[73] Such ex-post screening exists (e.g. in Germany, Hungary, Netherlands, Poland, Portugal, and Finland). Note that the German law only allows for such ex-post review if the deal has been carried out without being notified in the first place (cf. § 55(3) of the German Foreign Trade and Payments Ordinance (*Außenwirtschaftsverordnung*)).

[74] See Chap. 2 above.

[75] The existence of an investment is a general prerequisite under international investment agreements. See above.

[76] Pohl (2020).

equitable treatment, and full protection and security normally becomes applicable only once an eligible investor has invested (i.e. when the investor has established a new investment or acquired an existing investment from someone else).[77]

When a treaty is silent on the matter, a host state cannot be considered obligated to extend protection to prospective investments or investors.[78] Conversely, foreign individuals cannot be presumed to have a right to invest since states are inherently free, by virtue of their sovereign rights, to deny the entry or admission of foreign investors and their investments and to prohibit the establishment of foreign-controlled investments in their territories.[79]

In treaty practice, however, the exclusion of prospective investments and the making of investments from the scope of application of investment treaty obligations is often expressly reflected in a number of different ways: as an element of the definition of "investment" (4.3.1.1), specific exclusion clauses (Subsection 4.3.1.2), and the exclusion of specific activities involved in making of an investment (4.3.1.3). By way of exception, where future investments are excluded, investment treaties frequently include certain obligations which nevertheless apply to investments not yet undertaken (4.3.1.4). An interim summary of findings concludes the section (4.3.1.5).

4.3.1.1 Definitional Exclusion of Future Investments

IIAs may exclude prospective investments from the scope of application by excluding them from the definition of the term "investment" or "covered investment" to which the investment treaty obligations relate. By way of example, Article 8.2(1) of the CETA provides:

> This Chapter applies to a measure adopted or maintained by a Party in its territory relating to:
>
> (a) an investor of the other Party;
> (b) a covered investment; and
> (c) with respect to Article 8.5, any investments in its territory.

Here, the term "investor" is defined in Article 8.1 to mean "a Party, a natural person or an enterprise of a Party, other than a branch or a representative office, *that seeks to make*, is making or has made an investment in the territory of the other Party" [emphasis added]. Prospective investors are thus within the definition of "investor" and hence within the scope of the investment treaty obligations of CETA.[80]

---

[77] Ibid.

[78] See *Barcelona Traction* [1970] ICJ Rep 4, para. 33 and *Mihaly v Sri Lanka*, Award, 15 March 2002, para. 60. For further references, see Newcombe and Paradell (2009) 121–122; Salacuse (2013) 76.

[79] Ibid.

[80] See, for a similar reasoning, *Nordzucker v Poland*, para. 171.

By contrast, the term "covered investment" is limited to an investment that has already been made ("made in accordance with the applicable law at the time the investment is made" and "existing on the date of entry into force of this Agreement, or made or acquired thereafter").

It is thus clear from Article 8.2(1) that the scope of the CETA's obligations covers measures relating to investors in the pre- and post-investment phases, as well as measures relating to actual existing investments.[81] With respect to the prohibition against performance requirements in Article 8.5, the scope covers measures relating to existing and future investments.[82]

Once excluded from the definition of "covered investment", prospective investments fall outside substantive investment protection standards that incorporate the term, such as the absolute standard of protection referred to in Article 8.10(1):

> Each Party shall accord in its territory to covered investments of the other Party and to investors with respect to their covered investments fair and equitable treatment and full protection and security in accordance with paragraphs 2 through 6.

Hence, investment protection in the form of FET and full protection and security in the pre-investment phase is excluded in the CETA through the limitation of the scope of Article 8.10(1) to "covered investments" and "investors with respect to their covered investments".[83] Similar exclusions are found in Article 2.4 of the EU-Singapore Investment Protection Agreement (IPA),[84] which in addition limits the application of its investment protection standards to "covered investors" (i.e. investors that have made an investment) and Article 2.5 of the EU-Vietnam IPA.[85]

Other examples of definitions of "investment" that clarify that the act of investing must have taken place can be found in many treaties.[86] Many treaties

---

[81] Note, e.g. that the NT obligation in Article 8.6(1) CETA thus applies to the pre- and post-investment phase insofar as adverse discrimination of investors is concerned (per the definition of "investors") but only to the post-investment phase when it comes to adverse discrimination of investments (per the definition of "covered investments").

[82] Similar provisions are contained in Article 2.1 of the investment chapter of the draft EU-Australia Free Trade Agreement, published on 22 October 2018, available via: http://trade.ec.europa.eu/doclib/docs/2018/december/tradoc_157572.pdf (accessed 23 July 2022); and Article 2.1 of the investment chapter of the draft EU-New Zealand Free Trade Agreement, published on 25 September 2018, available via: http://trade.ec.europa.eu/doclib/docs/2018/december/tradoc_157580.pdf (accessed 23 July 2022).

[83] Note that with respect to the scope of application of Article 8.10(1), Article 8.2(1) does not add any further limitations.

[84] Investment Protection Agreement between the European Union and its Member States, of the one part, and the Republic of Singapore, of the other part, 15 October 2018 (pending ratification) available via: https://investmentpolicy.unctad.org/international-investment-agreements/treaty—files/5714/download. Accessed 23 July 2022.

[85] Investment Protection Agreement between the European Union and its Member States, of the one part, and the Socialist Republic of Viet Nam, of the other part, 30 June 2019 (pending ratification) available via: https://investmentpolicy.unctad.org/international-investment-agreements/treaty—files/5868/download. Accessed 23 July 2022.

[86] UNCTAD Investment Policy Hub (2022).

provide that investments must be "invested",[87] as illustrated by Article 1(1) of the China-Germany BIT:

> The term "investment" means every kind of asset invested directly or indirectly by investors of one Contracting Party in the territory of the other Contracting Party, and in particular, though not exclusively, includes: [. . .][88]

Another common formulation is that the investment must be "established or acquired", as exemplified by Article 1(1) of the Finland-Kazakhstan BIT:

> The term "investment" means every kind of asset established or acquired in connection with business and entrepreneurial activity by an investor of one Party in the territory of the other Party in accordance with the national legislation of the State of the latter Party, including in particular, though not exclusively: [. . .][89]

The difference between the "establishment" and "acquisition" of an investment is usually that the former refers to investments to establish a business, whereas the latter refers to investment in an established business.[90] However, the terminology is not uniform. Some treaties, such as the EU-Japan Economic Partnership Agreement (EPA)[91] and EU-Korea Free Trade Agreement (FTA),[92] define "establishment" to include acquisition.[93]

In arbitral practice, the issue of pre-investment obligations has surfaced in some cases in the context of the treaty definition of investment, although none have been a "clean" case of a prospective investment, in the sense of a denied opportunity to invest or a dispute as to the right to invest.[94] The emphasis of these cases has not

[87] See, e.g. *Nordzucker v Poland*, para. 184.

[88] Agreement between the People's Republic of China and the Federal Republic of Germany on the Encouragement and Reciprocal Protection of Investments, 1 December 2003, 2362 UNTS 253.

[89] Agreement between the Government of the Republic of Finland and the Government of the Republic of Kazakhstan on the Promotion and Mutual Protection of Investments, 9 January 2007, 2558 UNTS 585.

[90] See Juillard (2000) 332–333. Note that another frequent distinction is between, on the one hand "establishment" and "acquisition" and, on the other hand, "admission" (or, synonymously, "entry"), the latter terms being understood as occurring prior to the establishment, cf. Newcombe and Paradell (2009) 132; Gómez-Palacio and Muchlinski (2008) 229–232. References to "admission" or "entry" therefore signify a somewhat less far-reaching application of the relevant protection standard.

[91] Agreement between the European Union and Japan for an Economic Partnership, 17 July 2018 (not published in UNTS) OJ L330 of 27 December 2018, p.3.

[92] Free Trade Agreement between the European Union and its Member States, of the one part, and the Republic of Korea, of the other part, 6 October 2010 (not published in UNTS) OJ L 127 of 14 May 2011, p. 6.

[93] EU-Japan EPA Article 8.2(i) and EU-Korea FTA Article 7.9(a).

[94] *Mihaly v Sri Lanka*, Award dated 15 March 2002; *Nagel v Czech Republic*, Final Award, 9 September 2003; *Zhinvali v Georgia*, unpublished award, 24 January 2003; *Petrobart v Kyrgyz Republic*, Award, 29 March 2005; *Nordzucker v Poland*, Partial Award (Jurisdiction), 10 December 2008; *White Industries v India*, Final Award, 30 November 2011; *Bosca v Lithuania*, Award, 17 May 2013; *Deutsche Telekom v India*, Interim Award, 13 December 2017.

centred on whether an investment was "made" but whether certain pre-investment phase steps—communications or acts by the prospective investor—had progressed to the extent sufficient to constitute an "investment". In other words, the issue in principle of pre-investment application of investment treaty obligations has often veered into the more factual question of whether the substantive criteria for an investment have been satisfied.

4.3.1.2 Specific Exclusion of Future Investments

The substantive provisions of the IIAs may be expressly limited to investments that have been made by investors (i.e. to the exclusion of investments yet to be made). An example is contained in the Denmark-North Macedonia BIT,[95] which defines "investor" and "investment" in a manner that does not exclude prospective investors or investment but provides under Article 3(1) on "Treatment of Investments":

> Each Contracting Party shall in its territory accord to investments made by investors of the other Contracting Party fair and equitable treatment which in no case shall be less favorable than that accorded to its own investors or to investors of any third State, whichever is the more favorable from the point of view of the investor.

Here, it is clear that the treatment of investments excludes prospective investments by limiting the application of the provision to "investments *made* by investors" [emphasis added]. An example of another type of formulation is Article 4(1) of the France-Ethiopia BIT,[96] which limits the application of the NT and MFN treatment to investments "once admitted in accordance with the legislation" of the host state. Another example is found in Article III(1) of the Slovakia-Turkey BIT:

> Each Party shall in its territory accord investments of investors of the other Party, once established, and returns of investors of the other Party treatment which is fair and equitable and not less favourable than that which it accords to investments and returns of its own investors or to investments and returns of investors of any third State whichever is more favourable.[97]

Most IIAs do not have restrictive definitions that exclude prospective investments or exclude such investments expressly in the substantive provisions.[98] Nevertheless,

---

[95] Agreement between the Macedonian Government and the Government of the Kingdom of Denmark for the Promotion and Reciprocal Protection of Investments, 8 May 2015 (not published in UNTS) UN reg. no. 54486.

[96] *Accord entre le gouvernement de la République française et le gouvernement de la République démocratique fédérale d'Ethiopie sur l'encouragement et la protection réciproques des investissements*, 25 June 2003 (not registered in UNTS) available via: https://investmentpolicy.unctad.org/international—investment-agreements/treaty-files/3550/download.

[97] Agreement between the Slovak Republic and the Republic of Turkey Concerning the Reciprocal Promotion and Protection of Investments, 13 October 2013 (not published in UNTS) available via: https://investmentpolicy.unctad.org/international-investment-agreements/treaty—files/2266/download. Accessed 23 July 2022.

[98] UNCTAD Investment Policy Hub.

as mentioned above, this absence of an exclusion is an insufficient basis for interpreting the scope of application of these agreements so as to extend protection to the pre-investment phase.

4.3.1.3 Exclusion of Specific Activities Involved in Making Investments

The substantive provisions of the international investment agreement may be expressly limited to certain activities of an investor, which exclude references to the making of the investment, such as the entry, admission, establishment, or acquisition of the investment. This limitation usually applies to the NT and MFN treatment clauses insofar as they relate to the treatment of investors rather than investments, but it is also sometimes applied to the FET standard.[99] Article 3(2) of the Denmark-North Macedonia BIT is again illustrative:

> Each Contracting Party shall in its territory accord investors of the other Contracting Party, as regards their management, maintenance, use, enjoyment or disposal of their investment, fair and equitable treatment which in no case shall be less favorable than that accorded to its own investors or to investors of any third State, whichever of these standards is the more favorable from the point of view of the investor.

The standard of protection is here extended to investors, not with respect to the making of investments, but with respect to the "management, maintenance, use, enjoyment or disposal of their investment". What is not included is any mention of the making of investments, such as admission, establishment, acquisition, or expansion.[100] An example of a treaty that does include such references is the aforementioned Finland-Kazakhstan BIT, which in Article 3(2) provides,

> Each Contracting Party shall accord to investors of the other Contracting Party and to their investments, a treatment no less favourable than the treatment it accords to investors of the most favoured nation and to their investments with respect to the establishment, acquisition, expansion, operation, management, maintenance, use, enjoyment, and sale or other disposal of investments.

This provision extends MFN treatment to the pre-investment phase through the references to "establishment" and "acquisition". As in most investment treaties, "investor" here includes prospective investors.[101] Pursuant to Article 1(3), the term "investor" is defined as "subjects who invest in the territory of the State of the other Party in accordance with the national legislation of the State of the latter Party and the provisions of this Agreement" [emphasis added]. While only a minority of the

---

[99] Ibid.

[100] This point was highlighted by the arbitral tribunal in *Nordzucker v Poland*, para. 177. For further analysis of the pre-investment stage application of NT and MFN treatment, see Bonnitcha et al. (2017) 103–104; Gómez-Palacio and Muchlinski (2008) 242–245.

[101] UNCTAD Investment Policy Hub.

IIAs of the Member States, which have screening mechanisms, extend NT and MFN treatment to the pre-investment phase, most that do are of this type.[102]

In contrast with the pre-Lisbon treaty practice of the Member States,[103] the NT and MFN treatment clauses in the EU's post-Lisbon IIAs normally cover the making of investments. An example is Article 7.12 of the EU-Korea FTA:

> In the sectors inscribed in Annex 7-A, and subject to any conditions and qualifications set out therein, with respect to all measures affecting establishment, each Party shall accord to establishments and investors of the other Party treatment no less favourable than that it accords to its own like establishments and investors.[104]

Here, the term "establishment" is defined to comprise "the constitution, acquisition or maintenance of a juridical person [. . .] within the territory of a Party for the purpose of performing an economic activity", including "capital participation in a juridical person with a view to establishing or maintaining lasting economic links". When considering that "investor" is defined as "any person *that seeks to perform* or performs an economic activity through setting up an establishment" [emphasis added], it becomes clear that the application of the provision extends to the pre-investment phase. A somewhat similar formulation is contained in Article 8.8(1) of the EU-Japan EPA:

> Each Party shall accord to entrepreneurs of the other Party and to covered enterprises treatment no less favourable than that it accords, in like situations, to its own entrepreneurs and to their enterprises, with respect to establishment in its territory.[105]

The definition of "establishment" in this treaty means

---

[102] Ibid. Of the international investment agreements concluded externally by the EU and those of its Member States that have screening mechanisms in force, 31 apply NT to the pre-investment phase, whereas 38 apply MFN treatment to the pre-investment phase. In particular, agreements concluded by Finland and Italy are of these types.

[103] On 1 December 2009, the Lisbon Treaty entered into force, which brought about the latest major amendment and recodification of the founding treaties of the European Union. These amendments included the extension of Union competences to the area of FDI as part of the common commercial policy of the EU, cf. Article 206 TFEU. This became the departure point for the EU's investment treaty programme. It is therefore convenient to distinguish between treaty practice before and after the Lisbon Treaty.

[104] A similar provision is contained in Article 4 of the investment chapter of the draft EU-Mercosur Association Agreement, published 12 July 2022, available via: http://trade.ec.europa.eu/doclib/cfm/doclib_section.cfm?sec=151. Accessed 23 July 2022.

[105] Similar provisions are contained in Articles 7(1) and 8(1) of the investment chapter of the draft modernised EU-Mexico Global Agreement, published 25 April 2018, available via: http://trade.ec.europa.eu/doclib/cfm/doclib_section.cfm?sec=132; Article 2.3(1) of the investment chapter of the draft EU—Australia Free Trade Agreement, published on 22 October 2018, available via: http://trade.ec.europa.eu/doclib/docs/2018/december/tradoc_157572.pdf, and Article 2.3(1) of the investment chapter of the draft EU-New Zealand Free Trade Agreement, published on 25 September 2018, available via: http://trade.ec.europa.eu/doclib/docs/2018/december/tradoc_157580.pdf.

> the setting up or the acquisition of a juridical person, including through capital participation, or the creation of a branch or representative office, in the European Union or in Japan respectively, with a view to establishing or maintaining lasting economic links.

Again, considering that "entrepreneur" refers to "a natural or juridical person of a Party *that seeks to establish*, is establishing or has established an enterprise in accordance with subparagraph (i), in the territory of the other Party" [emphasis added], the application is also extended to cover the national treatment of investors (entrepreneurs) in making (establishing) future investments in this case.[106]

A similar formulation appears in Article 8.6(1) of the CETA on NT:

> Each Party shall accord to an investor of the other Party and to a covered investment, treatment no less favourable than the treatment it accords, in like situations to its own investors and to their investments with respect to the establishment, acquisition, expansion, conduct, operation, management, maintenance, use, enjoyment and sale or disposal of their investments in its territory.

Pursuant to this provision, investors and their investments are to be accorded NT. However, concerning the NT of investors, there is no distinction between the pre- and post-investment phases. Investors are protected with respect to the establishment and acquisition of their investments, as well as the expansion, conduct, operation, management, maintenance, use, enjoyment and sale or disposal of their investments.[107] By contrast, NT of investments only covers investments that have already been made and exist.[108] As such, treatment of investments (as opposed to investors) regarding the establishment or acquisition of such investments would cover matters pertaining retrospectively to the making of the investment but not a denied opportunity to invest in the first place. On the other hand, such denial would be covered as treatment of the investor.

In contrast to Article 8.8(1) of the EU-Japan EPA and Article 8.6(1) of CETA discussed above, the provisions in Article 2.3 of the EU-Singapore IPA and Article 2.3 of the EU-Vietnam IPA exclude references to the making of investments and restrict the application of the NT standard to "covered investments" and "covered investors", both of which are defined to apply exclusively to the post-investment phase.

---

[106] For another example, see Article 88 of the EU-Ukraine Association Agreement, see further UNCTAD Investment Policy Hub (2022).

[107] Note that Section B of Chapter 8 of CETA contains provisions that apply specifically to establishment, although the application of other provisions of the chapter also extend to establishment, notably Section C (which can also be gleaned from Article 8.2(2) and from the text of Articles 8.6 and 8.7). Note also that Section B is excluded from the investor-state arbitration provisions [cf. Article 8.18(1)]. See further Subsection 4.3.1.2 herein.

[108] Cf. the formulation of Article 8.10(1) of CETA, discussed above, which applies to "covered investments of the other Party *and* to investors with respect to their covered investments" [emphasis added]. Here, it is clear that the treatment of investments and the investor is limited to investments already in existence.

4.3.1.4 Provisions That Include Future Investments

Certain other investment treaty obligations frequently apply to investments that have yet to be made. Notably, it is not uncommon that obligations may apply with respect to the transfer of investment capital prior to the making of an investment. Some treaties also contain specific obligations to provide market access or not to impose performance requirements, both of which affect prospective investments. However, none of these provision types entails significant potential for disputes under investment treaties, as further explained below. While claims based on these provisions are not excluded and could proceed to the merits stage, they are not further analyzed in this study.

First, transfer-of-funds provisions often cover the free transfer of capital to establish the investment but primarily address the repatriation of funds.[109] Post-Lisbon EU IIAs either limit the transfer clause to existing investments[110] or provide for a general free movement of capital clause common to transfers related to both trade and investment.[111] However, even where transfer-of-funds provisions obligate the host state not to restrict the funds required to make the investment, it does not follow that the investment as such is admitted and subject to investment protection.

Second, market access provisions are included in most post-Lisbon EU investment agreements but are virtually non-existent in Member State agreements.[112] This type of treaty provision, based on Article XVI of the General Agreement on Trade in Services (GATS), prohibits the imposition of quantitative restrictions on the establishment of investments and restrictions on the types of legal entities through which economic activity may be carried out.[113] Thus, the subject matter of these clauses differs from the essentially qualitative restrictions on investment that may result from investment screening, which aims to control investments on the basis of their implications on matters of security and public order.[114] Market access clauses are found, for instance, in Article 8.4 of the CETA, Article 8.7 of the EU-Japan EPA, and Article 7.11 of the EU-Korea FTA.

Third, provisions prohibiting performance requirements are found in some post-Lisbon treaties, including Article 8.5 of the CETA and Article 8.11 of the

[109] See, e.g. Article 7.1(g) of the Slovakia-Iran BIT and Article 8.1(a) of the BLEU—Panama BIT, see further Investment Policy Hub (2022).

[110] See, e.g. Article 8.13(1) of CETA and Article 2.7(1) of the EU-Singapore IPA.

[111] See, e.g. Article 9.2(1) of the EU-Japan EPA and Article 8.2(1) of the EU—Korea FTA.

[112] UNCTAD Investment Policy Hub.

[113] Hahn (2015) 659–666; Van den Bossche and Zdouc (2017) 516–521.

[114] This does not exclude the possibility of an application of market access provisions to investment screening mechanisms in particular situations, such as if the mechanism were to be designed to impose a maximum limit to foreign capital participation or a restriction in the type of legal entity or joint venture that may engage in particular investments, e.g. sovereign wealth funds or other state-owned enterprises.

EU-Japan EPA, as well as in some Member State treaties.[115] This type of clause, which originates from the illustrative list of inconsistent measures set forth in the annex to the Agreement on Trade-Related Investment Measures, applies specifically to future investments.[116] The clause prohibits making investments conditional on certain trade practices, which often include subsidies that typically have discriminatory effects, such as mandated levels of exports or domestic content and mandated technology transfers.[117]

In the context of investment screening, an investment authorization could be made conditional on such performance requirements. However, it is questionable how likely it would be in practice since the policy interests at stake in investment screening fundamentally differ from those underpinning prohibitions against performance requirements. The former concerns, at least nominally, security and public order, whereas the latter concerns purely economic interests.

Thus, while performance-requirements clauses are applicable to future investments and could be engaged in ex-ante investment screening, it is fair to assume that the potential for investment disputes is limited.

4.3.1.5 Interim Summary

In the complex landscape of international investment law, the applicability of treaty obligations to future investments presents a nuanced area of debate and legal interpretation. Investment treaties predominantly do not extend core investment protection standards, such as NT, MFN treatment, FET, and full protection and security, to investments that have not yet been made. These protections typically only activate after an investor has established a new investment or acquired an existing one. This stipulation underscores the principle that the protections afforded by investment treaties are not pre-emptive in nature; they are reactive and contingent upon the actual establishment of a tangible economic commitment within the host state's territory.

Many treaties explicitly delineate that protections apply to established or acquired investments, which suggests that the entry, admission, and pre-establishment activities of prospective investors fall outside their scope. For example, various formulations in treaties may define "investment" as assets that have been "invested" or "established" while excluding activities that merely constitute intentions or preliminary actions towards making an investment. This definition ensures that only substantive economic engagements, rather than prospective plans or unexecuted intentions, receive protection under the law. Such distinctions are crucial in maintaining the integrity of investment treaties as mechanisms for managing actual, not potential, foreign investments.

---

[115] UNCTAD Investment Policy Hub.

[116] See, e.g. Article 8.5(1)(c) of CETA and Article 8.6(1)(c) of the EU-Japan EPA.

[117] Hahn (2015) 657–659; Van den Bossche and Zdouc (2017) 381.

However, certain treaty provisions specifically address or even accommodate future investments, particularly in contexts where capital transfer and market access are concerned. Provisions facilitating the free movement of capital for establishing an investment or that prohibit performance requirements prior to an investment's actual establishment demonstrate an acknowledgement of the pre-investment phase within the treaty framework. These provisions, though limited, indicate a nuanced recognition of the stages of investment and the different protections or obligations that may apply at each stage.

Despite these accommodations, the primary legal challenge in applying treaty protections to future investments lies in the inherent tension between the need to protect investors and the sovereign right of states to regulate the entry and nature of foreign investments. This tension is particularly palpable in treaties where explicit exclusions of pre-investment activities are absent, which leaves room for interpretation and potential dispute. Arbitral practice has shown that while the definitive acts of investing are covered, the anticipatory stages often remain legally ambiguous and subject to the interpretative approaches of individual tribunals.

In summary, while later-generation investment treaties occasionally extend certain obligations to prospective investments, the general scope of these treaties remains predominantly focused on investments that have already been made. The distinction between pre- and post-establishment phases in treaty obligations is significant for clarifying the temporal scope of protections and for understanding the legal status of investment actions at different stages. This distinction helps in delineating the boundary between the sovereign regulatory powers of states and the protections afforded to foreign investors to ensure that the balance of rights and obligations under international investment law is maintained.

4.3.2 Future Investments and the Expansion of Existing Investments

Frequently, screening concerns the expansion of an existing investment rather than a separate, future investment. From the moment an investment has been established or acquired, the provisions of IIAs normally apply. In principle, they encompass increases and decreases in the economic value of the investment.[118] In the case of expansion, an investment has already been admitted and established (or acquired). If further increases of an existing investment are considered an expansion and not a new investment (e.g. in the case of subsequent capital contributions or reinvestments of business profits), then they fall within the scope of investment treaty obligations. The situation mirrors decreases of the investment, such as the divestment of capital or the distribution of dividends.

[118] Dolzer et al. (2022) 85–99.

When screening concerns a future expansion of an existing investment—because an investment already exists for purposes of investment treaties—investment treaty obligations apply. From the perspective of investment treaties, such ex-ante screening occurs in the post-investment phase. On the other hand, where a future expansion is considered a separable fresh investment, the treaty obligations may not apply, depending on the formulation of the "investment" definition or the relevant protection standards (see Sect. 4.3.1).

In treaty practice, the distinction between the initial making of an investment (i.e. establishment or acquisition) and the expansion of an investment is often made clear in the treaty provision that provides for pre-investment treatment, such as Article 8.6(1) of the CETA quoted above. Pursuant to a footnote to Article 8.8(1) of the EU-Japan EPA, also quoted above, the definition of "establishment" also covers expansion. However, the distinction between expansion of investments and new investments is equally relevant in the context of treaties that do not explicitly cover expansion.[119] Often, such treaties include provisions that investments are admitted in accordance with the domestic law of the host state (e.g. as part of the definition of "investment").[120]

Normally, screening laws do not apply to all investments but only to those that satisfy certain quantitative or qualitative criteria, such as a minimum percentage of the shares or voting rights of a company (i.e. a screening threshold). An investment that was not notified for screening when it was originally made because it was below the screening threshold stipulated by the applicable screening law would have been admitted in accordance with the law. Hence, an "investment" already exists, so investment treaty obligations already apply to the screening of an expansion of such a previously admitted investment. Moreover, an investment originally not subject to screening would not necessarily lose its investment treaty protection just because the expansion of such an investment was subject to screening and eventually prohibited. Even if a national screening authority requires the unwinding of an entire investment (i.e. not only the acquisition that brought the investment over the screening threshold), it does not follow that the investment must be deemed never to have existed or otherwise must be deprived of protection for purposes of international investment law.

In the context of ex-ante investment screening, there are significant practical implications of distinguishing expansion from the establishment or acquisition of an investment. The fact that most mechanisms provide for (often high) quantitative or qualitative screening criteria means that investors may make investments and derive rights under investment treaty obligations—such as under the NT or MFN standards—prior to reaching the screening threshold.[121] If an investor already has

[119] See, e.g. *Nordzucker v Poland*, paras. 143–162.

[120] Post-Lisbon EU treaties and most pre-Lisbon treaties between Member States with screening mechanisms and third countries are of this type. UNCTAD Investment Policy Hub.

[121] Firm or indicative screening thresholds are applied by Germany, Spain, France, Italy, Latvia, Lithuania, Hungary, Austria, Portugal, Romania, and Finland.

made an investment that is not subject to screening, the ex-ante screening of a contemplated expansion of that investment over and above the screening threshold would result in the screening being deemed to have occurred in the post-investment phase for purposes of the applicable international investment agreement.

Whether the screening of future investments would be capable of resulting in investment treaty claims also depends on whether the future investment in question can be considered an expansion of an existing investment. Some treaties clarify that their provisions cover expanded investments. In the absence of such clarifying provisions, no settled case law determines whether an expanded investment is treated as a separable new investment or as a part of an existing investment.

4.3.3 Summary

The assessment of subject-matter jurisdiction in the context of investment treaty arbitration revolves significantly around the definition and scope of what constitutes an "investment". This issue becomes particularly pertinent when considering the effects of ex-ante and ex-post screening mechanisms on the status of an investment.

Investment treaties typically define "investment" to include assets that have been formally established or acquired according to the host state's laws and regulations. This definition ensures that only substantive and lawful economic engagements are recognized as investments and thereby activate the treaty's protection mechanisms. The emphasis on compliance with domestic laws as a precondition for recognizing an investment underscores the treaties' deference to sovereign regulatory frameworks while ensuring that investments meet a standard of legality before qualifying for protection.

However, the complexities of investment screening, especially ex-ante mechanisms, pose unique challenges. Ex-ante screening refers to the evaluation of investments before they are fully realized. This pre-emptive scrutiny can lead to situations where the legal status of what may constitute an "investment" under a treaty is ambiguous, particularly if the investment is modified or denied as a result of the screening process. Nonetheless, the prevailing view in international arbitration is that the legality of an investment under national law does not necessarily determine its recognition as an investment for treaty purposes unless explicitly stated in the treaty. Arbitral tribunals often treat compliance with domestic laws as a substantive issue rather than a jurisdictional one, which suggests that the fundamental character of an investment can withstand changes in domestic legal interpretations so long as the initial consent to arbitrate under the treaty is granted.

Further complexity arises when considering investments that may be nullified or required to be unwound due to screening decisions. Even in such cases, for the purpose of determining jurisdiction, an investment may still be deemed to exist under international law, particularly if it was initially made in compliance with the applicable treaty. This scenario underscores a crucial aspect of investment arbitration: the notion that the existence of an investment, once established, can transcend subsequent domestic actions to nullify or modify it, provided that the initial establishment met the treaty's requirements.

The screening of investments often requires prospective investors to notify and obtain authorization before proceeding, particularly when investments meet specific quantitative or qualitative thresholds that may invoke national security or public policy considerations. This notification and approval process, while prudent from a regulatory perspective, introduces a layer of uncertainty regarding the temporal scope of treaty protections—whether and how these protections extend to the pre-investment phase or are confined strictly to post-establishment activities.

In the realm of ex-post screening, where investments are scrutinized after being made, treaty protections generally apply without ambiguity, as the investments are already recognized under the treaty. This situation contrasts sharply with ex-ante screening, where the investment has not yet materialized, so the applicability of treaty protections is debatable.

For investments considered as expansions of existing ones, the delineation between what constitutes a new investment versus an expansion of an existing one is critical. Expanded investments may continue to benefit from the treaty's protections as they are deemed part of the initial investment, which has been recognized under the treaty. This continuity in protection plays a vital role in fostering investor confidence and stability in international investment flows.

In conclusion, the existence of an investment, crucial for establishing jurisdiction in investment treaty arbitration, remains primarily governed by the definitions and conditions set forth in the relevant investment treaty, independent of domestic law outcomes, including any nullification or unwinding orders. Investment treaties tend to exclude future investments from their scope explicitly to ensure clarity about what stages of investment are covered. Expanded investments are not generally excluded if they constitute part of an initially admitted investment, which aligns with the principle that the protections of investment treaties are designed to encourage and safeguard substantive economic engagements rather than merely prospective or planned activities. This framework supports a stable and predictable investment environment, which is critical for investors and states engaged in the global economic landscape.

4.4 Conclusion

Investor-state arbitration is typically designed to address disputes between private investors and states and may be interpreted to exclude sovereign investors involved in non-commercial activities from its purview. This exclusion stems from the nature of such activities, which may not meet the investment definitions under conventional international treaties. SOEs and SWFs, when acting beyond commercial purposes to fulfil broader strategic or policy objectives, often do not qualify under many treaties aimed at depoliticizing economic disputes between states and foreign private investors.

Investment screening mechanisms, particularly those implemented before the completion of an investment (i.e. ex-ante screening), introduce significant legal challenges. These mechanisms can determine whether a potential investment qualifies for protection under international treaties. To better align the expectations of contracting states with the realities of arbitration practices, it is critical to enhance the precision in defining "investment" and "investor". Clear definitions can ensure that sovereign and private investors are adequately covered under the treaties, especially when investments are subjected to ex-ante screening.

The fundamental distinction between commercial and non-commercial activities is highlighted by several arbitral decisions where the investor's intent and the nature of the investment were in focus. Investments aimed at achieving political or strategic objectives, especially those aligned with state functions, may often fail to meet the stringent definitions found in many treaties. Case law, such as *CSOB v Slovakia*, illustrates how tribunals focus on the nature of the activity rather than its purpose to clarify these distinctions, which emphasizes the need for explicit treaty language that can guide such interpretations.

To address the complexities identified, recommendations for treaty negotiators include enhancing the precision of treaty language, particularly in defining "investment" and "investor." Such precision is essential to clearly distinguish between sovereign and private investments and between investments made for commercial purposes versus those for governmental or strategic reasons. Negotiators could consider incorporating provisions that clarify the applicability of treaty protections to investments at various stages, including those undergoing ex-ante screening.

Arbitral tribunals frequently face jurisdictional challenges when encountering investments affected by national screening mechanisms or involving sovereign entities acting in non-commercial capacities. These challenges necessitate nuanced interpretations of treaty provisions to determine what constitutes an investment and who qualifies as an investor. Tribunals must balance the letter of the law with the economic and political realities underpinning international investments. They navigate through dense factual scenarios to uphold the principles of international investment law while ensuring equitable dispute resolution.

The complexities posed by sovereign investors and investment screening mechanisms require careful and informed approaches from arbitral tribunals. By balancing the legal framework with the economic and political realities of international investments, these tribunals play a critical role in maintaining the integrity and efficacy of the international investment arbitration system. This chapter underscores the resilience of investment treaty protections, which affirms the existence of investment despite contrary national rulings and highlights the need for clearer treaty language to manage disputes involving sovereign investors and pre-investment phase activities effectively.

References

Aggarwal V, Reddie A (2021) Economic statecraft in the twenty-first century: implications for the future of the global trade regime. World Trade Rev 20(2):137–151
Amerasinghe CF (1979) The jurisdiction of the International Centre for the Settlement of Investment Disputes. Indian J Int Law 19:166–227
Annacker C (2011) Protection and admission of sovereign investment under investment treaties. Chin J Int Law 10(3):531–564
Bischoff JA, Happ R (2015) The notion of investment. In: Bungenberg M, Griebel J, Hobe S, Reinisch A, Kim Y-I (eds) International investment law: a handbook. C. H. Beck/Hart/Nomos, pp 495–544
Blyschak P (2011) State-owned enterprises and international investment treaties: when are state-owned entities and their investments protected? J Int Law & Int Relat 6(2):1–52
Bonnitcha J, Skovgaard Poulsen LN, Waibel M (2017) The political economy of the investment treaty regime. Oxford University Press
Boute A (2018) Economic statecraft and investment arbitration. Univ Pa J Int Law 40:383–411
Broches A (1972) The convention on the settlement of investment disputes between states and nationals of other states. Recueil Des Cours 136(2):331
De Mestral A (2015) Pre-entry obligations under international law. In: Bungenberg M, Griebel J, Hobe S, Reinisch A, Kim Y-I (eds) International investment law: a handbook. C. H. Beck, pp 685–699
Diel-Gligor K, Hennecke R (2015) Investment in accordance with the law. In: Bungenberg M, Griebel J, Hobe S, Reinisch A, Kim Y-I (eds) International investment law: a handbook. C. H. Beck, pp 566–576
Dolzer R, Kriebaum U, Schreuer C (2022) Principles of international investment law, 3rd edn. Oxford University Press
Douglas Z (2003) The hybrid foundations of investment treaty arbitration. Br Yearb Int Law 74:151–289
Du M (2021) The status of Chinese state-owned enterprises in international investment arbitration: much ado about nothing? Chin J Int Law 20(4):785–815
Dugan C, Wallace Jr D, Rubins N, Sabahi B (2008). Investor-state arbitration. Oxford University Press
Feldman M (2016) State-owned enterprises as claimants in international investment arbitration. ICSID Rev Foreign Invest Law J 31(1):24–35
Francioni F (2009) Access to justice, denial of justice and international investment law. Eur J Int Law 20(3):729–747
Gómez-Palacio I, Muchlinski P (2008) Admission and establishment. In: Muchlinski P, Ortino F, Schreuer C (eds) The Oxford handbook of international investment law. Oxford University Press, pp 229–256
Hagemeyer-Witzleb TM (2021) The international law of economic warfare. Springer International Publishing
Hahn M (2015) WTO rules and obligations related to investments. In: Bungenberg M, Griebel J, Hobe S, Reinisch A, Kim Y-I (eds) International investment law: a handbook. C. H. Beck, pp 653–670
Juillard P (2000) Freedom of establishment, freedom of capital movements, and freedom of investment. ICSID Rev Foreign Invest Law J 15(2):322–339
Kaufmann-Kohler G, Potestà M (2020) Why investment arbitration and not domestic courts? The origins of the modern investment dispute resolution system, criticism, and future outlook. In: Kaufmann-Kohler G, Potestà M (eds) Investor-state dispute settlement and national courts: current framework and reform options. Springer, pp 7–29

Kriebaum U (2019) Evaluating social benefits and costs of investment treaties: depoliticization of investment disputes. In: Gómez KF, Gourgourinis A, Titi C (eds) International investment law and the law of armed conflict. Springer, pp 23–42

McLaughlin M (2019) Defining a state-owned enterprise in international investment agreements. ICSID Rev Foreign Invest Law J 34(3):595–625

McLaughlin M (2020) State-owned enterprises and threats to national security under investment treaties. Chin J Int Law 19(2):283–327

Mirabbasi SB, Siavashpour H (2020) Diplomatic protection under international investment treaties. Public Law Stud Q 49(4):1109–1125

Muchlinski PT (2005) Policy issues. Transnatl Disput Manag 2(5)

Newcombe AP, Paradell L (2009) Law and practice of investment treaties: standards of treatment. Kluwer Law International BV

Paparinskis M (2010). The limits of depoliticisation in contemporary investor-state arbitration. In: Crawford J, Nouwen S (eds) Select proceedings of the European Society of International Law, Volume 3: International law 1989–2010: A performance appraisal pp 271–289. Hart/ Bloomsbury.

Pohl JH (2020) The impact of investment treaty commitments on the design and operation of EU investment screening mechanisms. In: Hindelang S, Moberg A (eds) YSEC yearbook of socio-economic constitutions 2020. Springer, pp 725–768

Polanco RL (2019) The return of the home state to investor-state disputes: bringing back diplomatic protection? Cambridge University Press

Reinisch A, Malintoppi L (2008) Methods of dispute resolution. In: Muchlinski P, Ortino F, Schreuer C (eds) The Oxford handbook of international investment law. Oxford University Press, pp 691–720

Salacuse JW (2013) The three laws of international investment: national, contractual, and international frameworks for foreign capital. Oxford University Press

Sasson M (2010) Substantive law in investment treaty arbitration: the unsettled relationship between international law and municipal law. Kluwer Law International

Schreuer CH (2009) The ICSID convention: a commentary. Cambridge University Press

Sornarajah M (1997) Power and justice in foreign investment arbitration. J Int Arbitr 14:103–140

United Nations Conference on Trade and Development (2022) Investment Policy Hub [Database]. Retrieved Month Day, 2022, https://investmentpolicy.unctad.org/

Van den Bossche P, Zdouc W (2017) The law and policy of the World Trade Organization: text, cases, and materials, 4th edn. Cambridge University Press

Wang W (2017) The non-precluded measure type clause in international investment agreements: significances, challenges, and reactions. ICSID Rev Foreign Invest Law J 32(2):447–456

Chapter 5
National Security-Related Defences and Treaty Exceptions Applied to Investment Screening

Abstract This chapter investigates the intersection of investment screening, the necessity defence under customary international law, and investment treaty exceptions. The chapter critically examines the feasibility of employing the necessity defence, as highlighted in case law, to justify investment screening measures under national security considerations. The chapter also analyses the complexity and diverse application of treaty exception clauses while noting the challenges posed by the non-transparent and discretionary nature of investment screening. Furthermore, it discusses the significant role of arbitral tribunals in ensuring host states' compliance with the good faith obligation when invoking security exceptions. The chapter concludes by highlighting the intricate balance required between state sovereignty in national security and obligations under international investment law by emphasizing the case-by-case approach necessary in international investment dispute resolution.

5.1 Introduction

As discussed at the outset of this enquiry, an arbitral tribunal may limit itself to adopting or endorsing a decision by the host state with respect to a measure in dispute. In so doing, the tribunal submits to the host state's authority without questioning the basis for its decision. The previous chapter investigated the principal mechanisms through which this submissive deference is achieved at the pre-merit stage of a dispute by declining jurisdiction. The present chapter successively explores the main legal techniques or devices that operate at the merits stage to achieve submissive deference to state national security determinations by limiting the effect of investment treaty obligations on national security screening.

J. H. Pohl, *Arbitration of Disputes related to National Security Screening of Foreign Investments*, EYIEL Monographs - Studies in European and International Economic Law 50,
https://doi.org/10.1007/978-3-032-26342-1_5

The inherent flexibility of international law facilitates submissive deference.[1] As a general concept, international law has adopted the notion that every treaty contains an implicit provision that, subject to numerous conditions and limitations, its effectiveness will lapse if a fundamental change in circumstances occurs.[2] This idea acknowledges that the future scenarios to which any treaty applies are indeterminate. Hence, no treaty can exhaustively list all situations that may justify its non-application in practice.[3] In its simplest form, this idea is expressed in the doctrine of clausula rebus sic stantibus, which is part of international law and is rooted in customary international law and the VCLT.[4] This notion ensures that the application of legal obligations imposed by a treaty becomes more flexible and encourages states to submit to the discipline of an international legal regime that may otherwise appear too cumbersome.[5]

Indeed, the vagueness of the doctrine of fundamental change of circumstances and Article 62 of the VCLT may introduce an element of uncertainty and instability into the world of international treaty law.[6] However, its general acceptance is a clear indication of its indispensability and reflects the fact that the law must provide a limited number of options for circumventing treaty obligations.[7] Without these

---

[1] See Koskenniemi (2011).

[2] Heintschel von Heinegg (2006).

[3] See Binder (2012).

[4] Heintschel von Heinegg (n. 2).

[5] Ibid.

[6] Article 62 VCLT provides,

1. A fundamental change of circumstances which has occurred with regard to those existing at the time of the conclusion of a treaty, and which was not foreseen by the parties, may not be invoked as a ground for terminating or withdrawing from the treaty unless:

(a) The existence of those circumstances constituted an essential basis of the consent of the parties to be bound by the treaty; and
(b) The effect of the change is radically to transform the extent of obligations still to be performed under the treaty.

2. A fundamental change of circumstances may not be invoked as a ground for terminating or withdrawing from a treaty:
   (a) If the treaty establishes a boundary; or
   (b) If the fundamental change is the result of a breach by the party invoking it either of an obligation under the treaty or of any other international obligation owed to any other party to the treaty.
3. If, under the foregoing paragraphs, a party may invoke a fundamental change of circumstances as a ground for terminating or withdrawing from a treaty it may also invoke the change as a ground for suspending the operation of the treaty.

[7] Suraputra (2013).

options, treaties risk being ignored even more frequently.[8] Clear loopholes, while difficult to achieve, provide the respite necessary for the exercise of state sovereignty.[9]

The concept of essential interest goes beyond the flexibility clauses set forth above. Like them, the concept is a function of state sovereignty.[10] However, it goes much further: by invoking essential interests, a state is granted the freedom to exempt itself from international legal norms when a particular set of circumstances affects its survival and existence.[11] Substantively, the concept of essential interests is largely reminiscent of the notion of vital interests discussed in Chap. 3 and is at the heart of the necessity defence discussed in this chapter.

As a type of device to achieve submissive deference of the kind just discussed,[12] the necessity defence limits ex post the effects of a breach of applicable treaty obligations and is potentially of particular relevance in the case of arbitration arising from national security screening. Another type of device is (true) exceptions, which limit the effects of applying treaty obligations and affect how those obligations are applied.[13] In any event, an arbitrator who concludes that an investment treaty applies to a situation involving investment screening may nevertheless find provisions in the treaty that either limit the scope of application of the treaty's substantive investment protection standards or disapply legal consequences regarding measures to protect the host state's national security. The present chapter examines the extent to which such exceptions may apply to national security screening. The most important type of exception in the context of investment screening is (essential) security exceptions, including non-precluded measures (NPM) clauses. Another type is general exceptions, which may also apply to matters of national security.

Given that necessity is a defence under customary international law, while treaty exceptions are normally understood as lex specialis,[14] it is appropriate, for present purposes, to begin with the situation that applies in general. Notably, however, arbitral practice is not settled as to the exact relationship between the customary necessity defence and essential security exceptions in treaties, with some tribunals

---

[8] Ibid. See Blanco and Pehl (2020) 8.

[9] See Werner (2004).

[10] Galvez (2013), Hahn (1991).

[11] See Udich (2013).

[12] However, another type of device is exclusions, which delimit ex ante the scope of application of treaty obligations (see Chap. 4 above). For a comprehensive review of devices to achieve deference, of which exceptions are only a notable example, see Viñuales (2016). Defences and other devices range from those that operate at the application stage, including rules on burden of proof, choice of applicable law, and exhaustion of domestic remedies, to those that operate at the post-application stage, such as excuses or preclusions of responsibility, and circumstances precluding wrongfulness.

[13] Viñuales (n.12), Agius (2009).

[14] See *El Paso Energy International Company v Argentine Republic*, ICSID Case No ARB/03/15, Award (31 October 2011) paras. 614–15. The *El Paso* tribunal considered the NPM clause as a special case (lex specialis) of the plea of necessity under customary international law. However, since the NPM clause provided scant guidance as to its application, the tribunal proceeded to apply the conditions for the necessity defence.

holding that the necessity defence applies secondarily as an interpretive tool or in the absence of a specific provision, while other tribunals apply both sources equally.[15]

This chapter begins with the customary international law defence of necessity (5.2) before analysing possible treaty exceptions that may apply in a particular case depending on the treaty (5.3). The conclusions are summarized at the end (5.4).

5.2 The Necessity Defence Applied to Investment Screening

Customary international law provides legal flexibility to states in exceptional situations, as discussed above. Necessity is one of several secondary rules of customary international law that the state can invoke to preclude the wrongfulness of an act in breach of an international obligation of that state, including a breach of its obligations under an investment treaty.[16] The conditions under which wrongfulness of conduct may be precluded under international law are confirmed in the ILC Articles on State Responsibility (ARSIWA). They include

---

[15] *CMS v Argentina*, Decision on the Application for Annulment, 25 September 2007, paras. 145–147. The annulment committee observed that the tribunal's analysis did not distinguish between the application of the plea of necessity with the interpretation of the NPM clause found in the relevant investment treaty. While the NPM clause is subject to the treaty's exclusion of certain non-derogable measures from the scope of the treaty in certain circumstances (and therefore should be considered first), the necessity exception requires that treaty obligations apply and that the respondent state's conduct is found to be contrary to the applicable norms of the treaty, but that the conduct in question is not unlawful because of necessity. The relevant exclusion clause, Article X, reads:

This Treaty shall not derogate from:

(a) laws and regulations, administrative practices or procedures, or administrative or adjudicatory decisions of either Party;
(b) international legal obligations; or
(c) obligations assumed by either Party, including those contained in an investment agreement or an investment authorization, that entitle investments or associated activities to treatment more favorable than that accorded by this Treaty in like situations.

Although the *CMS* tribunal conflated the necessity defence and the NPM clause, the annulment committee did not consider this a "manifest excess of powers" (paras. 135–136). In the tribunal's view, the arbitral tribunal did not fail to apply the NPM clause fully, which would have justified annulling the award under Article 52(1)(b) of the ICSID Convention. See also *Enron Creditors Recovery Corporation (formerly Enron Corporation) and Ponderosa Assets LP v Argentina*, ICSID Case No ARB/01/3, Decision on Jurisdiction (2 August 2004); *Sempra Energy International v Argentine Republic*, ICSID ARB/02/16, Award (28 September 2007). The annulment committees in both cases noted that the Argentine Republic in its pleadings had conflated the necessity defence and the NPM clause.

[16] International Law Commission (ILC), Draft Articles on Responsibility of States for Internationally Wrongful Acts, with Commentaries. In *The Yearbook of the International Law Commission*, 2001, vol. II, Part Two, as corrected (2001) (ILC Articles Commentary) 31. See Burke-White and von Staden (2007).

force majeure,[17] distress,[18] and necessity,[19] each of which may relieve a state of international responsibility.

In the context of the present study, necessity is of particular interest and describes the situation in which a state has no other means to protect an essential interest and can do so without harming an essential interest of another state.[20] The defence of necessity was recognized in the ICJ case of *Gabčíkovo-Nagymaros*[21] and in the investment arbitration of *CMS v Argentina*,[22] *LG&E v Argentina*,[23] *Continental Casualty v Argentina*,[24] *Impregilo v Argentina*,[25] *Von Pezold v Zimbabwe*,[26] and *Unión Fenosa v Egypt*,[27] to name a few.

Regarding the necessity defence, the obvious question is, what, more precisely, are the consequences with respect to the application of investment treaty protection standards when a respondent state has successfully argued necessity under customary international law? Considering this question, the consensus understanding is that, if applicable, the necessity defence would preclude international responsibility even if a violation of the treaty provisions is found for as long as the state of necessity prevails.[28] When the period of necessity has ended, the international responsibility for breaching treaty obligations is restored.[29] In principle, once the state of necessity has come to an end, a state may no longer rely on that defence to preclude the wrongfulness of its actions or omissions.[30] However, in practice, when applied to investment screening, the effects of measures taken in connection with investment screening are permanent, such as the prohibition of a contemplated investment, and cannot be meaningfully undone.[31]

---

[17] Article 23 of the Articles on Responsibility of States for Internationally Wrongful Acts, with Commentaries (ARSIWA).

[18] Article 24 of the ARSIWA.

[19] Article 25 of the ARSIWA.

[20] Ibid. See Burke-White and von Staden (n. 16).

[21] *Gabčíkovo-Nagymaros Project* (Hungary/Slovakia), Judgment, 25 September 1997, I.C.J. Reports 1997, 7.

[22] *CMS Gas Transmission Company v Argentine Republic*, ICSID Case No ARB/01/08, Award, 12 May 2005.

[23] *LG&E v Argentine Republic*, ICSID Case No. ARB/02/1, Decision on Liability, 3 October 2006.

[24] *Continental Casualty v Argentine Republic*, ICSID Case No. ARB/03/9, Award, 5 September 2008.

[25] *Impregilo v Argentine Republic*, ICSID Case No. ARB/07/17, Final Award, 21 June 2011.

[26] *Von Pezold v Zimbabwe*, ICSID Case No. ARB/10/15, Award, 28 July 2015.

[27] *Unión Fenosa Gas, S.A. v Arab Republic of Egypt*, ICSID Case No. ARB/14/4, Award, 31 August 2018.

[28] ILC Articles Commentary, 80–81; Tanzi (2013) 7.

[29] Agius (n.13) 95–135.

[30] See Reinisch (2007) 191–214.

[31] See Chap. 2 above.

More specifically, the conditions that apply to necessity are codified in Article 25, as further explained by the ILC's commentary:

1. Necessity may not be invoked by a State as a ground for precluding the wrongfulness of an act not in conformity with an international obligation of that State unless the act:
   (a) is the only way for the State to safeguard an essential interest against a grave and imminent peril; and
   (b) does not seriously impair an essential interest of the State or States towards which the obligation exists or of the international community as a whole.
2. In any case, necessity may not be invoked by a State as a ground for precluding wrongfulness if:
   (a) the international obligation in question excludes the possibility of invoking necessity; or
   (b) the State has contributed to the situation of necessity.[32]

The burden of proof for the necessity defence under customary international law, as a positive allegation, rests with the respondent in investment arbitration, in accordance with the principle of *actori incumbit onus probandi*.[33] Since the elements of the necessity defence, as set forth in Article 25 of the ARSIWA, are cumulative, it is for the respondent to prove each of the relevant elements.[34]

Of particular interest for the present study, as applied to the factual context of investment screening, the necessity defence requires that (1) the state's "essential interest" is at stake,[35] (2) the act serves the purpose of safeguarding such interest against a "grave and imminent peril" (emergency situation),[36] (3) the act is the only way to achieve such a purpose,[37] and (4) the act does not seriously impair the essential interest of any other state.[38] The requirement of Article 25(2)(a) of the ARSIWA may also be relevant in the event that a relevant investment treaty excludes the possibility of invoking necessity.[39] Moreover, in practice, the facts of a case may indicate that the state invoking necessity may have contributed to the situation of necessity, in which case the defence would not be available.[40]

Essential interest. The requirement that the interest at stake is "essential" is a matter of fact-specific enquiry.[41] The notion of essential interest parallels the term 'vital interest' discussed above in the preceding chapter without necessarily being

[32] Article 25 of the ARSIWA.

[33] *Unión Fenosa v Egypt*, para. 8.38.

[34] See the tribunal in *Unión Fenosa* para. 8.38 referring to "the negative formulation of Article 25(1) and 25(2) ('may not be invoked', 'unless' and 'if'), together with elements that fall almost exclusively within the actual knowledge of the State invoking the defence of 'necessity.'" See also Crawford (2002), 162, 183.

[35] Article 25(1)(a) of the ARSIWA.

[36] Ibid.

[37] Ibid.

[38] Article 25(1)(b) of the ARSIWA.

[39] Article 25(2)(a) of the ARSIWA.

[40] Article 25(2)(b) of the ARSIWA; cf. Article 39 of the ARSIWA.

[41] Schill and Briese (2009).

identical.[42] It encompasses the "political and economic survival" of the state,[43] the (continued) "existence of a state, as well as the maintenance of public order of a State."[44] As such, safeguarding against threats to a state's "national security" or, more broadly, its "essential security interests", has frequently been cited as one of the "essential interests" of the state.[45] Moreover, in arbitral practice, investment arbitration tribunals have determined that essential interests also include economic and social stability, as well as the maintenance of essential public services.[46] What remains to be analysed below is what constitutes a state's "national security" or "essential security" in the context of investment screening.

Emergency. The necessity defence further requires an emergency situation. In other words, the contested measure must be taken to safeguard the essential interest in question against "grave and imminent peril".[47] In the *Gabčíkovo-Nagymaros* case, the ICJ established,

> a peril appearing in the long term might be held to be "imminent" as soon as it is established, at the relevant point in time, that the realisation of that peril, however far off it might be, is not thereby any less certain and inevitable.[48]

In other words, the peril can occur far in the future and yet be "imminent", provided that its occurrence is triggered with sufficient certainty in advance.[49] With respect to the "gravity" of the peril in question, tribunals have maintained a very high bar; the survival of the state must be in jeopardy.[50] How the emergency criterion applies in the context of investment screening is discussed below in conjunction with the requirement that the state must not have contributed to the emergency in question.

No alternative. The necessity defence is only available if there are no otherwise lawful means to safeguard the essential interest in question, regardless of whether such alternative measures are less expedient.[51] If it is assumed in the context of national security screening that the screening safeguards an essential interest of the host state under emergency circumstances, then such screening would not be protected by necessity if an alternative to investment screening existed, which

---

[42] See Chap. 3 above. See also Tanzi (n. 28), Udich (n. 11) para. 19.

[43] *LG&E Energy Corp et al. v Argentine Republic* (LG&E) (see ICSID Case No. ARB/02/1, Decision on Liability, 3 October 2006, paras. 246, 251) and *Continental Casualty Company v Argentine Republic* (Continental Casualty) (see ICSID Case No. ARB/03/9, Award, 5 September 2008, para. 175).

[44] *Von Pezold v Zimbabwe*, para. 628.

[45] Subramanian (2012) 68; Di Benedetto (2023) 65.

[46] See Thiga (2019).

[47] Paddeu and Waibel (2022) 160–191.

[48] *Gabčikovo-Nagymaros Project (Hungary v Slovakia)* Judgment [1997] ICJ Rep 7.

[49] Ibid.

[50] Ibid.

[51] Article 25(1)(a) of the ARSIWA. See Crawford (n. 34) 184; Paddeu and Waibel (n. 47) 160–191, 176; Rosenne (1991) 351 et seq.

would equally safeguard the same interest and would not result in the host state breaching international obligations. It would be for the aggrieved investor to argue that the host state had such alternatives at its disposal.[52] For example, an alternative to an investment screening measure in the form of an investment ban could be conditional approval, commonly known as "mitigation", such as an approval conditional on partial divestment of problematic assets, the appointment of external directors, or other bespoke security arrangements.[53]

Non-impairment of other essential interests. A state may not invoke the necessity defence if the measure in question seriously impairs an essential interest of the state(s) vis-à-vis which the breached obligation exists.[54] Nor must it seriously impair the essential interest of the international community as a whole.[55]

If the investor's home state were arguing that an investment screening measure would impair its (i.e. the home state's) non-economic essential interests, it would come very close to the home state acknowledging that there indeed was a good reason for the host state to subject the investment to investment screening.[56] It is precisely investments projecting home state geopolitical or geoeconomic ambitions that motivate investment screening in the first place.[57]

It is also difficult, but perhaps not impossible, to imagine that a tribunal could be persuaded that merely economic interests linked to one home state investor's investment activity abroad would amount to a serious impairment of an essential interest of the home state.[58] However, as the examples from Argentina's financial crisis richly illustrate,[59] the bar is quite high in regard to economic interests constituting essential interests. Following several subsequent awards, the tribunal in *Impregilo v Argentina* found that the interests of one or more foreign investors did not amount to the essential interests of their home state for the purposes of Article 25 of the ARSIWA.[60] The ILC Commentary notes that "the interest relied on must outweigh all other considerations, not merely from the point of view of the

---

[52] See n. 33 above.

[53] See Chap. 2 above.

[54] Article 25(1)(b) of the ARSIWA.

[55] Ibid.

[56] Although not a case of investment screening, the recent Huawei saga vividly demonstrates how the interests of a single foreign investor could matter greatly to a home state, perhaps even to the extent of engaging the essential interest of the investor's home state.

[57] See Chap. 2 above.

[58] See n. 51 above.

[59] See Section 5.2.2 below.

[60] *Impregilo v Argentina*, ICSID Case No. ARB/07/17, Final Award, 21 June 2011, Paragraph 354; *Suez v Argentina*, ICSID Case No. ARB/03/17, Decision on Liability, 30 July 2010, Paragraph 239; *LG&E v Argentina*, ICSID Case No. ARB/02/1, Decision on Liability, 3 October 2006, Paragraph 257; *Enron v Argentina*, ICSID Case No. ARB/01/3, Award, 22 May 2007, Paragraph 341; *Sempra v Argentina*, ICSID Case No. ARB/02/16, Award, 28 September 2007, Paragraph 390; *CMS v Argentina*, ICSID Case No. ARB/01/8, Award, 12 May 2005, Paragraph 358.

acting State but on a reasonable assessment of the competing interests, whether these are individual or collective".[61] The Impregilo tribunal found that the "interests of a small number of a contracting State's nationals or legal entities are not consistent with, and do not qualify as, an 'essential interest' of that State" and could not be considered in the balancing required under Article 25(1)(b) of the ARSIWA.[62]

The necessity defence, when applied to the breach of an investment treaty obligation in the context of national security screening, would not be available to justify a screening measure if an essential interest of the home state was seriously impaired. In light of *Impregilo* case law, it can be concluded that the non-impairment criterion is not typically involved in the context of investment screening in a case of pleading the necessity defence.[63]

From the previous discussion, two important questions require closer scrutiny with regard to the interpretation and application of the necessity defence to excuse breaches of investment treaty obligations in the context of national security screening. These are whether the alleged national security interests at stake in foreign investments qualify as "essential interests" (5.2.1) and whether national security screening constitutes an emergency measure in the sense that it is the "only way" for the host state to protect against a "grave and imminent peril" (to such interests) to which the host state itself has "not contributed" (5.2.2). Interim conclusions are summarized at the end (5.2.3).

5.2.1 Investment Security as an Essential Interest of the Host State

Investment screening involves restricting—whether by prohibiting or placing conditions on and thus even effectively restructuring—an investment and subjecting it to a potentially thorough and intrusive investigation. The justification for this restriction is that the investment may pose a threat to national security and, in some cases, potentially broader notions such as "security or public order".[64] The host state would have to prove that the screening safeguarded an "essential interest" of the host state to avail itself of the necessity defence in the context of a claim by a foreign investor on the basis of a host state's investment screening.

---

[61] ILC Commentary to Article 25, at para. 17.

[62] *Impregilo v Argentina*, ICSID Case No. ARB/07/17, Final Award, 21 June 2011, para. 354.

[63] Cf. *Von Pezold v Zimbabwe*: The defence of necessity was precluded because the contested measure impaired an essential interest of the international community as a whole by breaching an obligation erga omnes through the implementation of a policy of racial discrimination against landowners on the basis of their skin color and foreign ancestral heritage.

[64] Cf. Article 4 of the FDI Screening Regulation.

The notion of "essential interest" does not lend itself to a precise and exhaustive definition. According to the ILC Commentary,

> [T]he extent to which a given interest is essential depends on all the circumstances, and cannot be prejudged. It extends to particular interests of the State and its people, as well as of the international community as a whole.[65]

Because of its imprecise scope, notions such as essential interests and essential security interests serve as devices on which an adjudicator can rely to defer to national decision-making.[66] In its starkest form, such deference is at odds with the conception of international law as a binding set of rules that can be modified only through a certain pre-agreed-upon procedure and according to substantive conditions.[67] The ability of those to whom the rules apply to unilaterally modify the rules whenever they deem the rules to be at odds with their interests is incompatible with legal order.[68] Because such devices subject the binding nature of international obligations to a unilateral and potentially arbitrary decision by one state, the scope of essential interests and the concomitant deference is not and cannot be limitless.[69]

To what extent essential interests are the subject matter of international judicial or arbitral scrutiny is linked to the allegedly self-judging character of the concept.[70] Exclusions for essential interests from international arbitration have a long history.[71] The well-known reservation of the Anglo-French Treaty of 1903, discussed in Chap. 3, concerning "vital interests, independence, honour, and the interests of third parties", became a widely copied model for treaty clauses that exclude sensitive issues from arbitration, which left it to the state concerned to unilaterally decide whether a particular dispute is appropriate for submission to final and binding arbitration.[72]

In contemporary general international law, the extreme notion of essential security interests as self-judging, has given way to a more nuanced understanding.[73] Notably, as an outer limit of state discretion, essential security interests do not justify the use of force beyond the strictures of the UN Charter and customary international law.[74] Essential interests are only exceptionally valid justifications for suspending treaty norms under current international law.[75] In the context of

---

[65] Crawford (n. 34) 184.

[66] ILC Commentary to Article 25, at para. 16.

[67] See Hahn (n. 10), citing Partsch (1987).

[68] Ibid.

[69] Ibid.

[70] Schill and Briese (n. 41) 61–140, 113–119.

[71] See Hahn (n. 10).

[72] 1903 France-U.K. Agreement for the Settlement by Arbitration of Certain Classes of Questions Which May Arise Between the Two Governments, Fr.-Gr. Brit., Oct. 14, 1903, 194 Consol. T.S. 194.

[73] Hahn (n. 10).

[74] Ibid. 562. Also, Schachter (1984).

[75] U.N. CHARTER art. 2, para. 4; see Military and Paramilitary Activities in and Against Nicaragua, (Nicaragua v United States), 1986 I.C.J. 14, 187 (June 22).

investment treaties, vital interest clauses have largely been superseded by the balanced NPM clauses modelled on Article XXI of the GATT, as further discussed in Subchapter 5.3.[76] However, the concept of essential interests has not entirely disappeared and remains relevant, even more so in recent years. States continue to invoke—increasingly so—essential interests, including to avoid ICJ proceedings on alleged treaty violations.[77] The continued practice of attaching domestic jurisdiction clauses to declarations under Article 36 of the Statute of the ICJ is another example of states remaining reluctant to arbitrate matters involving their essential interests.[78]

While not self-judging, arbitral tribunals have been extremely reluctant to reject a state's contention as to what constitutes its essential interests.[79] In fact, while disinclined to accept essential interests as self-judging, tribunals have shown remarkable deference to states' substantive delimitation of such interests.[80] In the hands of international adjudicators, earlier tendencies to relate the application of the notion of essential interests to the "[continued] existence of the State itself, its political or economic survival"[81] have, over time, given way to much more expansive interpretations in arbitral practice.[82] Several ICSID tribunals have held that the "essential interest" of a state and its "existence" extend to the social, economic, financial and political interests of the state, which may include the maintenance of the state's public order and stability, as well as the maintenance of its basic services, such as water and sewage services.[83] Notably, the tribunal in *Continental Casualty v Argentina* found that the "essential security interests" of a host state may be affected not only by military and international security matters but also by a serious economic crisis[84]:

> As to "essential security interests," it is necessary to recall that international law is not blind to the requirement that States should be able to exercise their sovereignty in the interest of their population free from internal as well as external threats to their security and the maintenance of a peaceful domestic order. It is well known that the concept of international security of States in the Post World War II international order was intended to cover not only political and military security but also the economic security of States and of their population. The Preamble to the Charter of the United Nations and, even more relevant for the present case, that of the International Monetary Fund support this approach. As noted by the International Law Commission, States have invoked necessity "to protect a wide variety of interests, including safeguarding the environment, preserving

---

[76] Hahn (n. 10).

[77] Udich (n. 11) paras. 5–11. Cf. Blanco and Pehl (n. 8) 10–12.

[78] Akande and Williams (2002) 365, Briese and Schill (2009) 308–328.

[79] Ibid.

[80] Ibid.

[81] Paddeu (2018) 339–386, 391.

[82] *LG&E v Argentina* (2006); *Impregilo v Argentina* (2011); *Von Pezold v Zimbabwe* (2015).

[83] Ibid.

[84] *Continental Casualty Company v Argentine Republic*, ICSID Case No ARB/03/09, Award (5 September 2008), para. 151.

the very existence of the State and its people in time of public emergency, or ensuring the safety of a civilian population".[85]

In principle, a state's security—whether encompassing national or public security, external or internal security, and economic security—speaks to the "stability and public order" of the state[86] and may call into question the state's "political and economic survival" or the very "existence of the State".[87] As such, the security interests of the state may indeed be essential interests (i.e. essential security interests) for purposes of the necessity defence, per the discussion above. Thus, the question of debate is not whether national security, in principle, could qualify as an essential interest but what exactly suffices to qualify as a national security interest, let alone an essential one. In other words, not every state interest is a security interest, and not all security interests are essential security interests. Nevertheless, an interest that does not qualify as a security interest may still be essential.

Thus, the concept of essential interests is not identical to a state's security; it encompasses much more. Not only the national (external) and public (internal) security of the state but also the safety and social welfare of a state's civilian population, such as the safeguarding of the environment, are contemporary interests that could legitimately be designated "essential" for the purpose of seeking protection by means of invoking the defence of necessity.[88] It has been argued that, in the context of cybersecurity, there is "growing consensus as to the recognition of secure and functioning 'critical infrastructures' as essential to a society's welfare".[89] With similar reasoning applied to investment screening, "critical infrastructure" as well as "critical technologies", "critical inputs", the protection of personal data, and the freedom and plurality of the media (i.e. factors potentially affecting "security or public order", as listed in Article 4(1) of the FDI Screening Regulation) may currently be successfully invoked as essential interests in the context of the necessity defence.[90] In theory, an essential interest could be anything that the respondent host state can prove is "critical" to its political and economic survival and existence.

As discussed in Chap. 2, screening mechanisms, such as those modelled on the EU FDI Screening Regulation, apply non-international law notions (i.e. domestic law or, in the case of the EU, EU law—such as the EU law concept of "security or public order") to such an array of investment situations as to stretch the international law notion of national security.[91] For example, investments that threaten the "freedom and plurality of the media" (cf. Article 4[1][e] of the FDI Screening Regulation) could arguably invoke essential interests in their own right but also conceptions of

---

[85] *Continental Casualty Company v Argentine Republic*, ICSID Case No ARB/03/09, Award (5 September 2008), para. 175.

[86] *LG&E v Argentina* (2006); *Impregilo v Argentina* (2011); *Von Pezold v Zimbabwe* (2015).

[87] Ibid.

[88] Ibid. Paddeu (n. 81); see also Lahmann (2023).

[89] Lahmann, Ibid., 429.

[90] Article 4 of the FDI Screening Regulation.

[91] Chap. 2 above.

political security, such as in the prevention of public misinformation.[92] An international tribunal may not be willing to defer to such a broad conception of national security for purposes of international law but may nevertheless acknowledge such interests as being within the broader ambit of essential interests for purposes of applying the necessity defence. However, the more expansive the concept of essential interests, the greater emphasis rests upon other criteria for a successful plea of necessity, chiefly whether the essential interests in question would be in "grave and imminent peril" but for the contested measure, as explored in the next subsection.

Critically, the respondent has to prove that the measure truly serves such an essential interest of the host state rather than another purpose (e.g. the interest of the state's incumbent government, the ruling party or political supporters,[93] or indeed the interest of a country's domestic exporters, industry, or business community). In *Unión Fenosa v Egypt*, the tribunal concluded that the contested measure was unrelated to circumstances that might otherwise have constituted "essential interests" of the state, notably the Egyptian revolution and the global financial crisis of 2008, but rather to structural economic circumstances that predated the revolution and crisis.[94] Again, in practice, the question of what constitutes an essential interest of a host state can easily be conflated with the question of whether such interests are in "grave and imminent peril", as discussed in the subsection below.

To sum up, essential security interests are historically strongly linked to the use of force. As contemporary international law does not consider the use of force legal except in very limited situations, essential security interests are subject to the rule of law and can only exceptionally justify non-compliance with international obligations. The same is true with respect to other essential interests. However, apart from the necessity defence, a specific essential security defence has not emerged in customary law. Instead, it is in treaties that the specific notion of essential security interests has evolved, to which this chapter returns in Subchapter 5.3.

5.2.2 Investment Screening as an Emergency Measure

To avail itself of the necessity defence in the context of investment screening, the screening would have to protect the host state's essential interest against "grave and imminent peril",[95] which must not be of its own making and against which screening must be the "only way" to do so.[96]

[92] Cf. Article 4(1)(e) of the FDI Screening Regulation.

[93] *Von Pezold* para. 631.

[94] *Unión Fenosa v Egypt,* para. 8.57–8.58.

[95] Article 25(1)(a) of the ARSIWA.

[96] Ibid.

The points of departure for analysing the necessity defence in the context of investment arbitration are the cases emanating from the Argentine sovereign debt crisis of the early 2000s, which were touched on above.[97] Among these cases, as discussed immediately below, the tribunal in *CMS* considered that the relevant investment treaty (between the United States and Argentina)[98] was clearly intended to protect investment in times of economic difficulty or challenges prompting governmental countermeasures.[99] The core issue explored was the extent of economic adversity required for these protections to remain operative.[100]

According to the *CMS* tribunal, a severe crisis does not necessarily equate to a total collapse that may excuse the non-performance of treaty obligations.[101] Without such extreme circumstances, the obligations stipulated by the treaty for a limited period prevail over any argument of necessity.[102] The *CMS* tribunal's analysis of necessity was sharply criticized by the ad hoc committee, which, however, refrained from annulling it.[103]

In the deluge of subsequent awards against Argentina, the tribunal in the *Continental Casualty* case[104] upheld this interpretation of the defence of necessity. In contrast, the tribunal in the *El Paso* case held that the necessity exception was not available because of Argentina's contribution to its economic crisis.[105] Notably, two other Argentina awards, *Enron* and *Sempra*, were annulled due to methodological flaws in their necessity analysis.[106] However, in another case, the *BG* award was overturned on appeal in the United States because it was found that the arbitral tribunal had erroneously ignored the exhaustion clause of the domestic remedies clause of the U.K.-Argentina investment treaty.[107]

Apart from the Argentina cases, the notions of "grave and imminent peril" and "only way" were also analysed by the tribunal in *Von Pezold v Zimbabwe*.[108] The tribunal found that the respondent failed to adduce evidence of a threat to the

[97] See 5.2.1 above.

[98] Article XI of the Argentina-United States of America Bilateral Investment Treaty (1991).

[99] *CMS Gas Transmission Company v Argentine Republic*, ICSID Case No ARB/01/08, Award (12 May 2005), para. 354. See Sacerdoti (2013).

[100] Bjorklund (2008) 462–465. See Sacerdoti (n. 99).

[101] *CMS Gas Transmission Company v Argentine Republic*, ICSID Case No ARB/01/8, Decision of the ad hoc Committee for Annulment (25 September 2007) para. 354.

[102] Ibid. See Sacerdoti (n. 99).

[103] Ibid. paras. 101–150.

[104] Ibid. paras 180, 181.

[105] *El Paso Energy International Company v Argentine Republic*, ICSID Case No ARB/03/15, Award (31 October 2011) paras 614–15.

[106] *Enron Creditors Recovery Corporation (formerly Enron Corporation) and Ponderosa Assets LP v Argentina*, ICSID Case No ARB/01/3, Decision on Jurisdiction (2 August 2004); *Sempra Energy International v Argentine Republic*, ICSID ARB/02/16, Award (28 September 2007).

[107] *BG Group Plc v The Republic of Argentina*, UNCITRAL, Award (24 December 2007) paras. 258–266.

[108] *Von Pezold v Zimbabwe*, ICSID Case No. ARB/10/15, Award, 28 July 2015, paras. 633 et seq.

survival of the state and specifically failed to prove that the contested measure was implemented for the long-term economic interests of the state rather than to appease the government's political supporters.[109]

Overall, the picture emerging from this early case law centres on the *CMS* award. To outline the contours of the "emergency" criterion (starting with the "grave and imminent peril" criterion) emerging from early case law, the departure point is the *CMS* award (5.2.2.1). The analysis below turns to the other elements of the necessity defence relevant for present purposes: whether the measure at issue was the "only way" to protect against the peril (5.2.2.2) and whether the state invoking it contributed to the same peril (5.2.2.3).

5.2.2.1 Grave and Imminent Peril

For purposes of the necessity defence, it is insufficient that investment screening protects the essential interest of the host state, namely, its national security. The screening host state must prove that the screening protects such interest against "grave and imminent peril".[110] Even more than "essential interests", the requirement of "grave and imminent peril" entrusts arbitrators with a generous margin of discretion as to the degree of threat posed to such interests to trigger an application of the necessity defence.

The "grave and imminent peril" requirement, according to the ILC Commentary, should be established "objectively" in the sense of being assessed otherwise than by the state concerned, albeit with the state being granted a certain margin of appreciation.[111] If an investment subject to screening is deemed to endanger the availability of critical technologies, infrastructures, inputs, or other critical functions of the state, the preconditions are likely to be met.[112] The inherent indeterminacy of outcomes with respect to threat assessment may play an even more prominent role in determining the availability of alternative measures, as discussed below.

According to the *CMS* tribunal, the "grave and imminent peril" requirement in the context of essential economic interests can take on a different meaning only when economic difficulties "lead to catastrophic conditions in terms of disruption and disintegration of society or are likely to lead to a total collapse of the economy".[113] In doing so, the tribunal transferred its conclusions as to the existence of a grave

---

[109] Ibid. para. 637.

[110] See n. 33.

[111] ILC commentary, 311.

[112] See Foster (2008).

[113] See Sacerdoti (n. 99) discussing *CMS Gas Transmission Company v Argentine Republic*, ICSID Case No ARB/01/08, Award (12 May 2005), para. 354. As a further consequence, the tribunal therefore declined to apply the relevant treaty's NPM clause (Article XI) because it was convinced that "the crisis in Argentina was serious but did not lead to total economic and social collapse" (para. 306).

(serious) and imminent peril to interpret the "essential security interest" element inherent in the emergency clause.[114] The tribunal noted that the crisis in Argentina could be "compared to other contemporary crises affecting countries in different regions of the world"[115] and "ha[s] not led to a derogation of international contractual or treaty obligations. Renegotiation, adaptation, and postponement have occurred, but the essence of the international obligations has been kept intact".[116]

Further decisions evaluating the Argentine crisis in light of the necessity defence took different approaches and reached opposite conclusions.[117] As further discussed in Subchapter 5.3, in contrast to the earlier awards, the *LG&E* tribunal held that the "highest degree of public disorder" prevailed, which "threatened Argentina's essential security interests" to the point of a risk of "total collapse of the Government and the State".[118]

In the context of investment screening, extant case law appears to put a very high bar in terms of the threat that a screened investment would have to pose to the host state's essential interests. Although not unimaginable, the type of investment that may involve "grave and imminent peril" would appear to be limited to particularly sensitive areas. For example, one could imagine an investment in the form of an acquisition of a manufacturer of a critical technology, such as nuclear weapons technology or artificial intelligence, as being of this type. However, even in such cases, it would appear to be practically highly problematic for a host state to argue that an individual foreign investment may jeopardize its national security (i.e. its political or economic survival) without providing extensive evidence to support such an assertion. Understandably, a host state would be reluctant to do this unless it were to disclose secret intelligence relating to its threat assessments and security concerns.

5.2.2.2 No Alternatives

For investment screening to qualify for the necessity defence, the host state would also have to satisfy the tribunal that the screening would be the "only way" to

---

[114] Article XI provides:

> This treaty shall not preclude the application by either Party of measures necessary for the maintenance of public order, the fulfilment of its obligations with respect to the maintenance or restoration of international peace or security, or the protection of its own essential security interests.

[115] *CMS Gas Transmission Company v Argentine Republic*, ICSID Case No ARB/01/08, Award (12 May 2005), para. 355. See Sacerdoti (n. 99).

[116] Ibid.

[117] *LG&E Energy Corp, LG&E Capital Corp and LG&E International Inc. v Argentine Republic*, ICSID Case No ARB/02/1, Award (3 October 2006), para. 260 et seq. Unlike the tribunals in the *CMS* and *Enron* cases, which had erroneously analysed the NPM clause of the US-Argentina investment treaty as part of the pleas of necessity, the *LG&E* tribunal considered a state of necessity under the NPM as a distinct, treaty-based defence.

[118] Ibid. para. 231. See Sacerdoti (n. 99).

safeguard the essential interest from "grave and imminent peril". This argument could be particularly difficult to support, in part because investment screening is only one of several types of investment restriction and in part because investment screening itself can result in several measures at the end of the screening procedure—investment prohibition or approval—subject to a virtually unlimited number of possible individualized conditions (e.g. a condition to appoint independent directors to the board of directors or to divest a product line or division or restructure the investment in one or other way). As discussed below, this "only way" requirement has undergone significant evolution in case law.

The *CMS* tribunal explored the necessity of the Argentine measures[119] and determined that they did not fulfil the stringent criteria of Article 25 of the ARSIWA.[120] Therefore, they were not the sole means to protect the country's interests.[121] On the other hand, the *Sempra* tribunal acknowledged the severity of Argentina's economic downturn, which potentially justified emergency status.[122] However, it argued that the Argentine Emergency Law was unnecessary for maintaining public order or safeguarding essential security interests as defined by the NPM clause since alternative strategies were feasible.[123] The annulment proceedings that followed led to the committee nullifying this decision.[124]

The *Enron* tribunal, by contrast, did not find the crisis severe enough to justify reliance on the customary necessity defence, which it again—like the *CMS* and *Sempra* tribunals—erroneously conflated with the NPM clause.[125] Like the annulment committee in *Sempra*, the *Enron* committee found an error in the tribunal's approach to the "only way" requirement.[126] The *Enron* tribunal relied solely on expert testimony that the Argentine Emergency Law, which sought the "balancing" (i.e. de-dollarizing) of the economy of the Argentine Republic, was "the only way to protect an essential interest from serious consequences and imminent danger" under Article 25(1)(a) of the ARSIWA.[127] By solely relying on that expert

[119] *CMS Gas Transmission Company v Argentine Republic*, ICSID Case No ARB/01/08, Award (12 May 2005), para. 323.

[120] Ibid. para. 331.

[121] Ibid. para. 324.

[122] *Sempra Energy International v Argentine Republic*, ICSID ARB/02/16, Award (28 September 2007), para. 348.

[123] Ibid., para. 350–351. See Sacerdoti (n. 99).

[124] Ibid. Sacerdoti (n. 99) elaborates that the *Sempra* annulment committee concluded the tribunal completely failed to engage with the NPM clause, instead of misapplying it, by conflating it with the customary law defence of necessity (para. 218). Consequently, the committee annulled the award citing a manifest excess of power under Article 52(1)(b) of the Washington Convention (para. 219).

[125] *Enron Creditors Recovery Corporation (formerly Enron Corporation) and Ponderosa Assets LP v Argentina*, ICSID Case No ARB/01/3, 30 July 2010, Decision on the Application for Annulment, para. 359.

[126] Ibid., para. 378.

[127] Ibid., para. 377. See Sacerdoti (n. 99).

testimony, the *Enron* committee found that the tribunal had committed a manifest excess of power when applying the "no alternative" condition of the customary necessity defence.[128] The annulment was also based on a failure to state reasons under Article 52(1)(e) of the Washington Convention, as the tribunal's reasoning on the "no alternative" condition was not apparent.[129]

Regarding the requirement that the actions taken by the Argentine Republic must be "the only means available" to manage the crisis, the *LG&E* tribunal diverged from both *CMS* and *Enron*, which had identified feasible policy alternatives to the crisis measures.[130] The arbitrators in the *LG&E* case recognized several potential approaches to formulating a stimulus plan yet accepted Argentina's plan as the exclusive viable solution under the prevailing conditions.[131] Additionally, it was determined that the Article XI defence could only be invoked for a restricted timeframe, pertinent to threats against public order and essential national security interests.[132] During this interval, the tribunal attributed the measures of de-dollarization and the non-adjustment of regulated tariffs to circumstances beyond the control of the Argentine Republic.[133]

Even though the *LG&E* tribunal ultimately adopted a pragmatic approach to the "only way" requirement, what is clear from thc early Argentina cases is the lack of a clear yardstick to assess the merits of available alternative measures. In a sense, even the availability of a clearly inappropriate alternative measure could be enough to conclude that the measure at issue was not the "only way" to protect against grave and imminent peril. As evident in the discussion below, WTO law offers such a yardstick, although investment tribunals have found its application to investment treaties less than straightforward. See further Subchapter 5.3.

5.2.2.3 No Contribution

A final point worth noting is the requirement that the state invoking necessity must not have contributed to the situation of grave and imminent peril against its essential interests.[134] The *Continental* tribunal analysed the Argentine Republic's alleged contribution to the emergency situation, which distinguished the analysis in that respect for purposes of the NPM clause from the analysis conducted for purposes of satisfying the criteria under Article 25 of the ARSIWA.[135] In this regard, the tribunal accepted that if a host state contributed to endangering its

[128] *Enron*, Ibid.

[129] Ibid., para. 378. See Sacerdoti Ibid.

[130] See Sacerdoti Ibid.

[131] Ibid., also *Enron*, para. 250.

[132] *Enron*, para. 257. See Sacerdoti Ibid.

[133] *Enron*, para. 258. See Sacerdoti Ibid.

[134] See n. 40 above.

[135] Ibid.

essential security interests, which it subsequently took the contested measures to protect, those measures could not be said to be "necessary" within the meaning of the NPM clause since the host state could have adopted a different policy that would have rendered them unnecessary.[136]

The tribunal acknowledged that a country invariably holds ultimate responsibility for its economic policies and their outcomes, both politically and economically.[137] Nonetheless, it determined that the Argentine Republic's actions did not prevent it from invoking the NPM clause of the BIT: "We do not consider that the Argentine Republic is precluded from invoking the NPM clause of the BIT on the basis of its own conduct".[138]

In differentiating the application and scope of the NPM clause from that of customary-law necessity defence, the tribunal noted that certain elements are pertinent to both frameworks.[139] Indeed, both seek flexibility in the application of international obligations and recognize that the need to protect overriding national interests may justify the abrogation or suspension of an obligation or the disclaimer of liability for its breach.[140] Furthermore, the tribunal identified that employing the NPM clause, as opposed to the necessity exception, could lead to identical outcomes: it could legitimize actions that would otherwise breach legal obligations and thereby absolve the state of responsibility.[141]

The analysis by the *Continental* tribunal starkly differed from that in *CMS*, where it was determined that the requirement that the state not contribute to the emergency was not satisfied.[142] The *CMS* tribunal attributed significant blame for the crisis and resulting emergency situation to the Argentine government's policies and failures.[143] Conversely, the *LG&E* tribunal found insufficient credible evidence to suggest that the Argentine Republic had significantly contributed to the crisis precipitating the emergency.[144]

The Argentina cases again illustrate the lack of clear guidelines for assessing the role of contribution. The *Continental* tribunal was right to observe the truism that all policies are the result of the state's contribution and thus to any emergency arising therefrom, which was true for actions and omissions: policies that actively contributed to an emergency as well as policies not pursued that, if pursued, would have avoided an emergency. This point emphasizes the need for a certain high

[136] *Enron*, para. 235. See Sacerdoti (n. 99).

[137] *Enron*, para. 236. See Sacerdoti Ibid.

[138] *Enron*, para. 168. See Sacerdoti Ibid.

[139] See *Continental Casualty v Argentine Republic*, ICSID Case No. ARB/03/9, Award, 5 September 2008. See Sacerdoti Ibid.

[140] Ibid. *Continental Casualty*.

[141] Ibid. See Sacerdoti (n. 99).

[142] *CMS Gas Transmission Company v Argentine Republic*, ICSID Case No ARB/01/08, Award (12 May 2005), para. 328–329. See Sacerdoti Ibid.

[143] Ibid.

[144] Ibid. CMS para. 257. See Sacerdoti Ibid.

degree of relevant contribution for a state to be denied the necessity defence. Customary international law has not developed to provide clarity as to which situations a state ought to be responsible for foreseeing and preventing in its policymaking and, if it fails to do so, could be deemed to have contributed to. Moreover, some policies that end up contributing to an emergency may nevertheless be justified, which adds an element of uncertainty to the application of the necessity defence.

In the context of national security screening, it is appropriate to recall that security risks related to investments are often the result of a permissive, liberal investment policy. By allowing relatively free movement of capital, e.g. allowing investments in privatized "critical" infrastructure such as transportation networks, a host state may invite similar arguments (i.e. that the host state could have contributed to a national security risk through privatization and lack of appropriate oversight and regulation), even though a liberal investment policy may be justified as a matter of policy. Perhaps such a contribution would not suffice to deny the host state the plea of necessity, but as of today, case law does not provide clear answers.

5.2.3 Summary

At first glance, the necessity defence appears well suited to inviting submissive deference to investment screening. Being motivated by national security concerns, investment screening appears very much like a measure adopted to protect an "essential interest" of the state. However, as the string of cases emanating from the 2001 Argentine debt crisis illustrates, a high bar is required for a "grave and imminent peril", and much uncertainty remains as to whether investment screening would be the "only way" to protect against such peril. For purposes of applying the necessity defence to national security screening, the question remains whether the interests at stake in an individual FDI transaction could reach such a high bar. In limited cases, it is certainly imaginable that the facts might support the conclusion that the survival of the host state is at stake. In most investment screening cases, the bar would surely be too high to reach for all practical purposes.

5.3 Treaty Exceptions Applied to Investment Screening

Most investment treaties do not contain specific exception clauses, let alone exceptions applicable to national security matters.[145] Those that do contain one of two types of clauses: essential security exceptions, often although not uniformly enumerating NPM clauses, and general public policy exceptions that may apply to

[145] Data retrieved from UNCTAD Investment Policy Hub.

national security matters. Although rare, security exceptions are more common and are discussed first (5.3.1) before turning to general exceptions (5.3.2) and interim conclusions (5.3.3).

5.3.1 Security Exception Clauses in Investment Treaties

Exceptions for essential security interests or national security, sometimes by reference to or incorporation of the corresponding exception in WTO law, Article XXI of the GATT, are found in treaty clauses under which certain measures taken by a state that would otherwise deviate from a treaty obligation are not precluded (NPM). Therefore, they are commonly referred to, in the context of investment treaties, as NPM clauses.[146]

A clause of this type is limited to certain stated policy objectives to which the measure in question must relate (i.e. the nexus),[147] which are listed in the clause (i.e. the overriding objectives).[148] The clause also specifies its scope of application, which may be the entire treaty or limited to specific treaty provisions.[149]

NPM clauses often provide that the treaty does not preclude measures taken by the state to safeguard its national security interests, often referred to as "public security" or "essential security interests".[150] These measures may also extend to the fulfilment of obligations with respect to the maintenance of international peace and security.[151] Another overriding policy objective mentioned in NPM clauses is "public order", which is commonly understood as "internal security" or the maintenance of "law and order".[152] Other overriding policy objectives include "public health"[153] and occasionally environmental protection or economic emergencies.[154] A broader, contemporary understanding of the concept of security may overlap with other overriding objectives, particularly the notions of "environmental security" and "health security".[155]

---

[146] For a comprehensive treatment on the subject of security exceptions in investment treaties, see inter alia Newcombe and Paradell (2009) 488–500; Henckels (2019); Pathirana and McLaughlin (2021); Burke-White and von Staden (n. 16) 307–410; Schill and Briese (n. 41) 61–140; Schill and Vidigal (2021) 503–508; Vidigal and Schill (2021); Hagemeyer-Witzleb (2021); Wang (2017) 447–456; Alschner and Hui (2018).

[147] Pathirana and McLaughlin (n. 146) 492–496.

[148] Burke-White and von Staden (n. 16).

[149] Ibid.

[150] Ibid. 326–329.

[151] Schill and Briese (n. 41), 61–140, 71–72.

[152] Burke-White and von Staden (n. 16).

[153] Ibid. 334.

[154] Ibid. 334–335.

[155] See generally Baylis et al. (2022); Buzan et al. (1998).

Given the breadth of situations that can give rise to investment screening and the type of investments covered, as well as the multifaceted elements of security (including environmental security, food security, and energy security), the variously defined scope of NPM clauses is potentially broadly applicable to investment screening (5.3.1.1).

An important question that arises regarding the interpretation and application of security exception clauses in investment treaties is whether the clauses exclude the relevant subjects from the scope of the treaty (or specified provisions thereof, i.e. exemptions) or are merely a means of defence against treaty violations (i.e. defence). Another point of interpretation is the relationship between the clauses and the customary necessity defence.

The interpretation and application of such a clause are fact-specific and vary with the formulation of the clause. Even the same clause can result in widely varying interpretations. For example, in the context of arbitrations against Argentina following the Argentine economic crisis in the early 2000s, several arbitral tribunals took starkly different approaches and reached results that were difficult to reconcile. However, they interpreted the same NPM clause, which expressly did not preclude the application by a party of measures necessary to maintain public order, to carry out its obligations to maintain or restore international peace or security, or to protect essential interests of the state's national security.[156] Drawing firm conclusions on how NPM clauses and other security exceptions are generally interpreted and applied is thus very difficult. With that caveat, in the following paragraphs, an outline is provided (5.3.1.2).

These and other questions of interpretation are subject to the overarching question as to the extent to which security exception clauses are self-judging. The answer to these questions ultimately depends less on the precise formulation of the clause in question and more on the evolution of the WTO case law on Article XXI of the GATT, from which investment tribunals have taken inspiration, even where the exception clause in the relevant treaty is not closely modelled on Article XXI (5.3.1.3).

5.3.1.1 Security Exceptions in Treaty Practice

Although security has long been a key element of NPM clauses in investment treaties, the link to WTO law (or GATT law) is a comparatively late evolution, which reflects the absence of cases and case law until the *Russia-Traffic in Transit* case in 2019.[157] A look at some examples of security exception clauses provides an overview of their form and structure.

The earliest bilateral investment treaty between Germany and Pakistan, which was concluded in 1959,[158] included the following clause in a protocol to the treaty:

---

[156] Schill and Briese (n. 41).

[157] Pathirana and McLaughlin (n. 146); Burke-White and von Staden (n. 16).

[158] *Treaty between the Federal Republic of Germany and Pakistan for the Promotion and Protection of Investments*, signed 25 November 1959 (entered into force 28 April 1962).

> [M]easures taken for reasons of public security and order, public health or morality shall not be deemed as discrimination within the meaning of Article 2.[159]

This formulation excludes measures taken for reasons of public security and order (among other things) from the scope of the discrimination clause. Thus, such measures are exempted and cannot give rise to a breach. The standard of "non-discrimination" to which the exception refers has, however, been replaced in subsequent German treaties by the now prevailing standards of NT and MFN treatment. Thus, the standard clause in modern German investment treaties now reads as follows:

> Measures that have to be taken for reasons of public security and order, public health or morality shall not be deemed "treatment less favorable" within the meaning of Article 3 [the article containing the NT and MFN treatment standards].[160]

Here, it can be noted that the words "have to be taken" are included, which appear to introduce a necessity requirement that limits the scope for submissive deference by arbitrators.

In U.S. investment treaty practice, beginning in the early 1980s, a different type of security exception, the NPM clause, was included, which was originally formulated as follows:

> [T]his treaty shall not preclude the application by either Party of any and all measures necessary for the maintenance of public order, the fulfilment of its obligations with respect to the maintenance or restoration of international peace and security, or the protection of its own essential security interests [emphasis added].[161]

The formulation "shall not preclude" results in ambiguity as to whether the clause operates as an exemption or a defence. Note also that the formulation is not expressly self-judging because it refers to measures that are necessary for, among other things, the protection of the invoking party's essential security interests, rather than measures that the party "considers" necessary for such purpose.

Applied to investment screening, formulations such as those of the previous two clauses leave the host state with the burden of arguing and proving that investment screening is necessary. Thus, the formulation invites a fact-specific inquiry that likely runs counter to the host state's interest in keeping national security determinations away from public scrutiny.

Over the years, the United States has developed new versions of its model bilateral investment treaty. As a result, variations in the form and structure of the NPM clause have emerged over time.[162] One of the most notable changes occurred in the late 1990s when the United States clarified its position on the self-judging

---

[159] Article 2 of the *Protocol to the Treaty between the Federal Republic of Germany and Pakistan for the Promotion and Protection of Investments*, signed 25 November 1959 (entered into force 28 April 1962).

[160] See Burke-White and von Staden (n. 16), see also Yannaca-Small (2007).

[161] Gazzini (2010).

[162] Burke-White and von Staden (n. 16).

nature of the security exception.[163] Subsequent treaties thus indicate that a party is not precluded from taking measures that it "considers" necessary to protect the relevant overriding objective.[164] In the most recent 2004 U.S. model BIT, the NPM clause reads as follows:

> Nothing in this Treaty shall be construed: [. . .] to preclude a Party from applying measures that it considers necessary for the fulfilment of its obligations with respect to the maintenance or restoration of international peace or security, or the protection of its own essential security interest [emphasis added].[165]

This type of formulation easily excludes investment screening from the scope of the investment treaty's substantive obligations. However, as discussed below, the clause gives great discretion to the host state invoking it, yet it is unlikely to be interpreted as self-judging.

Many other states routinely include security exception clauses in their investment treaties.[166] A typical such clause is formulated as an exemption from a relevant standard of protection:

> Except for measures required to maintain public order, such investments shall enjoy continuous protection and security, i.e. excluding any unjustified or discriminatory measure which could hinder, either in law or in practice, the management, maintenance, use, possession or liquidation thereof.[167]

This clause is not expressly self-judging while exempting measures required (cf. necessary) for the maintenance of public order. Concerning investment screening, this formulation places the same burden on the host state as the non-self-judging clauses discussed above, only heavier since the sweeping reference to "public order" provides less basis for exempting investment screening compared to formulations that separately list "essential security interests" or similar. While many treaties mention only an overriding policy objective, such as "public order", others mention the "security of the state" as an additional objective.[168] Another common reference is "emergency":

> Notwithstanding paragraph (1) of this Article nothing in this Agreement precludes the host Contracting Party from taking action for the protection of its essential security interests or in circumstances of extreme emergency in accordance with its laws normally and reasonably applied on a non-discriminatory basis.[169]

Although this example does not include a necessity requirement, the inclusion of "circumstances of extreme emergency" as an alternative basis for preclusion tilts the balance of the entire clause further towards exceptionality for purposes of

---

[163] Ibid. 393.

[164] Schill and Briese (n. 41).

[165] Yannaca-Small (n. 160).

[166] Ibid.

[167] Article 3(2) of the 2002 Belgian-Luxembourg Economic Union (BLEU) Model BIT.

[168] Burke-White and von Staden (n. 16) 307–410, 328.

[169] UK-India BIT 1994, cited in Burke-White and von Staden (n. 16).

interpretation. Fitting investment screening into such a clause may be easy while inviting the counterargument from the claimant that a necessity requirement is implied in the clause's formulation.

Although security exceptions were infrequently included in earlier investment treaties, they are now a standard feature of IIAs, particularly in the case of investment treaty provisions included in free trade agreements.[170]

Security exceptions included in newer investment treaties are frequently more closely modelled on Article XXI(b) of the GATT and Article XIV bis(1)(b) of the GATS and exempt certain actions related to the protection of the host state's essential security interests. The structure is exemplified by Article 28.6(b) of the CETA, and similar exceptions are found in CPTPP, RCEP, and USMCA, which also allow for the protection of essential security interests[171]:

> Nothing in this Agreement shall be construed: [. . .]
>
> (b) to prevent a Party from taking an action that it considers necessary to protect its essential security interests:
> (i) connected to the production of or traffic in arms, ammunition and implements of war and to such traffic and transactions in other goods and materials, services and technology undertaken, and to economic activities, carried out directly or indirectly for the purpose of supplying a military or other security establishment;
> (ii) taken in time of war or other emergency in international relations; or
> (iii) relating to fissionable and fusionable materials or the materials from which they are derived.[172]

The exception in clause (b) above covers certain enumerated types of "actions" (i.e. not just legal acts or "measures" but potentially any type of treatment).[173] These enumerated kinds of actions are excepted subject to the chapeau of the clause, which provides that the host state considers the action in question necessary for the protection of the host state's essential security interests. This necessity thus appears on its face as subjective or "self-judging," which is a question that became subject to qualification in case law with the WTO Panel Report in *Russia-Traffic in Transit* (as discussed below in Subsection 5.3.1.3).[174] Thus, the material scope of the exception is difficult to delimit ex ante. It is, however, not unlimited in scope, as shown below, in accordance with WTO jurisprudence, in part, because the "actions" to which it applies must be of the kinds enumerated in subclauses (i),

---

[170] Pathirana and McLaughlin (n. 146) 492–496.

[171] The CPTPP contains similar general exceptions for public security (Chapter 29, Article 29.2). The USMCA includes general exception clauses that allow for measures necessary to protect essential security interests (Chapter 32, Article 32.2). The RCEP provides for general exceptions, including measures for the protection of national security.

[172] Article 28.6(b) of the CETA.

[173] On the meaning of "treatment", see Salacuse (2013) 228; Newcombe and Paradell (n. 146) 182, 203, 261.

[174] Note that some pre-Lisbon treaties have non-self-judging essential security exceptions.

(ii) and (iii),[175] and, in part, because the host state's discretion is subject to the general obligation of good faith.[176]

Three kinds of actions exist for which the security exception may be invoked. They need to be "relating to",[177] "connected with",[178] or "taken in time of"[179] certain other objectively ascertainable material or temporal facts or circumstances. Actions "relating to fissionable or fusionable materials or the materials from which they are derived" in clause (b)(iii) of Article 28.6 of the CETA pose scant interpretive difficulty. Actions "taken in time of war or other emergency in international relations" in clause (b)(ii) offer some more space for disagreement, particularly with respect to what counts as an "emergency" in this context.[180] Rather, it is the first prong of the clause that is the widest in scope. A footnote to clause (b)(i) clarifies that "[t]he expression 'traffic in arms, ammunition and

[175] This conclusion was endorsed in Panel Report, *Russia-Traffic in Transit* (2019), para. 7.101. Also, DS544: *United States-Certain Measures on Steel and Aluminium Products*; DS556: *United States-Certain Measures on Steel and Aluminium Products*; DS564: *United States-Certain Measures on Steel and Aluminium Products*. See Muchlinski (2009) 59–60.

[176] Newcombe and Paradell (n. 146) 484, 492, 494–495; Muchlinski (n. 175) 57, 74; Salacuse (n. 173) 381; Van den Bossche and Zdouc (2017) 620. By way of reaching the same conclusion, note also that actions of the enumerated kinds are not excepted without qualification under Article 28.6(2) of the CETA, in which case the necessity requirement would have been superfluous (e.g. the clause could have stated that all actions related to fissionable and fusionable materials were excepted). Nor are all actions of the enumerated kinds excepted that are objectively necessary for the purpose of protecting its essential security interests. For these reasons, the clause is not a pre-application exemption, for instance, a (preliminary) exclusion from (or delimitation of) the treaty's scope of application, the applicability of which would have been the claimant's burden of proof. See Viñuales (n. 12) section 1.2. Cf. Article XI of the Argentine-US BIT (not published in UNTS, UN reg. no. 54935), which was at issue in a number of cases arising out of Argentina's economic crisis of 2001–2002, including *CMS v Argentina*. The security exception of that treaty has an objective necessity requirement and is thus a pre-application exemption, operating as a "threshold requirement", see *CMS v Argentina*, Decision on the Application for Annulment, 25 September 2007, para. 129.

In contrast, Article 28.6(2) of the CETA only excepts such actions of the enumerated kinds that the host state determines to be necessary for the purpose of protecting its essential security interests (i.e. the necessity requirement is subjective). Absent such a determination—and invocation of the exception by the host state—full effect will be given to the application of the substantive treaty obligations. This security exception is therefore a post-application exemption (i.e. an exception stricto sensu), which precludes a finding of breach. See Viñuales (n. 12) section 1.6. This is to be distinguished from an excuse, which operates to preclude liability, Ibid. section 1.7. Muchlinski (n. 175) 67 rightly pointed out that the security exception at issue in the Argentina cases is not an exemption that operates to preclude liability. However, nor are all security exceptions exclusions (i.e. scope-of-application clauses). The self-judging ones apply only at the option of the host state and are thus to be invoked and proven (to the extent required) by that state.

[177] Cf. Article XXI(b)(i) of the GATT.

[178] Cf. Article XXI(b)(ii) of the GATT.

[179] Cf. Article XXI(b)(iii) of the GATT.

[180] It is evident from the negotiating record of the GATT that the potential for abuse in this respect was acknowledged. See United Nations Conference on Trade and Employment (1947) 19–21. Cf. Panel Report, *Russia-Traffic in Transit* (2019), section 7.5.5.

implements of war' in this Article is equivalent to the expression 'trade in arms, munitions and war materials' in Article 19.3 of the CETA".

In the context of investment screening, the screening of investments of the kind referred to in Article 4(1)(b) of the FDI Screening Regulation may be covered by Article 28.6(b)(i) of the CETA,

> critical technologies and dual use items as defined in point 1 of Article 2 of Council Regulation (EC) No 428/2009, including artificial intelligence, robotics, semiconductors, cybersecurity, aerospace, defence, energy storage, quantum and nuclear technologies as well as nanotechnologies and biotechnologies.

With respect to the other factors listed in Article 4(1) of the Screening Regulation, the screening of investments affecting critical infrastructure and the supply of critical inputs could also be covered to the extent that there is a direct or indirect purpose of supplying a military or other security establishment. In contrast, the screening of investments affecting other critical infrastructure, the supply of other critical inputs, food security in general, access to sensitive information, or the freedom and pluralism of the media would appear to fall outside the scope of the exception. However, the screening of such investments may fall within the ambit of exceptions such as in Article 24(3)(c) of the ECT, which applies to "any measure which [a Contracting Party] considers necessary [. . .] for the maintenance of public order".

It is less than clear what the scope is of "such other traffic and transactions in other goods and materials, services and technology undertaken, and to economic activities, carried out directly or indirectly for the purpose of supplying a military or other security establishment". The potential for abusive application of the clause is significantly greater with respect to the broad category of actions covered by this wording. In particular, the "indirect" purpose of supply may cause interpretive difficulties, especially in the context of investment screening. It is arguable that "dual use" goods and services (i.e. goods and services with military and civilian applications) fall within this formulation. If so, and if other requirements are fulfilled, the implication would be the applicability of the security exception to investment screening involving dual-use goods or services.

In summary, the interpretation and application of NPM clauses vary with the widely divergent formulations encountered in treaty practice. While WTO-style clauses benefit from the persuasive precedents of WTO case law, the same is not true for other types of clauses. However, where these latter clauses are narrower in scope because they apply to specific standards of protection, there is not the same risk of abuse (i.e. breach of good faith) as with more broadly phrased exceptions. With respect to WTO-style clauses (and non-WTO-style clauses of similar breadth), the scope of application to investment screening is relatively limited. The "normal" case of investment screening (i.e. that would apply in the normal course of business and not in the case of heightened tension in international relations) would not readily fit into the application of WTO-style clauses, except where military or dual-use investments are concerned. Even then, the application and interpretation of the clause are not self-judging as to requirements that correspond to the enumerated subparagraphs in Article XXI(b) of the GATT.

5.3.1.2 Security Exceptions in Arbitral Case law

As discussed in Subchapter 5.2, early arbitral case law struggled with keeping the interpretation and application of NPM clauses separate from the necessity defence under customary international law. A breakthrough came when a new interpretive approach to the "no alternatives" requirement of the necessity defence was introduced by the tribunal in *Continental Casualty v Argentina,* which bridged the divide between the necessity defence and treaty NPM clauses while, interestingly, linking these to notions of "necessity" under WTO law.

Partially following the *LG&E* tribunal's approach, the *Continental* tribunal arrived at different findings and reached different conclusions. First, as referenced in Section 5.2.1, the tribunal acknowledged that a severe economic crisis could impact the "essential security interests" of a host state. However, initially, the United States likely intended this clause within the NPM clause to address international security and military concerns.[181]

Second, the *Continental* tribunal addressed the conflation of customary and treaty laws in earlier Argentine cases by emphasizing the distinct conceptual frameworks between the scope of the NPM clause and the defence of necessity under customary international law.[182] This approach aligned with the *CMS* annulment committee's perspective. Specifically, the NPM clause in Article XI of the US-Argentina investment treaty serves as an exception, rendering the protections and remedies of investment treaties inapplicable only when their conditions are met.[183] In contrast, the defence under Article 25 of the ARSIWA aims to preclude the wrongfulness of actions once a breach of substantive obligations is established.[184]

Third, drawing on these distinctions, the *Continental* tribunal clarified that the strict conditions typically associated with necessity as a defence against liability for breaches of international obligations do not govern the NPM clause.[185] The origins, language, and contextual background of this clause, inspired by the American Friendship, Commerce, and Navigation treaties and reflected in Article XXI of the GATT, suggest that interpretation standards should align with those used by the WTO.[186] This tribunal noted the comprehensive treatment of the necessity concept within WTO jurisprudence, particularly relating to Article

XX of the GATT and its application to domestic economic measures that diverge from GATT obligations.[187]

[181] *Continental Casualty Company v Argentine Republic*, ICSID Case No ARB/03/09, Award (5 September 2008), para. 151. See Sacerdoti (n. 99).

[182] Ibid. *Continental Casualty* paras. 160–168. See Sacerdoti Ibid.

[183] Ibid. *Continental Casualty.*

[184] Ibid. *Continental Casualty. See* Sacerdoti (n. 99).

[185] *Continental Casualty* para. 192. See Sacerdoti Ibid.

[186] *Continental Casualty* para. 193. See Sacerdoti Ibid.

[187] Ibid.

Building on this groundwork, the Continental tribunal introduced a refined approach to evaluating "necessity" within the scope of the NPM clause, influenced significantly by WTO case law. According to this tribunal, WTO interpretations of Article XX of the GATT suggest that a "necessary" measure exists closer on the continuum to "indispensable" rather than merely making a "contribution".[188] Importantly, the term "necessary" extends beyond the confines of "indispensable", "absolutely necessary", and "unavoidable".[189]

To assess whether a non-indispensable measure is still considered "necessary", the Continental tribunal adopted and adapted a method from WTO rulings on Article XX of the GATT, involving a "process of weighing and balancing factors".[190] This assessment typically considers three critical elements: (1) the relative significance of the interests or values that the challenged measures support, (2) the effectiveness of the measure in achieving its intended goals, and (3) the measure's impact on international trade.[191] The tribunal noted,

> The reach of the word "necessary" is not limited to that which is "indispensable" or "of absolute necessity" or "inevitable". [. . .] A "necessary" measure is, in the continuum, located significantly closer to the pole of "indispensable" than to the opposite pole of simply "making a contribution". [. . .] In order to determine whether a measure which is not indispensable may nevertheless be "necessary", the Tribunal relied again on the WTO case law: "The necessity of a measure should be determined through 'a process of weighing and balancing of factors' which usually includes the assessment of the following three factors: the relative importance of interests or values furthered by the challenged measures, the contribution of the measure to the realization of the ends pursued by it and the restrictive impact of the measure on international commerce".[192]

The tribunal reasoned that "[w]ithin the WTO a measure is not necessary if another treaty consistent, or less inconsistent alternative measure, which the Member State concerned could reasonably be expected to employ is available".[193] Citing *US-Gambling*, the tribunal concluded that an alternative measure may be found not to be "reasonably available." An alternative may be not reasonably available where it is merely theoretical in nature, for instance, where the host state is not capable of taking it or where the measure imposes an undue burden on that state, such as prohibitive costs or substantial technical difficulties.[194]

The tribunal proceeded to assess whether the measures at issue were materially conducive to achieving their legitimate objectives under Article XI of the BIT,

---

[188] Ibid.

[189] Ibid.

[190] *Continental Casualty* para. 194. See Sacerdoti Ibid.

[191] Ibid.

[192] *Continental Casualty Company v Argentine Republic*, ICSID Case No ARB/03/09, Award (5 September 2008), para. 193–194.

[193] Ibid. para. 195.

[194] Ibid. para. 195. See also Sacerdoti (n. 99) 1–33, 29. It should be noted that under WTO law, there are two more conditions/requirements for the alternative to be acceptable: less trade restrictive and at least equally effective.

namely, the protection of the essential security interests of the Argentine Republic in the economic and social crisis it faced.[195] The tribunal conducted a detailed examination of the origins, characteristics, and effects of the crisis in the Argentine Republic. It concluded that the crisis met the requirements of Article XI and that the measures challenged by the claimant were necessary to meet them.[196]

The tribunal also considered whether the Argentine Republic had reasonably available alternatives that were less conflicting or more consistent with its international obligations while making an equivalent contribution to the achievement of the objective pursued by the measures challenged by the claimant, which were found to be inconsistent with the BITs.[197] The arbitral tribunal concluded that the alternatives to the contested measures (notably de-dollarization) proffered by the claimant[198] would not have been feasible to protect the investor's assets from the alleged loss.[199]

The analysis pioneered by the *Continental* tribunal managed to introduce a more nuanced assessment of the "necessity" of a contested measure as the only reasonably available means of protecting the essential interest in question. However, although the analysis somewhat approached the necessity analysis elaborated in Appellate Body case law under the general exception in Article XX of the GATT, it did not achieve alignment with such case law. In fact, such alignment would already be difficult since the necessity under the latter article is specific to its context and the provisional justifications enumerated therein. It is not readily transferable in unmodified form to an analysis of necessity under NPM clauses in investment treaties. Nevertheless, the *Continental* tribunal embarked on an evolutionary route towards closer alignment with WTO law, which could be expected to continue.

[195] *Continental Casualty Company v Argentine Republic*, ICSID Case No ARB/03/09, Award (5 September 2008), para. 197.

[196] Ibid. See Sacerdoti (n. 99).

[197] Ibid.

[198] Ibid. *Continental Casualty* paras. 223–234. "In the Claimant's submission, Argentina could have avoided the devaluation and the pesification if it had adopted a different economic policy, specifically if it had implemented in a timely manner those accompanying policies and measures (especially relating to budgetary and fiscal discipline) required for the sustainability of the parity arrangement, convertibility and the currency board" (para. 223). See further Sacerdoti (n. 99).

[199] Ibid. Continental Casualty para. 231: "Even if practicable, these 'alternatives' cannot however be invoked fruitfully by the Claimant as measures that would have respected its dollar-denominated investments in Argentina whilst being sufficient to avoid the crisis. If Argentina had abandoned the parity and convertibility at 1:1 before 2000, Continental could not have made those U.S. dollars denominated investments exchanging at par CNA's income made in peso that it complains have been affected by Argentina devaluation/pesification. If the convertibility board system had been abandoned later, the probability is, as indicated above, that the Claimant would have been subject to the same losses that it challenges here. Therefore, the alternative would not have put it in any better situation." See further Sacerdoti (n. 99).

Applying the *Continental* case law to investment screening would mean that a screening host state would have to demonstrate that its investment screening was "necessary" for the protection of its essential security interests as the outcome of a three-pronged weighing and balancing of (1) the national security interests at issue with respect to the investment being screened (e.g. whether the investment involved a security threat to certain critical infrastructure, critical technology or input of critical supplies), (2) the contribution of the screening to the achievement of the objective it pursues (i.e. the extent to which the screening addresses the security threat posed by the investment), and (3) the restrictive effect of the investment screening on international investment.

In the absence of other guidance, such a weighing and balancing approach to necessity in the context of investment treaty security exceptions adds to legal certainty and ensures that the discretion of the host state is not unrestricted while limiting the scope for submissive deference of the tribunal to the determinations of the host state. However, as discussed next, the interpretation of Article XXI of the GATT that recently emerged in the WTO case law takes a rather different approach, which would likely take precedence in new arbitral cases relating to NPM clauses and other security exceptions in investment treaties.

5.3.1.3 Self-Judging Character of Security Exceptions

While the *Continental* tribunal took inspiration from WTO case law on Article XX of the GATT, there was at the time no further inspiration to be taken with respect to the WTO law interpretation of Article XXI, which article, as the tribunal noted, had served as a model for the NPM clause of the US-Argentina investment treaty.[200] Today, WTO case law is even more relevant for the purposes of investment arbitration in interpreting investment treaty security exceptions modelled on Article XXI of the GATT. However, rather than resorting to Article XX case law, it is likely that an investment tribunal would seek to apply the jurisprudence emerging around Article XXI itself.

In *Russia–Traffic in Transit* (2019), the panel held that the discretion of a WTO Member to take "any action which it considers necessary for the protection of its essential security interests" pursuant to the chapeau of Article XXI(b) of the GATT—which is nearly identical to Article 28.6(b) of the CETA—extends to the determination of the invoking Member's essential security interests and the necessity of the actions of the enumerated kinds taken for the protection of those interests.[201] The panel observed that "essential security interests" is a narrower concept than "security interests" and generally refers to "those interests relating to the quintessential functions of the State, namely, the protection of its territory and its population from external threats, and the maintenance of law and public

[200] Ibid. para. 192.

[201] Panel Report, *Russia-Traffic in Transit* (2019), paras. 7.131, 7.146 and 7.147.

order internally".[202] What constitutes essential security interests in a specific case depends on the particular situation and perceptions of the state in question and can be expected to vary with changing circumstances.[203]

The *Russia–Traffic in Transit* panel further observed that the obligation to act in good faith requires WTO Members not to invoke the security exception as a means to circumvent their GATT commitments.[204] States are under a duty to observe good faith in the application and interpretation of their international obligations.[205] Article 26 of the VCLT enshrines the customary principle of pacta sunt servanda—that "[e] very treaty in force is binding upon the parties to it and must be performed in good faith". As the ICJ explained in the Gabčíkovo-Nagymaros case, "[T]he principle of good faith obliges the [parties to a treaty] to apply it in a reasonable way and in such a manner that its purpose can be realised".[206] Interpreting the security exception in good faith thus implies that although the necessity requirement is self-judging and the discretion of the host state invoking the exception is very extensive, that discretion must nevertheless be exercised reasonably and not in a manner that defeats the purpose of the exception.[207]

From the obligation of good faith, the panel in *Russia–Traffic in Transit* distinguished between what a WTO Member considers an essential security interest and what measure is necessary to protect this interest. From this bifurcation, the panel derived (A) a duty of transparency—a duty to "articulate the essential security interests said to arise from the [alleged situation in the relevant enumerated subclause (i), (ii) or (iii) of the clause] sufficiently to demonstrate their veracity"[208]—and (B) a requirement that the actions at issue are "not implausible as measures protective of these interests".[209] This conclusion finds additional support in the recent ruling of the ICJ in *Certain Iranian Assets*,[210] which, as discussed in Chap. 3, reaffirmed that the standard of proof applicable to the essential security exception of the US-Iran Treaty of Amity required more than a mere assertion that a contested measure is necessary to protect essential security interests.[211]

For the level of transparency needed, the *Russia–Traffic in Transit* panel held that the essential security interests would have to be articulated with greater specificity the further the situation at issue is removed from external or internal threats and the less obvious the "defence and military interests, or maintenance of

---

[202] Ibid. para. 7.130.

[203] Ibid. para. 7.131.

[204] Ibid. para. 7.133.

[205] Art. 26 and 31.1 VCLT. See Panel Report, *Russia-Traffic in Transit* (2019).

[206] *Gabčikovo-Nagymaros Project* [1997] ICJ Rep 7, para. 142.

[207] Ziegler and Baumgartner (2015) 18–19; De Brabandere and van Damme (2015) 52–55.

[208] Ibid. para. 7.134.

[209] Ibid. para. 7.138.

[210] *Certain Iranian Assets (Islamic Republic of Iran v United States of America)*, Judgment of 30 March 2023.

[211] Ibid.

law and public order interests, that can generally be expected to arise".[212] The right of a party not to disclose information contrary to its essential security interests pursuant to Article XXI(a) of the GATT (cf. Article 28.6(1) of the CETA) could not be invoked to evade this duty of transparency.[213] For the implausibility requirement, the panel considered whether the measures at issue were so remote from, or unrelated to, the essential security interests in question that it was implausible that the measures protected these interests.[214]

The analysis of *Russia–Traffic in Transit* was confirmed later in the case law. The panel in *US–Origin Marking Requirements (2022)* reached a similar conclusion, which rejected the contentions of the United States that Article XXI(b) should be considered self-judging in its entirety. By concluding that the subparagraphs of that article were reviewable, the panel proceeded to analyse the invocation of subparagraph (iii) and its claim that the contested measure in question (origin markings indicating products from Hong Kong, China) was "taken in time of war or other emergency in international relations". The panel held that an "emergency in international relations" refers to a deterioration in relations between states or other participants in international relations, which amounts to a breakdown or near-breakdown of relations, irrespective of what caused that deterioration. The panel concluded that the situation in Hong Kong, China, had not escalated to the extent that it constituted an emergency in international relations.

In three cases emanating from the "Trump tariffs" on aluminium and steel,[215] the panels further endorsed the *Russia–Traffic in Transit* case law. Having found that the U.S. duties on steel and aluminium were inconsistent with Article II:1 of the GATT, as they exceeded the bound tariff rates in the United States' WTO Schedule of Concessions, the panels examined the United States' claim that the duties were "taken in time of war or other emergency in international relations" under Article XXI(b)(iii). The panels considered that an "emergency in international relations" under Article XXI(b)(iii) refers to situations of a certain gravity or severity and international tensions that are critical in nature in terms of their impact on the conduct of international relations. Having considered the evidence and arguments submitted in the dispute, the panels did not find that the measures at issue were "taken in time of war or other emergency in international relations" within the meaning of Article XXI(b)(iii) of the GATT. Therefore, the panels found that the inconsistencies of the duties with the GATT were unjustified under Article XXI(b)(iii).

If this interpretation of Article XXI(b) of the GATT were transferred to Article 28.6(b)(i) of the CETA (or similarly phrased BIT clauses) to except the screening

---

[212] Ibid. para. 7.135.

[213] Ibid. para. 7.129 in light of para. 7.134.

[214] Ibid. para. 7.139.

[215] DS544: *United States-Certain Measures on Steel and Aluminium Products*; DS556: *United States-Certain Measures on Steel and Aluminium Products*; DS564: *United States-Certain Measures on Steel and Aluminium Products.*

of an investment (e.g. relating to a critical technology), the duty of transparency would mean that the host state conducting the screening would have to articulate what essential security interest it considered to be threatened by the contemplated investment in the relevant technology. The scope of applying the security exception would be very limited in peacetime unless the screening applied to nuclear technology, infrastructure or inputs (cf. Article XXI(b)(iii)) or

> the production of or traffic in arms, ammunition and implements of war and to such traffic and transactions in other goods and materials, services and technology undertaken, and to economic activities, carried out directly or indirectly for the purpose of supplying a military or other security establishment. (cf. Article XXI(b)(ii))

Hence, for non-military security threats (cf. the type of security interests at issue in the Argentina cases), the security exception would not be readily available.

It remains to be seen how the *Russia–Traffic in Transit* case law may influence the interpretation of the kind of NPM clauses based on the 2004 U.S. model BIT, which does not contain enumerated kinds of essential security interests. The basic structure of the *Russia–Traffic in Transit* test may, in principle, still apply: a duty of transparency to articulate the essential security interest at stake in the investment screening (albeit not limited to enumerated situations) and a requirement to demonstrate that the investment screening measure (e.g. a prohibition or conditional approval) is "not implausible" as a measure "protective of these interests". The exception would then be available unless the screening measure were so remote from, or unrelated to, these articulated interests that it would be implausible that the screening was protecting the interests. However, it is also clear that the subclauses of the security exception would be justiciable and that, consequently, an investment tribunal would apply the facts of the case to ascertain whether the requirements of the exception were met. Thus, for practical purposes, the clause would not be self-judging in the corresponding respect.

5.3.2 General Exception Clauses in Investment Treaties

Newer investment treaties often include general exception clauses inspired to a greater or lesser extent by Article XX of the GATT and Article XIV of the GATS. Under WTO law, while the provisional justifications of Article XX of the GATT and Article XIV of the GATS are geared towards the character of the measure at issue, the "chapeau" of these articles addresses the manner in which the measure is applied.[216]

Mirroring these articles in the GATT and the GATS, the structure of general exception clauses in investment treaties is often that treatment that is inconsistent with the host state's treaty obligations may nevertheless be provisionally justified on the basis of enumerated policy objectives but that the exception is only effective

---

[216] Van den Bossche and Zdouc (n. 176) 646–656.

if the provisionally justified treatment is consistent with the chapeau of the clause, pursuant to WTO jurisprudence. Article 28.3(2) of the CETA is illustrative:

> For the purposes of [...] Sections B (Establishment of investments) and C (Non-discriminatory treatment) of Chapter Eight (Investment), subject to the requirement that such measures are not applied in a manner which would constitute a means of arbitrary or unjustifiable discrimination between the Parties where like conditions prevail, or a disguised restriction on trade in services, nothing in this Agreement shall be construed to prevent the adoption or enforcement by a Party of measures necessary:
>
> (a) to protect public security or public morals or to maintain public order;
> (b) to protect human, animal or plant life or health; or
> (c) to secure compliance with laws or regulations which are not inconsistent with the provisions of this Agreement including those relating to:
>
> (i) the prevention of deceptive and fraudulent practices or to deal with the effects of a default on contracts;
> (ii) the protection of the privacy of individuals in relation to the processing and dissemination of personal data and the protection of confidentiality of individual records and accounts; or
> (iii) safety.[217]

Given the policy objective of investment screening, the excepted situation in clause (a) of the provision above appears relevant.[218] A footnote to the clause provides that "[t]he public security and public order exceptions may be invoked only where a genuine and sufficiently serious threat is posed to one of the fundamental interests of society".[219] By way of comparative analysis, this requirement reflects the interpretation in case law of Article 65(1)(b) TFEU, which excepts from the free movement of capital Member State measures justified on grounds of "public policy or public security".[220] In EU case law, this requirement means that a measure so justified must not serve purely economic ends[221] and must be designed to give effect to such justification.[222]

---

[217] Article 28.3(2) of the CETA.

[218] Given the policy objective of investment screening, the excepted situation in clause (a) of the provision above appears relevant. Comparative analysis with CPTPP, RCEP, and USMCA reveals that these treaties also incorporate similar exceptions to address public security and public order. The CPTPP contains exceptions for public security in Chapter 29, Article 29.2, which provides general exceptions that allow for measures necessary to protect public security and essential security interests. The USMCA includes general exception clauses in Chapter 32, Article 32.2, which allow parties to adopt measures necessary to protect essential security interests. The RCEP provides for general exceptions, including measures for the protection of national security. While specifics may vary, the RCEP generally supports the ability of states to protect public security and order.

[219] Footnote to Article 28.3(2) of the CETA.

[220] See Hindelang (2009).

[221] See ECJ judgment of 7 June 2012, *VBV-Vorsorgekasse*, Case C-39/11, EU:C:2012:327, para. 29 and the case law cited.

[222] Ibid., para. 30 and the case law cited.

In view of Article 4(1)(d) of the FDI Screening Regulation, the excepted situation described in clause (c)(ii) of Article 28.3(2) of the CETA (and similar provisions in other treaties), related to data protection enforcement measures, may also be relevant, as well as—generally in view of Article 4(1) of the Regulation—the situation described in clause (c)(iii) of that article, related to safety enforcement measures. These clauses relate to measures necessary to secure compliance with laws or regulations which are not inconsistent with the provisions of the CETA, including those relating to data protection (clause (c)(iii)) and safety (clause (c)(iii)). Therefore, an initial step in assessing the applicability of these exception clauses to the screening of a specific investment is to determine whether the investment screening measure at issue falls within the range of policy objectives permitted by the excepted situation described in these clauses.

Importantly, in the next step, the measures at issue must be necessary for the achievement of the relevant policy objective, which generally implies that they must contribute to a sufficient degree to achieving that objective. In determining whether the necessity requirement is met, interpretive guidance is provided by a rich body of WTO case law,[223] which indicates a "weighing and balancing" relative to "reasonably available" alternative measures of (a) the degree to which the measure contributes to achieving the policy objective in question, (b) the relative importance of the values or interests that the measure aims to safeguard, and (c) the degree to which the measure restricts international commerce.[224] As stated by the Appellate Body in *US-Gambling* (2005):

> The requirement, under Article XIV(a), that a measure be "necessary"—that is, that there be no "reasonably available", WTO-consistent alternative—reflects the shared understanding of Members that substantive GATS obligations should not be deviated from lightly. An alternative measure may be found not to be "reasonably available", however, where it is merely theoretical in nature, for instance, where the responding Member is not capable of taking it, or where the measure imposes an undue burden on that Member, such as prohibitive costs or substantial technical difficulties. Moreover, a "reasonably available" alternative measure must be a measure that would preserve for the responding Member its right to achieve its desired level of protection with respect to the objective pursued under paragraph (a) of Article XIV.[225]

In the context of investment screening, it is sufficient to observe that WTO jurisprudence would be persuasive in interpreting investment treaty general exception clauses modelled on Article XIV(a) of the GATS. However, given that the provisional justifications in such clauses may deviate significantly from those of Article XIV(a) of the GATS, such as those in Article 28.3(2) of the CETA

---

[223] For a comprehensive analysis of GATT-style general exception clauses in investment treaties, see Mitchell et al. (2016).

[224] See Mitchell et al. (n. 223) 225–231; Newcombe and Paradell (n. 146) 503–506; Van den Bossche and Zdouc (n. 176) 609–611. The "weighing and balancing" is not necessarily limited to these three factors, see Van den Bossche and Zdouc Ibid. 614, citing Appellate Body Report, *United States-Gambling* (2005) paras. 306–307.

[225] Appellate Body Report, *United States-Gambling* (2005) para. 308.

discussed above, caution is warranted against relying too uncritically on GATS (or GATT) case law. That said, some insights surely remain relevant. For example, with respect to provisional justifications invoking "public order", the case law of *US-Gambling* would appear relevant insofar as the "public order" exception "may be invoked only where a genuine and sufficiently serious threat is posed to one of the fundamental interests of society" and that "public order" thus refers to "the preservation of the fundamental interests of society, as reflected in public policy and law" relating, inter alia, to "standards of law, security and morality".[226]

Moreover, the necessity test of Article XIV(a) of the GATS remains instructive in giving meaning to similarly phrased general exception clauses in investment treaties, subject to certain caveats. Here, again, *US-Gambling* case law provides guidance as a starting point. Whether a contested investment screening measure would be deemed "necessary" to maintain "public order" would begin with "an assessment of the 'relative importance' of the interests or values furthered by the challenged measure". In the context of an investment treaty, an arbitral tribunal applying WTO jurisprudence analogously would then "weigh and balance" the relative importance of those interests or values against other factors, including the "contribution of the measure to the realisation of the ends pursued by it" and "the restrictive impact of the measure" on the flow of investments between the contracting parties to the investment treaty. Moreover, a tribunal may next compare the contested measure with any equally effective, less trade-restrictive and reasonably available alternatives and consider the results of such comparisons in light of the importance of the interests at issue. The "possible alternatives" that come readily to mind in the context of investment screening are so-called "mitigation measures" (i.e. the proposed restructuring of an investment transaction to mitigate possible threats to national security or public order). Specifically, a mitigation measure may consist of the appointment of host state delegates on the board of directors of an acquired enterprise, the divestment of certain sensitive business operations, or government inspections.[227]

However, transferring the WTO necessity analysis of Article XIV(a) of the GATS to investment screening also requires reflecting upon certain key differences between what the general exception clauses in investment treaties are meant to accomplish compared to the GATS or the GATT. Mitchell et al. argued that Appellate Body jurisprudence has been interpreted to imply that the determination of "necessity" is the entry point for multifaceted scrutiny of the measure at issue, involving both a relative assessment of international and domestic policy interests (trade-restrictiveness versus the importance of the policy objective of the domestic measure at issue, cf. (b) and (c) above) and a relative assessment of the measure's policy effectiveness (contribution to the objective, cf. (a) above).[228] Mitchell et al. further argued that the necessity test is principally characterized by substantial

[226] Panel Report, *United States-Gambling* (2005) para. 6.467.

[227] See Chap. 2.

[228] Mitchell et al. (n. 223) 329–330.

deference to the level of protection chosen by a host state to achieve the policy objective in question.[229]

With respect to investment screening, unlike the context of the GATT and the GATS, investment treaties are normally not international commitments to liberalize the entry of investments.[230] As discussed in Chap. 3, states normally do not commit to investors' pre-entry rights.[231] Therefore, there is no straightforward equivalent to the "trade restrictiveness" analysis inherent in the *US-Gambling (2005)* case law. However, using the analytical prism of Mitchell et al., one may consider adding to the balancing of other international policy interests typically included in investment treaties, such as non-discrimination and FET. Following that logic, the balancing of international versus domestic policy interests would entail balancing the restrictiveness of the investment screening towards the host state's investment treaty commitments against the "relative importance of" the host state's essential security interests inherent in investment screening.

Thus, the policy interests of security and public order, interpreted in light of the list of factors in Article 4(1) of the FDI Screening Regulation, would have to be scrutinized concerning their relative importance. Given the diverse nature of these policy interests, one could expect them to be assigned different levels of importance. For instance, military security interests may be considered more important than the supply security of certain raw materials, or food security and critical financial infrastructure may not be deemed at the same level of importance. Moreover, the restrictive impact of the screening measure on investment treaty commitments would possibly be limited, in which case the necessity test would focus more on the contribution of the screening measure at issue to the policy objectives and the "reasonable availability" of alternative measures. For example, a screening decision consisting of the imposition of a condition (cf. Article 2(3) of the Screening Regulation) may be a "reasonably available" alternative to prohibiting the investment (ibid.). It may contribute to an equivalent (or even greater) degree to the realization of the policy interests at stake.

Turning to the "chapeau" of GATT/GATS-style general exception clauses, exceptions must be applied in good faith and not discriminate in their application arbitrarily or unjustifiably between "the Parties where like conditions prevail".[232] The GATT/GATS chapeau serves to prevent abuse or misuse by providing that provisionally justified measures may not be used as arbitrary or unjustifiable discrimination or disguised restrictions on trade.[233] The GATT/GATS case law

[229] Ibid.

[230] See Chap. 3.

[231] Ibid.

[232] Appellate Body Report, *Brazil-Retreaded Tyres* (2007) paras. 215 and 224. See Van den Bossche and Zdouc (n. 176) 594–595; Newcombe and Paradell (n. 146) 504–505.

[233] See generally Mitchell et al. (n. 223) 331, 347–348; Van den Bossche and Zdouc Ibid. 594–595; Newcombe and Paradell Ibid. 502–503. Note that, in addition to general exceptions modelled on Article XIV bis of the GATS relating to trade in services, Article 28.3(1) of the CETA, Article 2.22 of the EU-Japan EPA and Article 2.15 of the EU-Korea FTA incorporate Article XX of the GATT, addressing trade in goods, as applicable also to the investment chapters of each treaty.

can again provide a useful persuasive precedent for interpreting general exception clauses in investment treaties.

Specifically, if an investment screening measure has been deemed to satisfy the requirements of a provisional justification, such as public security or public order as per Article 28.3(2)(a) of the CETA, the chapeau of that article would, pursuant to GATS/GATT case law, require an assessment of whether the application of the measure constitutes neither arbitrary or unjustifiable discrimination between countries where like conditions prevail nor a disguised restriction on (in this case) international investments.[234] In this assessment, the absence of consistency in the application of the measure may lead to the conclusion that the measure is applied in a manner that amounts to arbitrary and unjustifiable discrimination or a disguised investment restriction.

With respect to investment screening, the manner in which the host state's investment screening authority consistently applies its discretionary screening powers could be called into question. The more consistently the host state conducts investment screening, the less likely it is that a provisional justification would be considered "capricious" or "random" and thus not satisfy the chapeau.[235] According to the Appellate Body case law, "arbitrary or unjustifiable discrimination" is one where the cause or rationale for the discrimination arising in the application of a provisionally justified measure "bear[s] no rational connection to the objective falling within the purview of a paragraph of Article XX, or would go against that objective".[236]

Variations in screening frequency and intensity between, for example, investments originating in states that are allies versus geopolitical rivals could invite challenges on the basis of inconsistent application. Thus, an investment screening authority could theoretically apply the regime rigidly without proper reflection on differences in conditions and without genuine engagement. However, this scenario seems rather far-fetched in practice but is not inconceivable (e.g. if investments originating in the People's Republic of China were rigidly screened by the United States and prohibited without proper analysis of the security issues involved). However, if the host state could demonstrate that the application of the screening regime follows a foreseeable procedure, even though there may be elements of discretion in its application, the likelihood that the screening would be deemed rigid, capricious, or random would be limited. The remaining problem is that there are limits to how transparent and foreseeable an investment screening procedure can be made, given the security interests involved and the need to maintain secrecy and rely on secret intelligence in conducting the screening. This inherent challenge exists in passing the chapeau stage when invoking the general exception in the context of investment screening.

---

[234] Appellate Body Report, *United States-Shrimp* (1998) para. 166.

[235] Panel Report, *Brazil-Retreaded Tyres* (2007) paras. 7.281, 7.294; Appellate Body Report, *Brazil-Retreaded Tyres* (2007) para. 225.

[236] AB Report, *Brazil-Retreaded Tyres* (2007) para. 227.

5.3.3 Summary

Treaty exception clauses are an obvious avenue for removing investment screening measures from the effects of investment treaty standards of protection. As shown in this subchapter, reality is not so simple. First, only a minority of treaties include exception clauses of any kind. Second, with respect to security exceptions, the design of the clauses varies greatly across treaties, which makes any application quite case-specific. Third, security exceptions are not self-judging in their entirety, even if arbitrators may defer extensively to the host state's national security determinations. Fourth, the necessity analysis that must be undertaken in the application of many security exceptions is far from straightforward and not subject to any established arbitral case law. Fifth, with respect to some security exceptions, the effective scope is objectively limited to military security matters, emergency situations, and nuclear matters. Sixth, with respect to general exceptions, many significant problems exist in transferring the case law of Article XX of the GATT or Article XIV of the GATS to except investment screening measures from the application of investment treaty standards of protection.

Another possible complication stems from the relationship between security and general exceptions. While it is possible to invoke both types of exceptions simultaneously under existing legal frameworks since no explicit prohibition exists, they nevertheless inherently target different situational criteria and policy goals. Security exceptions, particularly those employed in the context of investment screening, are designed to address explicit threats to national security, which are usually well-defined and often pertain to military and emergency scenarios. On the other hand, general exceptions are broader and cater to a range of public interest considerations like health, environment, and public morals, which do not necessarily align with the stringent requirements of a security threat. Therefore, the strategic invocation of these exceptions in investment arbitration must be approached with caution to maintain consistency and legitimacy in argumentation. This issue is especially pertinent since mixing these exceptions could potentially dilute the force of the security-based rationale and lead to a scenario where if a measure did not unequivocally fit within a security exception, it would be considered under a general exception. This approach, however, would necessitate a clear delineation of policy objectives to avoid overlapping applications that could undermine the arguments made under each category. Reflecting on these distinctions is crucial, particularly given the absence of specific case law addressing the simultaneous application of these exceptions. Thus, the logical structuring of arguments is an essential element in their invocation.

That said, WTO case law—whether in the context of the security exception in Article XXI of the GATT/Article XIV bis of the GATS or the general exception in Article XX of the GATT/Article XIV of the GATS—provides a rich source of persuasive guidance for how security and general exceptions in investment treaties may be interpreted and applied. The two-tiered structure of GATT/GATS-style general exception clauses allows for an analysis of a measure as such. Moreover, its application is theoretically well suited to the context of investment screening as a means of effecting deference to host state authority. In principle, general exception clauses also obviate the need to substantiate a security threat by providing classified information, which allows the host state to rely instead on policy arguments, such as the importance of interests and values, contribution, and restrictive impact. However, the inherently discretionary nature of investment screening, coupled with the equally inherent non-transparency of investment screening procedures, makes general exceptions a difficult avenue in practice.

5.4 Conclusion

Several key insights emerge in concluding this chapter on the intricate relationship between investment screening, the necessity defence, and treaty exceptions in the context of national security.

First, the application of the necessity defence to investment screening, particularly under the ambit of national security, presents a significant challenge. The stringent requirements of establishing a "grave and imminent peril", as demonstrated in the Argentine debt crisis cases, impose a high threshold. This challenge is further compounded by the host state's understandable reluctance to disclose sensitive national security information, which is essential to justify the essential security interests at stake and the gravity and imminence of the peril associated with the investment in question.

Second, the overview of treaty exception clauses reveals that while WTO case law offers useful guidance, the diversity in the design of these clauses and the discretionary nature of investment screening measures create difficulties in their practical application. The non-transparent procedures inherent in investment screening add another layer of complexity, specifically to the use of general exceptions in this context.

Third, the chapter highlights the important role of the host state's contribution to the situation that necessitates the invocation of the necessity defence. The wide-ranging application of investment screening measures, which extend beyond traditional military security concerns, suggests that the host state's regulatory and risk management decisions can significantly influence the security risks cited as a justification for these measures.

Fourth, the chapter underscores that the term "essential interest" in the context of international jurisprudence is a self-judging categorization yet bounded by the duty of good faith and the prohibition against abuse of rights. This understanding is pivotal in considering treaty exceptions related to national security, which are not entirely self-judging and remain subject to the general obligation of good faith in public international law.

Fifth, in terms of arbitral tribunals' roles, the need for transparency is emphasized. For a host state to successfully invoke a security exception, it must clearly articulate the security interest at issue and demonstrate the plausibility of the investment screening measure as a protective mechanism. The extent of this implied transparency obligation and its development in arbitral practice is an area ripe for further exploration.

In summary, while international law theoretically equips arbitral tribunals with tools for substantial deference to state authority in national security matters, the practical application of the necessity defence and treaty exceptions is fraught with challenges. These mechanisms, as analysed, leave considerable room for dispute outcomes to be determined on their individual merits. This concluding analysis underscores the inherent tension between state sovereignty in national security and the principles of international investment law while highlighting the intricate balancing act that states and tribunals must navigate in this evolving legal landscape.

References

Agius M (2009) The invocation of necessity in international law. Neth Int Law Rev 56(2):95–135

Akande D, Williams S (2003) International adjudication on national security issues: what role for the WTO? Va J Int Law 43:365–404

Alschner W, Hui K (2019) Missing in action: general public policy exceptions in investment treaties. In: Sachs LE, Johnson L, Coleman J (eds) Yearbook on international investment law & policy. Oxford University Press, pp 363–393

Baylis J, Wirtz JJ, Johnson JL (eds) (2022) Strategy in the contemporary world. Oxford University Press

Binder C (2012) Stability and change in times of fragmentation: the limits of Pacta Sunt Servanda revisited. Leiden J Int Law 25(4):909–934

Bjorklund AK (2008). Emergency exceptions. In: Muchlinski P, Ortino F, Schreuer C (eds) The Oxford handbook of international investment law. Oxford University Press, pp 459–523

Blanco SM, Pehl A (2020) National security exceptions in international trade and investment agreements: justiciability and standards of review. Springer

Briese R, Schill SW (2009) Djibouti v France: self-judging clauses before the International Court of Justice. Melb J Int Law 10(1):308–328

Burke-White WW, von Staden A (2008) Investment protection in extraordinary times: the interpretation and application of non-precluded measures provisions in bilateral investment treaties. Va J Int Law 48:307–410

Buzan B, Wæver O, de Wilde J (1998) Security: a new framework for analysis. Lynne Rienner Publishers

Crawford J (2002) The International Law Commission's articles on state responsibility: introduction, text and commentaries. Cambridge University Press

De Brabandere E, van Damme I (2015). Good faith in treaty interpretation. In: Mitchell AD, Sornarajah M, Voon T (eds) Good faith and international economic law. Oxford University Press

Di Benedetto S (2023) The national security clauses in international economic agreements: a loophole for states to escape their obligations? In: Mauro MR, Pernazza F (eds) State and enterprise: legal issues in the global market. Springer, pp 53–72

Foster C (2008) Necessity and precaution in international law: responding to oblique forms of urgency. NZ Univ Law Rev 23:265

Galvez CC (2013) Necessity, investor rights, and state sovereignty for NAFTA investment arbitration. Cornell Int Law J 46:143

Gazzini T (2010) Interpretation of (allegedly) self-judging clauses in bilateral investment treaties. In: Fitzmaurice M, Elias OA, Merkouris P (eds) Treaty interpretation and the Vienna Convention on the Law of Treaties: 30 years on, vol 1. Brill, pp 239–254

Hagemeyer-Witzleb TM (2021) The international law of economic warfare. Springer

Hahn M (1991) Vital interests and the law of GATT: an analysis of GATT's security exception. Mich J Int Law 12:558

Heintschel von Heinegg W (2021) Treaties, fundamental change of circumstances. Max Planck Encycl of Public Int Law

Henckels C (2019) Investment treaty security exceptions, necessity and self-defence in the context of armed conflict. In: Fach Gómez K, Gourgourinis A, Titi C (eds) International investment law and the law of armed conflict: European yearbook of international economic law. Springer, pp 319–340

Hindelang S (2009) The free movement of capital and foreign direct investment: the scope of protection in EU law. Oxford University Press

Koskenniemi M (2011) The politics of international law. Bloomsbury Publishing

Lahmann H (2023) The plea of necessity in cyber emergencies: unresolved doctrinal questions. Nord J Int Law 92(3):422–445

Mitchell, A. D., Munro, J., & Voon, T. (2019). Importing WTO general exceptions into international investment agreements: Proportionality, myths and risks. In L. E. Sachs, L. Johnson, & J. Coleman (Eds.), Yearbook on international investment law & policy 2017. Oxford University Press, pp 305–355

Muchlinski PT (2009) Trends in international investment agreements: balancing investor rights and the right to regulate. The issue of national security. In Sauvant KP (ed) Yearbook on international investment law and policy. Oxford University Press, pp 35–78

Newcombe AP, Paradell L (2009) Law and practice of investment treaties: standards of treatment. Kluwer Law International BV

Paddeu F (2018) Justification and excuse in international law: concept and theory of general defences. Cambridge University Press

Paddeu F, Waibel M (2022) Necessity 20 years on: the limits of Article 25. ICSID Rev Foreign Invest Law J 37(1–2):160–191

Partsch KJ (1987). Vital interests. In Bernhardt R (ed) Encyclopedia of public international law (Vol. 10), North-Holland, pp 526–529

Pathirana D, McLaughlin M (2021) Non-precluded measures clauses: regime, trends, and practice. In: Chaisse J, Choukroune L, Jusoh S (eds) Handbook of international investment law and policy. Springer, pp 483–505

Reinisch A (2007) Necessity in international investment arbitration—an unnecessary split of opinions in recent ICSID cases – comments on CMS v. Argentina and LG&E v. Argentina. J World Invest Trade 8:191–214

Rosenne S (ed) (1991) The International Law Commission's draft articles on state responsibility: part 1, Articles 1–35 vol 1. Martinus Nijhoff Publishers

Sacerdoti G (2013) BIT protections and economic crises: limits to their coverage, the impact of multilateral financial regulation and the defence of necessity. ICSID Review-Foreign Investment Law Journal 28(2):351–383

Salacuse JW (2013) The three laws of international investment: national, contractual, and international frameworks for foreign capital. Oxford University Press

Schachter O (1984). The right of states to use armed force. Mich Law Rev, 82:1620

Schill SW, Briese R (2009) "If the state considers": self-judging clauses in international dispute settlement. Max Planck Yearb UN Law 13(1):61–140

Schill SW, Vidigal G (2021) National security, private actors, and political risk: judicial and non-judicial responses: an introduction. J World Invest Trade 22(4):503–508

Subramanian SR (2012) Too similar or too difficult: state of necessity as a defence under customary international law and the bilateral investment treaty and their relationship. Manch J Int Law 9:68–91

Suraputra DS (2013) Doctrine of rebus sic stantibus and law of international treaty. Indonesian J Int Law 11:462
Tanzi A (2013) Necessity, state of. Max Planck Encycl Public Int Law
Thiga JM (2019) The state of necessity as a contractual defence in investment disputes between states and individuals: an evaluation. [Doctoral dissertation, University of Nairobi]
Udich J (2013) Vital interests. In: Wolfrum R (ed) Max Planck Encyclopedia of Public International Law. Oxford University Press
Van den Bossche P, Zdouc W (2017) The law and policy of the World Trade Organization: text, cases, and materials, 4th edn. Cambridge University Press
Vidigal G, Schill SW (2021) International economic law and the securitization of policy objectives: risks of a Schmittean exception. Leg Issues Econ Integr 48(2):109–118
Viñuales JE (2020) Seven ways of escaping a rule: of exceptions and their avatars in international law. In: Bartels L, Paddeu F (eds) Exceptions in international law. Oxford University Press, pp 65–87
Wang W (2017) The non-precluded measure type clause in international investment agreements: significances, challenges, and reactions. ICSID Rev Foreign Invest Law J 32(2):447–456
Werner WG (2004) State sovereignty and international legal discourse. In: Dekker IF, Werner WG (eds) Governance and international legal theory. Brill Nijhoff, pp 125–157
Yannaca-Small K (2007) Essential security interests under international investment law. In: International investment perspectives: freedom of investment in a changing world. Organisation for Economic Co-operation and Development, pp 94–134, 113
Ziegler AR, Baumgartner J (2015) Good faith as a general principle of (international) law. In: Mitchell AD, Sornarajah M, Voon T (eds) Good Faith and International Economic Law. Oxford University Press, pp 9–36

Chapter 6
Investment Screening and the Right to Regulate Investments

Abstract This chapter examines the relationship between national security considerations and the substantive application of international investment treaties by focusing on how these treaties balance host state sovereignty with investor protections. It examines the treaty frameworks that allow host states to invoke national security to regulate foreign investments while preventing arbitrary or discriminatory practices. Through a detailed analysis of treaty provisions and arbitral jurisprudence, the chapter illustrates a pattern of deference granted to host states in the interpretation and application of key treaty standards. It enquires into the procedural challenges arbitrators face in maintaining transparency while respecting confidentiality in security-sensitive matters.

6.1 Introduction

Regarding matters of national security, the tension between state sovereignty and investor rights introduces a uniquely challenging complexity. The principal contention in this discourse is the extent to which national security considerations are accommodated within the framework of international investment treaties. While these treaties typically ensure substantial protection for investments, they also need to allow host states the sovereign right to regulate or intervene in foreign investments that pose security threats.

This chapter examines how the legal protections afforded by investment treaties meet the often opaque field of national security decision-making. A close examination of multiple treaties reveals that outright exclusions of substantive treaty guarantees in the context of national security are rare. Instead, what has emerged is a pattern where treaties are crafted to maintain a delicate balance: they neither fully preclude host states from invoking national security considerations nor allow them

J. H. Pohl, *Arbitration of Disputes related to National Security Screening of Foreign Investments*, EYIEL Monographs - Studies in European and International Economic Law 50,
https://doi.org/10.1007/978-3-032-26342-1_6

an unfettered hand that could lead to arbitrary or discriminatory practices against foreign investors.

Notably, these treaties frequently incorporate general exclusion clauses, which are then supplemented by specific restrictions that tailor the applicability of key treaty standards such as NT and MFN treatment. These provisions can accommodate the unique and sensitive nature of national security, which arguably necessitates a departure from the norms applicable in less sensitive areas.

International adjudicators have consistently recognized the special status of national security. This recognition manifests in a jurisprudence that is distinctly deferential to states when interpreting and applying the principal standards of treatment in contexts that implicate important national interests.

This chapter builds on the intricate analyses presented in previous chapters and extends the discussion on the delicate balance between state sovereignty and investor rights by focusing on the specific aspect of national security. Throughout the discourse on international investment law, a recurrent theme has been the scope of arbitral deference towards host states. This deference is not confined to the jurisdictional stage (see Chaps. 3 and 4) or the application of necessity defences and NPM clauses (see Chap. 5). Instead, it manifests even more profoundly during the merits phase of arbitration. Here, arbitrators' discretion is critical, especially in the application of both relative and absolute standards of treatment.

In earlier discussions, we observed instances where tribunals did not defer to host states at the jurisdictional stage or fully submit to host state determinations through necessity defences. However, the concept of deference resurfaces and is intricately applied at the merits stage through the interpretation and application of substantive legal requirements. This re-emergence is particularly evident through the careful and often intricate application of treatment standards. Such standards, which are relative standards (e.g. NT and MFN) and absolute standards (e.g. FET), require arbitrators to uphold treaty obligations while respecting a host state's security imperatives.

A critical intersection in this balancing act is the principle of due process, particularly related to procedural transparency. The transparency required in arbitration proceedings often collides with the confidentiality vital to national security interests. Ergo, arbitrators find themselves in a conundrum: how to maintain procedural transparency and ensure due process while simultaneously respecting the host state's fundamental interest in keeping certain matters of national security confidential.

This challenge poses significant questions about the limits of arbitration as a mechanism for dispute resolution in contexts involving sensitive security issues. Can arbitrators ensure a fair and transparent process without compromising the confidentiality critical to national security? How do they defer to the host state's assessment of sensitive facts without abdicating their duty to scrutinize—and afford the investor an opportunity to scrutinize—the state's actions critically?

The ensuing discussion probes how arbitrators recognize and interpret the special status accorded to national security under various treaties by specifically focusing on the deference given during the interpretation of principal standards of treatment (6.2). It illustrates how these standards are modulated when vital national interests (i.e. national security) are at stake by using examples from a range of arbitral decisions to show how arbitrators address the tension between treaty obligations and the host state's security imperatives.

Further, the chapter examines the practical application of these interpretive strategies, particularly how arbitrators defer to the host state's assessment of facts related to national security (6.3). This section looks into the procedural dynamics of arbitration, where the factual sovereignty of states in matters of security often leads to a layered, if not visibly restrained, arbitral scrutiny.

The insights gathered here can enhance an understanding of the law and inform future treaty formulations and arbitral decisions in the interface of investment law and national security. The concluding remarks reflect on these discussions and propose pathways for future research and policy development (6.4).

6.2 Investment Screening and the Right to Regulate in the Interest of National Security

The right to regulate appears in arbitral reasoning on the substance of a dispute as a device justifying termination of the enquiry into the merits of a state's decision-making on a particular matter.[1] The right to regulate may be reinforced by the argument that the state's domestic adjudication holds greater competence or legitimacy as a decision-maker.[2] Another reason may be that the issue involves a "political question" that, while not precluding arbitral jurisdiction, nevertheless is more authoritatively or legitimately decided by a domestic institution, such as a state's legislative or executive branch of government.[3]

This section examines the extent to which the host state's right to regulate matters concerning its national security imposes limitations on the interpretation and application of the principal obligations concerning national security screening. The potential for deferential interpretations of applicable investment treaty obligations, on the one hand, and the application of such interpretations to claims arising out of investment screening, on the other, depends greatly on the factual situation. Given the factual variety involved in investment screening, only a cursory outline of the application of investment treaty obligations can be provided here. The aim is limited to demonstrating that significant room for deferential interpretations exists.

The right to regulate is related to the principal standards of protection. The factual situations associated with investment screening may engage the relative

[1] The situation where an adjudicator invokes the right to regulate to decline jurisdiction to review matters it considers to be "political" on the basis that such matters are inappropriate for settlement by arbitration is discussed above in Chap. 3.

[2] Schill (2012) 599–600; van Harten (2013) 3–4; Henckels (2015) 36, 42.

[3] Katselas (2012) 147–148; Schill (2012) 600.

standards of protection, notably non-discrimination standards (6.2.1) and absolute standards of protection, including the FET standard and the protection against expropriation (6.2.2). The subchapter closes with a summary (6.2.3).

6.2.1 The Right to Regulate and the Relative Treaty Standards of Protection

The most common relative standards of protection in IIAs provide that a host state must treat investors of a certain home state and their investments no less favourable than it treats its own investors and their investments (i.e. NT) or foreign investors of a third country and their investments (i.e. MFN treatment).[4] Most international investment treaties include one or both of these non-discrimination standards.[5] In addition, many investment treaties provide for a general non-discrimination obligation (relating to distinctions not based on origin but on other grounds).

Formulations of these standards vary somewhat across treaties. However, in arbitral practice, their application has evolved into a comparison of treatments structured around a threefold enquiry: identifying the basis of comparison (6.2.1.1), assessing the existence of adverse difference in treatment (6.2.1.2), and evaluating whether any such discrimination is justified (6.2.1.3).[6]

6.2.1.1 Basis of Comparison

As for the first element, investment screening typically applies only to foreign investors.[7] Similar investments that domestic investors make are not subject to screening.

To assess whether a relevant differential treatment exists, the basis of comparison must be "apposite".[8] Hence, the situation or circumstances pertaining to the foreign investor concerned and its investment must be "like" (or similar to, but not necessarily identical to) the situation or circumstances pertaining to domestic investors or investors of other third countries with which the treatment is compared. Ergo, the investments by foreign investors and those by domestic investors

[4] See Bonnitcha et al. (2017) 93.

[5] See above Chap. 2.

[6] *UPS v Canada*, Award, 27 August 2009, para. 388; *Saluka v Czech Republic*, Partial Award, 17 March 2006, para. 313; *Marfin* v *Cyprus*, Award, 26 July 2018, para. 1237. See further Schefer (2016) pp 338–353; Reinisch (2015) 852–864; Dolzer and Schreuer (2012) 199–206; Newcombe and Paradell (2009) 158–188.

[7] See above fn 12.

[8] Bonnitcha et al. (2017) 101–102; Schefer (2016) 338–350; Newcombe and Paradell (2009) 163–169.

or other foreign investors must at least relate to the same economic sector or economic activity.[9]

Notably, investment treaties provide differently formulated bases of comparison. Some treaties, including the majority of the EU's post-Lisbon IIAs, specify that the treatment in question must be that which is accorded in "like situations".[10] Some Member State treaties also include wording to that effect.[11] Nevertheless, even if such qualifiers are meant to narrow the basis of comparison, perhaps to investors or investments in the same line of business (e.g. competitor or near-competitor industries), arbitral practice does not provide much support for the legal significance of such express comparator wording.[12]

In any event, it is plain from the design of investment screening mechanisms that similarly situated foreign and domestic investors and investments are inherently treated differently since investment screening exclusively applies to the former, not the latter. Moreover, it cannot be excluded that not all similarly situated foreign investors may be treated equally, but that the identity of the investors' home state may be considered in the screening process, as discussed next.

6.2.1.2 Adverse Differences in Treatment

Investment screening mechanisms impose on foreign investors the obligation to undergo screening of their investments on grounds of national security. These investors may be prohibited from establishing, acquiring, or expanding investments and can also be subjected to conditions or enforcement measures, including the unwinding of previously made investments. This treatment is, on its face, less favourable than the treatment accorded to similarly situated domestic investors who are not subject to screening.[13] In other words, investment screening inherently involves the adverse treatment of foreign investors or investments compared to similarly situated domestic investors or investments.

It is also conceivable that this treatment of foreign investors depends on the investor's home state. It could readily be imagined that, in practice, the treatment of foreign investors of a certain home state with which the host state does not maintain close security links is found to be less favourable than, for example, the treatment accorded to similarly situated investors of home states with which the

[9] Ibid. However, in some cases, tribunals went beyond this and compared investors in different sectors/economic activities; See the "totality of circumstances" approach in e.g. *Bilcon/Clayton v Canada*.

[10] UNCTAD Investment Policy Hub.

[11] Ibid.

[12] Newcombe and Paradell (2009) 159–161.

[13] It should be noted, however, that most national screening laws apply to Member State investors as well, although somewhat different rules apply to third-country investments under the screening laws of some Member States.

host state cooperates closely on security matters.[14] The former may be subject to more rigorous screening and more restrictive screening decisions than the latter, which can be seen as an adverse difference in treatment that would be at odds with the MFN treatment obligation. For purposes of the application of MFN provisions, it is sufficient that the treatment of investors or investments of a particular home state is de facto less favourable compared to the treatment of investors or investments of another home state; de jure discrimination is not required.

6.2.1.3 Justified Discrimination

Discriminatory treatment does not constitute a breach of the non-discrimination standards if the treatment can be appropriately justified. This additional requirement has emerged as a defence or implied exception in arbitral practice in the interpretation of the NT standard in IIAs.[15] Nonetheless, similar qualifications and implied exceptions have also emerged in the application of non-discrimination standards in other contexts.[16] It is fair to presume that the issue of justification would be central to the application of non-discrimination standards to disputes involving alleged NT violations or even MFN treatment violations related to investment screening.

Whether screening direct investments made by foreign investors while not screening investments of domestic investors in similar situations can be justified is an issue that cannot be determined abstractly. Indeed, the differentiation of treatment may, in principle, be readily justified on rational grounds by citing the fundamental societal interest of safeguarding security and public order. Nevertheless, with respect to the manner of application of investment screening, it can be questioned whether the differential treatment of the relevant foreign investor or its investment can be reconciled with, or is rationally related to, the policy objective with which the screening has been justified. In this respect, there is no shortage of inspiration for persuasive arguments that can be gleaned from other instances where non-discrimination standards have been applied, notably WTO jurisprudence.[17]

[14] Other possible bases for differential treatment may be the maintenance of economic sanctions against a third country or a third country's human rights record.

[15] *Saluka v Czech Republic*, Partial Award, 17 March 2006, para. 313; *Marfin v Cyprus*, Award, 26 July 2018, para. 1237; *SD Myers v Canada*, First Partial Award, 13 November 2000, para. 250. See Dolzer and Schreuer (2012) 202–204; Schefer (2016) 351–353; Bjorklund (2010) 419, 433–434; Salacuse (2013) 279–280.

[16] An example from the context to WTO law is the implied exception to the non-discrimination obligation in Article 2.1 of the Agreement on Technical Barriers to Trade (1994) with respect to de facto discrimination stemming exclusively from "legitimate regulatory distinctions". See *United States-Clove Cigarettes* (2012) paras. 182, 215. See further Van den Bossche and Zdouc (2017) 904–912.

[17] See e.g. *Olin v Libya,* paras. 200–203; *Pope & Talbott,* para. 78. See also above Chap. 5. With respect to the interpretation of general exceptions, the interpretive guidance provided by WTO jurisprudence may be particularly influential. See Newcombe and Paradell (2009) 503–505.

For example, drawing inspiration from WTO caselaw, unjustified discrimination can be argued if it is shown that the screening is applied arbitrarily, in the sense of random or capricious application or by being applied rigidly without allowing for an inquiry into its appropriateness for the situation of the relevant investor or its investment.[18] Likewise, a lack of justification may also be argued where the differential treatment can be avoided,[19] where a less intrusive alternative exists to imposing a condition for or denying investment authorization following a screening investigation,[20] and where the screening measure at hand lacks a sufficient degree of means-end relationship with the pursued policy objective.[21]

It follows from the previous paragraphs in this section that an implied exception with respect to the NT standard has been recognized in arbitral practice. To some extent, an overlap exists between this implied exception and the general exception based on the WTO law standard.[22] Stated differently, if a measure violates the NT standard and cannot be justified by the implied exception that forms part of that standard, then it is difficult to imagine that the measure can be justified by the general exception, which, if anything, is narrower, or at least more structured than the implied exceptions developed in practice.[23] In any event, the added value of the general exception clause is that it applies uniformly across all standards of protection. It is worth reflecting that the implied exception is a plausible reason why there are so extremely few successful claims of discrimination in investment arbitration.

6.2.2 The Right to Regulate and the Absolute Treaty Standards of Protection

Many international investment treaties include an FET clause,[24] which provides for a standard of protection that is not related to how the host state treats its own or other third-country investors. While there are different formulations of the standard, attempts at elaborating the contours of its contents can be found in arbitral practice.[25] For present purposes, it is sufficient to note that reference is commonly made to other legal concepts that are treated as a manifestation of the standard. These include the denial of justice, due process, transparency, non-arbitrariness,

---

[18] Ibid. See also Van den Bossche and Zdouc (2017) 595–597, 600–601.

[19] See above Chap. 5; see also Van den Bossche and Zdouc (2017) 597–598.

[20] Ibid.

[21] See further Newcombe and Paradell (2009) 503–505. For the relationship between proportionality and the rule of law, see generally Jacob and Schill (2015) 713–717 (in particular para. 36).

[22] See further Newcombe and Paradell (2009) 505–506.

[23] For a comprehensive discussion of the interplay between WTO general exceptions and investment treaty exceptions, see Mitchell et al. (2016).

[24] UNCTAD Investment Policy Hub.

[25] For a comprehensive review, see Jacob and Schill (2015).

non-discrimination, legitimate expectations, legal certainty, good faith, proportionality, and reasonableness.[26] As such, the standard is susceptible to a wide range of argumentative structures and models of legal discourse. This wide scope is somewhat balanced by certain tendencies in treaty and arbitral practice towards a restrictive application, which leaves a margin of discretion on the part of the host state and renders non-actionable potential errors within that margin.[27] Like similar provisions found in CPTPP, RCEP, and USMCA,[28] which also aim to balance investor protections with state regulatory autonomy, the FET clause in Article 8.10(2) and (4) of the CETA reflects this practice:

1. A Party breaches the obligation of fair and equitable treatment referenced in paragraph 1 if a measure or series of measures constitutes:
   (a) denial of justice in criminal, civil or administrative proceedings;
   (b) fundamental breach of due process, including a fundamental breach of transparency, in judicial and administrative proceedings;
   (c) manifest arbitrariness;
   (d) targeted discrimination on manifestly wrongful grounds, such as gender, race or religious belief;
   (e) abusive treatment of investors, such as coercion, duress and harassment; or
   (f) a breach of any further elements of the fair and equitable treatment obligation adopted by the Parties in accordance with paragraph 3 of this Article.

[...]

2. When applying the above fair and equitable treatment obligation, a Tribunal may take into account whether a Party made a specific representation to an investor to induce a covered investment, that created a legitimate expectation, and upon which the investor relied in deciding to make or maintain the covered investment, but that the Party subsequently frustrated.

The first two items on the list relate mainly to procedural justice, whereas the following three are also relevant to the protection of property. Paragraph 4 clarifies that a breach of legitimate expectations may also constitute a violation of the standard, even though it is not specifically mentioned in the closed list of paragraph 2.[29] Perhaps a breach of legitimate expectations involving property rights would most appropriately have to be construed as a case of manifest arbitrariness.

---

[26] Ibid. 717–743 and the caselaw cited. See also Bonnitcha et al. (2017) 108–112.

[27] For a comprehensive overview, see Schefer (2016) 381–426.

[28] The CPTPP includes similar FET provisions that balance investor protection with the right of states to regulate in the public interest (Chapter 9, Article 9.6). The USMCA also has FET provisions, but with more stringent requirements and specific limitations, balancing investor protection with state regulatory interests (Chapter 14, Article 14.6). The RCEP emphasizes state-to-state dispute resolution and includes investment protection standards, but its provisions on FET may not be as detailed as those in CETA, CPTPP, and USMCA. Overall, RCEP provides investment protections but focuses more on state-to-state mechanisms and less on detailed FET provisions.

[29] Notably, legitimate expectations in the new generation of treaties can no longer be a sole (independent) basis for finding an FET breach, unlike under caselaw developed for a traditional (undefined and unqualified) FET found in most old generation investment treaties.

This example illustrates that the items on that list are legal concepts of broad scope, the further elaboration of which is still expected from arbitral practice.

Investment screening decisions may have the effect of depriving the foreign investor of the possibility of making use of the property as expected.[30] A decision may involve the prohibition of a prospective or expanded investment or may result in its unwinding, modification, or nullification. In this case, screening decisions can amount to a "regulatory taking", "de facto" expropriation, or "indirect" expropriation.[31]

The protection against unlawful expropriation is commonly addressed in investment treaties.[32] Commonly, expropriation clauses include references to formal (direct) expropriation and "measures tantamount to expropriation" or "measures having equivalent effect to expropriation".[33] Article 8.12 CETA is illustrative:

> A Party shall not nationalise or expropriate a covered investment either directly, or indirectly through measures having an effect equivalent to nationalisation or expropriation ("expropriation") except:
>
> (a) for a public purpose;
> (b) under due process of law;
> (c) in a non-discriminatory manner; and
> (d) on payment of prompt, adequate and effective compensation.
>
> For greater certainty, this paragraph shall be interpreted in accordance with Annex 8-A. […]

Similar clauses are included in CPTPP, RCEP, and USMCA to protect against both direct and indirect expropriation.[34] The reference in Article 8.12 CETA to "measures having an effect equivalent to nationalisation or expropriation" in the expropriation clause is further elaborated on in Annex 8-A CETA:

> The Parties confirm their shared understanding that:
>
> 1. Expropriation may be direct or indirect:
>   (a) direct expropriation occurs when an investment is nationalised or otherwise directly expropriated through formal transfer of title or outright seizure; and

---

[30] For example, by means of conditions for authorizing the investment, which may include so-called mitigating measures aimed at addressing an identified national security issue. This could include restricting the owners' voting rights in an acquired enterprise while requiring certain independent directors to join the board of directors of the enterprise, the forced sale of certain divisions, etc.

[31] Kriebaum (2007).

[32] See generally Kriebaum (2015).

[33] Dolzer et al. (2022) 152–153.

[34] Similarly, the CPTPP contains expropriation clauses (Chapter 9, Article 9.8) that protect against direct and indirect expropriation, requiring prompt, adequate, and effective compensation. The USMCA includes similar expropriation provisions (Chapter 14, Article 14.8), offering protections against direct and indirect expropriation with detailed requirements for lawful expropriation. While the RCEP includes investment protection provisions, its exact treatment of expropriation is not as detailed as those in CETA, CPTPP, and USMCA.

(b) indirect expropriation occurs if a measure or series of measures of a Party has an effect equivalent to direct expropriation, in that it substantially deprives the investor of the fundamental attributes of property in its investment, including the right to use, enjoy and dispose of its investment, without formal transfer of title or outright seizure.

2. The determination of whether a measure or series of measures of a Party, in a specific fact situation, constitutes an indirect expropriation requires a case-by-case, fact-based inquiry that takes into consideration, among other factors:

(a) the economic impact of the measure or series of measures, although the sole fact that a measure or series of measures of a Party has an adverse effect on the economic value of an investment does not establish that an indirect expropriation has occurred;
(b) the duration of the measure or series of measures of a Party;
(c) the extent to which the measure or series of measures interferes with distinct, reasonable investment-backed expectations; and
(d) the character of the measure or series of measures, notably their object, context and intent.

3. For greater certainty, except in the rare circumstance when the impact of a measure or series of measures is so severe in light of its purpose that it appears manifestly excessive, non-discriminatory measures of a Party that are designed and applied to protect legitimate public welfare objectives, such as health, safety and the environment, do not constitute indirect expropriations.

Here, it is further explained that a measure qualifies as an indirect expropriation if it "substantially deprives the investor of the fundamental attributes of property in its investment, including the right to use, enjoy and dispose of its investment, without formal transfer of title or outright seizure". Arguably, such a description may aptly be applied to investment screening measures, which, depending on their design, impose conditions or limitations on the investor's control of an investment or require the divestment of certain operations.

A non-excessive, non-discriminatory regulatory taking that is justified by legitimate public purposes might not constitute an indirect expropriation, even if due process is not observed and the investor is not duly compensated. In other words, the failure to observe procedural justice does not automatically qualify a regulatory taking as an expropriation. Thus, the respondent host state must establish the legitimate purpose of its measure, which in the context of national security screening may be difficult, given the confidential nature of national security matters. For that reason, a host state may not be able to justify a screening decision as a legitimate interference with the foreign investor's investment.

6.2.2.1 Procedural Justice

Investment screening is an administrative procedure liable to result in legally binding acts. As such, screening mechanisms are subject to the customary principle prohibiting the denial of justice as well as principles of administrative due process that apply by virtue of treaty obligations, including judicial and administrative transparency.[35] More specifically, an administrative decision to prohibit an investment, to impose conditions, to deny an application for authorization, or to require an investment to be unwound would involve the application of the due process obligation to hear the investor concerned (the principle of audi alteram partem).[36] This principle involves administrative transparency and includes providing reasonable notice to the investor when the screening proceeding is initiated,[37] which should comprise the legal basis and a description of the nature of the proceedings and the facts and issues in question.[38] A failure to provide the investor concerned with an effective opportunity to present its views on the truthfulness or relevance of any fact relied upon in an adverse screening decision may violate the right to be heard.[39] In addition to responding to facts and arguments alleged against it, the investor can expect a reasonable opportunity to present facts and arguments of its own in support of its position.[40]

Administrative justice also requires the possibility for aggrieved investors to seek review and correction of administrative actions before impartial and independent tribunals and to support and defend their positions before such tribunals.[41] The principle of nemo iudex in sua causa also requires that the tribunal not have a substantial interest in the outcome of the proceedings.[42] Moreover, administrative and judicial decisions must be properly motivated and be based on evidence, facts, and arguments submitted in the record.[43] The elaboration of these and other fundamental principles of procedural law may be gleaned from a wide range of sources, including the caselaw of human rights tribunals and municipal legal systems.

---

[35] See generally Kläger (2011) 213–234; Della Cananea (2010) 56–74; Palombino (2018) 57–82; Paparinskis (2013) 181–216; Yannaca-Small (2010) 394–398.

[36] See further Kläger (2011) 214; Della Cananea (2010) 60–64; Palombino (2018) 61; Paparinskis (2013) 194, 213.

[37] See further Kläger (2011) 227–234, Della Cananea (2010) 65–67; Paparinskis (2013) 247–250; Yannaca-Small (2010) 388, 396–397.

[38] See e.g. Article 27.3(a) CETA; Article 17.5(2)(a) of the EU-Japan EPA; Article 12.5(a) of the Article EU-Korea FTA.

[39] A related question concerns the determination of the scope of the right to be heard required under investment treaty obligations. If, on the basis of the NT standard, the scope is determined by EU law, the *Hoffmann-La Roche* formula would be applicable ["*le respect des droits de la défense exige que l'entreprise intéressée ait été mise en mesure, au cours de la procédure administrative, de faire connaître utilement son point de vue sur la réalité et la pertinence des faits et circonstances alléguées et sur les documents retenus par la Commission*", ECJ Judgment of 13 February 1979, *Hoffmann-La Roche v Commission*, C-85/76, EU:C:1979:36, para. 11], which also extends to matters of external economic matters, see ECJ Judgment of 27 June 1991, *Al-Jubail Fertilizer v Council*, C-49/88, EU:C:1991:276, para. 17. For the relationship between the right to be heard in EU law and the international minimum standard, see also Pohl (2018).

[40] See e.g. Article 27.3(b) CETA; Article 17.5(2)(b) of the EU-Japan EPA; Article 12.5(b) of the EU-Korea FTA.

[41] See e.g. Article 27.4 CETA; Article 17.6 of the EU-Japan EPA; Article 12.6 of the Article EU-Korea FTA.

[42] Ibid.

[43] Ibid.

Regarding investment screening, the availability of domestic legal recourse is hampered by the confidential nature of national security matters. As illustrated by the *Ralls* case discussed above, a government may not be required to provide procedural transparency concerning sensitive information pertaining to national security matters, which deprives the investor of an opportunity to scrutinize and comment on such matters. While this deprivation may not be regarded as a breach of due process for domestic purposes, it nevertheless restricts the ability of the investor to pursue its arguments and bring relevant (counter)evidence.

6.2.2.2 Protection of Property

The FET standard also protects against the deprivation of property rights, in particular by incorporating the concept of legitimate expectations.[44] In this respect, the standard significantly overlaps with the protection of investor interests in connection with direct and indirect expropriation. However, it is broader in scope and also covers situations that involve less invasive interference with property rights than in the case of expropriation.[45]

A claim based on the protection of legitimate expectations requires that the host state's conduct creates

> reasonable and justifiable expectations on the part of an investor (or investment) to act in reliance on said conduct, such that a failure by the [host state] to honour those expectations could cause the investor (or investment) to suffer damages.[46]

In post-Lisbon treaties that include this standard, it is further qualified by wording such as that contained in Article 8.10(4) CETA quoted above.

The range of claims that can be raised on the basis of legitimate expectations cannot be easily generalized. A common type of expectation relates to the manner in which the screening is conducted. Expectations as to the non-discriminatory, non-arbitrary, proportional, and good faith application of screening appear more reasonable and justifiable. It may also be reasonably expected that the screening is applied in conformity with its policy objective and not, for example, as a disguised restriction on competition.

Investment screening can result in significant interference with the property rights of investors, particularly in the post-investment phase. The prohibition of an investment, the imposition of conditions for authorizing an investment, and, in particular, the unwinding of already consummated investments are prone to severely disturbing the affected investor's property rights.

---

[44] See generally Jacob and Schill (2015) 723–728; Kläger (2011) 164–186; Paparinskis (2013) 217–259; Yannaca-Small (2010) 396–407.

[45] See further Jacob and Schill (2015) 758–760; Kläger (2011) 281–302.

[46] *Thunderbird v Mexico*, Arbitral Award, 26 January 2006, para. 154. See further Jacob and Schill (2015) 725.

Nevertheless, absent special circumstances, protection from such disturbances would normally fall short of qualifying as a legitimate expectation created by the host state's conduct. In the post-Lisbon treaties, the argument that the introduction of the screening mechanism would per se frustrate the investor's expectations is neutralized by provisions such as Article 8.9(2) CETA:

> For greater certainty, the mere fact that a Party regulates, including through a modification to its laws, in a manner which negatively affects an investment or interferes with an investor's expectations, including its expectations of profits, does not amount to a breach of an obligation under this Section.

Although rare in pre-Lisbon treaties, this type of provision would exclude from the protection of legitimate expectations the mere fact that the host state introduced screening legislation or that the EU adopted the Screening Regulation.

As for the application of screening legislation in a particular case, an investor alleging legitimate expectations would have to elicit evidence of conduct attributable to the host state that created the expectation, such as explicit representations that were reasonably relied upon by the investor.[47] It is also possible that consistent host state conduct could amount to implicit representations in the context of investment screening, which depends on how the screening mechanism is administered in practice.[48]

6.2.3 *Summary*

This subchapter engaged in a detailed examination of the host state's right to regulate within the domain of national security and its impact on foreign investments. Central to this discourse is the recognition that while states possess an inherent sovereign right to regulate for national security reasons, this right must be exercised within the constraints set by IIAs.

The right to regulate allows states to implement measures that may adversely affect foreign investments, such as national security screenings. These measures, however, must adhere to principles of fairness and equity to be considered legitimate under international law and must ensure that any differential treatment of foreign investors, compared to domestic or other foreign investors, is justified, non-arbitrary, and proportional. The principle of non-discrimination is particularly important, as it demands that foreign investors from different states be treated equitably unless a compelling state interest dictates otherwise.

Moreover, the deprivation of the use, enjoyment, or disposal of an investment must not be excessive or discriminatory. It should align with the investor's

---

[47] See generally Dolzer and Schreuer (2012) 145–149; Newcombe and Paradell (2009) 279–289; Salacuse (2013) 253–260.

[48] See further Jacob and Schill (2015) 725–727; Yannaca-Small (2010) 400–402; Salacuse (2013) 260–261.

legitimate expectations, which are formed based on the host state's previous actions and commitments. These expectations are legally protected under the FET standard, which is a cornerstone of modern IIAs.

Due process also plays a critical role in maintaining the legality of national security screenings. Where screening measures amount to expropriation, they must also satisfy the applicable requirements of public purpose, due process, non-discrimination, and be implemented in a manner that provides prompt, adequate, and effective compensation to ensure that while states can act to protect national security, investors are not unduly prejudiced by such actions.

Procedural transparency is fundamentally linked to procedural justice. Transparency ensures that all actions and decisions are made openly and allows affected parties to understand the basis of decisions that impact their investments significantly. This transparency is essential for procedural justice and forms an integral part of the FET standard to ensure that investors are treated fairly and can anticipate and respond to state actions effectively.

6.3 Transparency and the Suitability of Arbitration to Settle Investment Disputes Relating to National Security Screening

As discussed in Chap. 2, in the increasingly interconnected global economy, FDI is essential in bridging economies and fostering economic development. However, as stated in previous chapters, the intersection of FDI with national security considerations presents unique challenges, particularly in the arbitration of investment disputes. This subchapter focuses on the critical issue of transparency within the framework of FDI screening against the backdrop of national security concerns. It examines the tension between the need for host states to protect their security interests and the imperative for procedural fairness and transparency in resolving investment disputes.

In investment screening, procedural transparency is specifically significant as it is closely linked with due process and, thus, FET, as it pertains to the timely disclosure of information that investors require to navigate the regulatory landscape effectively. This issue is particularly problematic when perceived threats to national security or public order justify screening mechanisms. The dilemma arises because detailing the nature of these threats can, paradoxically, undermine the security intended to be protected.

The geopolitical and geoeconomic domains, characterized by broadening concepts of national security, reflect a variety of threats that states must manage.[49]

[49] Vidigal and Schill (2021) 111, fn 8–10. The European Court of Justice has upheld the wide scope of the concepts of "public order" and "public security" with the resulting degree of freedom of Member States to invoke those grounds in light of their national needs, although it has

This complexity is compounded by the executive branch's predominant role in interpreting sensitive information—a function that courts typically avoid due to their lack of expertise in foreign relations and security matters. Even when the facts giving rise to the perception of a security threat are not sensitive or confidential, the state's executive branch of government normally has the last word in interpreting such facts since courts are ill-equipped and do not have the expertise to make factual determinations about foreign relations and national security.[50]

Transparency within the framework of investment screening encompasses multiple facets, each important to the legal and procedural environment faced by investors. It involves the comprehensive disclosure of (a) the existence of legal requirements, (b) prospective changes to these requirements, (c) the administration of existing laws, and (d) the clarity of these laws.[51] The objective is to ensure that information is accessible to the right addressee and is communicated effectively and in a timely manner that aligns with the needs of investors and stakeholders.[52]

The lack of procedural transparency introduces significant systemic risks and affects the effectiveness and efficiency of investment screening mechanisms. A non-transparent screening process may lead to several adverse outcomes: (a) Due to insufficient engagement with the investor, the executive authority may make uninformed decisions that lead to errors which could have been mitigated with better information exchange. (b) In the absence of robust procedural checks, there is a heightened risk that security measures may extend beyond necessary bounds, potentially harming the state's economic interests or leading to decisions where investments are unnecessarily blocked or modified. (c) Without the safeguard of judicial scrutiny, the application of screening mechanisms can be misused and serve interests unrelated to national security or public order. Political motives, personal gains, or other non-security-related objectives could drive this misuse.

Transparency is a fundamental principle for ensuring accountability and fairness in arbitration. However, the current system often lacks sufficient transparency, contributing to democratic deficits. The confidential nature of arbitral proceedings and the limited availability of arbitral awards hinder the development of a coherent body of legal precedents. Greater transparency can be achieved through the publication of arbitral decisions and increased access to arbitration proceedings. This would not only enhance the legitimacy of the arbitration process but also contribute to the development of consistent legal principles.

---

determined that these concepts may be relied on only if there is a "genuine and sufficiently serious threat to a fundamental interest of society" and that derogations on the basis of these concepts "must not be misapplied so as, in fact, to serve purely economic ends", see Judgment of 14 March 2000, *Association Eglise de scientologie de Paris and Scientology International Reserves Trust v The Prime Minister*, C-54/99, EU:C:2000:124, para 17.

[50] See further Eichensehr and Hwang (2023); Chesney (2009) 1361.

[51] Pohl (2017) 198.

[52] Ibid. 189.

Thus, the consequences of inadequate transparency are twofold: they jeopardize the integrity of investment screening processes and affect the broader investment climate by introducing uncertainty and potential arbitrariness into the decision-making process.

The discussion is organized as follows. First, the foundational issues surrounding transparency in the context of national security are examined. An analysis of how public policy and legal frameworks define and influence the practices of national security screening is included to emphasize the inherently discretionary nature of these processes (6.3.1). Second, using the role of the European Commission under the FDI Screening Regulation as a case study, the next section focuses on the procedural rights afforded to investors and the real-world challenges they encounter to provide a critical assessment of how the Regulation functions in practice while offering insights into the effectiveness of current procedural safeguards within the EU's legal landscape (6.3.2). Third, an alternative mechanism to enhance transparency in the screening process is proposed as a potential solution to uphold the required level of confidentiality for national security purposes while improving the transparency of the screening process, the feasibility, benefits, and potential limitations of which are critically analyzed (6.3.3). Finally, the key findings from the discussions in this section are summarized (6.3.4).

6.3.1 Procedural Transparency in Investment Arbitration and the Problem of National Security

The principle of procedural transparency serves as a standard to ensure that the arbitration processes are open, accountable, and fair. However, this pursuit of transparency often encounters significant challenges when juxtaposed against national security concerns, where states assert their sovereign rights to control foreign investments that pose potential threats to their security or public order. This fundamental tension underscores the necessity of balancing transparent legal processes with the protective measures a state may employ to guard its national interests.

This section begins by tracing the evolution of transparency from a domestic legal doctrine to a crucial component of international investment law by highlighting its inception with the U.S. Freedom of Information Act and its global dissemination through various national legislations (6.3.1.1). The discussion then transitions to how transparency has been embedded within the fabric of international investment law, particularly through BITs that stipulate clear mandates for the public disclosure of laws and regulations affecting investments (6.3.1.2).

Further exploration is dedicated to understanding how these transparency norms are integrated and interpreted within the arbitration framework by examining key arbitral decisions that have shaped the application of transparency related to the FET standard (6.3.1.3). This analysis provides insights into the varying degrees of transparency required by different tribunals and the impact of these interpretations on the jurisprudence of international investment arbitration.

The section concludes by addressing the critical issues arising from the intersection of transparency requirements with national security measures (6.3.1.4). It discusses how investment screening mechanisms employed by states to scrutinize and potentially restrict foreign investments on security grounds frequently rely on broad, sometimes ambiguous, definitions of national security and public order. This reliance introduces a layer of complexity and uncertainty for investors and complicates the enforcement and predictability of transparency standards in international investment law. This narrative opens for a deeper inquiry into the procedural rights of investors and the operational challenges they face under these regulatory frameworks, as detailed in the subsequent sections of the chapter.

6.3.1.1 Origin of Transparency as a Legal Concept

It is essential to trace the origin of transparency as a legal concept within international investment law back to its roots in domestic legal traditions before its adoption at the international level.[53] The U.S. Freedom of Information Act (FOIA) of 1966 is widely acknowledged as the catalyst for a global proliferation of transparency laws.[54] This legislation sparked a significant legislative trend, beginning from 1978 to 1991 with countries such as France, Australia, New Zealand, Canada, and Colombia, which continued through the 1990s with nations including the Netherlands, Belgium, South Korea, and Japan, and extended into the twenty-first century with further adoption by countries like South Africa, the United Kingdom, Romania, Angola, Zimbabwe, Ecuador, Argentina, Germany,

[53] For an account of the emergence of transparency as term unrelated to its original association with vision, see Michener and Bersch (2013), who trace its current figurative use to an academic article by Danish economist, Knud Erik Svendsen in 1962.

[54] The realization that disclosure inhibits wrongdoing and promotes good governance is age old. U.S. Supreme Court Justice Louis Brandeis famously captured this idea: "Publicity is justly commended as a remedy for social and industrial diseases. Sunlight is said to be the best of disinfectants; electric light the most efficient policeman", Brandeis (1914) 92. The earliest example of statutory initiative to this effect appears to be the Swedish Freedom of the Press Act 1766, which, in a bid to thwart royal usurpation of parliamentary power, established a presumption for publicity, whereby official documents could only by way of exception be withheld from public availability. This principle of publicity (Sw. *offentlighetsprincipen*) later obtained constitutional status in Swedish law, but was not widely emulated, not even in other Scandinavian legal systems. The FOIA and similar later initiatives did not introduce anything akin to a full principle of publicity but established orderly administrative procedures and criteria for granting access to government documents. On the international plane, an oft-quoted precursor is Article 19 Universal Declaration of Human Rights, which provides that "[e]veryone has the right to freedom of opinion and expression; this right includes freedom to hold opinions without interference *and to seek, receive and impart information and ideas* through any media and regardless of frontiers" [emphasis added].

India, China, Russia, Indonesia, and Brazil.[55] By 2014, over 100 countries had implemented some form of transparency legislation.[56]

By the early 2000s, the concept of "open government" had become well-established and encompassed freedom of information laws with broader practices. Advocates for transparency have successfully expanded its scope to include "open records", "open access", and "open meetings", where government deliberations occur publicly. This expansion has extended to openness in public procurement, conflict of interest rules, ethical codes, financial disclosures for politicians and public servants, protections for journalistic sources and whistle-blowers, anti-corruption measures, and corporate transparency.[57]

Additionally, transparency is closely linked with principles of due process and fair procedure, such as the rights to be informed and to access files, the equality of arms, and being heard (audi alteram partem).[58] These principles were evident in early parliamentary procedures, which mirrored judicial processes and emphasized the need for transparent, orderly dissemination of draft laws to facilitate parliamentary consultations prior to enactment.[59]

Thus, the concept of transparency has evolved into a comprehensive framework centred on the systematic disclosure of information by various governmental branches. It serves as an umbrella term encapsulating a diverse range of legal practices aimed at enhancing the openness of legal regimes and their procedures.

6.3.1.2 Transparency in International Investment Law

In the area of international investment law, the concept of transparency began to gain prominence in the 1980s with the inclusion of explicit clauses mandating the publication of laws and regulations affecting investments. The first formal

---

[55] List maintained by freedominfo.org, retrieved from http://www.freedominfo.org. See also, Banisar (2006). For a historical overview, see Metcalfe (2014).

[56] Cf. list maintained by freedominfo.org ibid.

[57] See, e.g. Schauer (2011) 1349. OECD (2005), cf. Piotrowski and Borry (2010) 141; Schudson (2015). The wide array of policies under the transparency umbrella often builds upon existing legal practices. For instance, the foundational notion of transparency in the public sector aligns with the ancient legal principle that laws must be known to those they govern. Historical examples include Rome's Law of the Twelve Tables, prominently displayed in public spaces, and the Napoleonic Code's stipulations that laws take effect post-promulgation and operate only prospectively.

[58] See, e.g. Harlow (2006) 190; Fisher (2010) 290; Cassese (2005) 111; Vaughn (2014) 247–250.

[59] Patnode (2013) 18, 65; Waldeck (1972); Levmore (1989), 976. Consultation open to the public or sections thereof is arguably a later evolution, although legislative com-missions involving external experts and certain representatives of the general public appear to have been well known in seventeenth century Sweden, which can be gleaned from the King's Resolution ratifying the Law of the Swedish Realm 1734 (1736) (Sw. *Konungens stadfästelseresolution till Sveriges rikes lag [1734 års lag*; 1736]) and may stretch as far back as the Late Middle Ages, see Lockwood (1967) 197.

inclusion of a "transparency of laws" clause appeared in Australia's inaugural BIT with China in 1988, as encapsulated in Article VI of the Australia-China BIT. Previously, a similar mandate existed in the U.S. BIT framework, although not explicitly labelled as "transparency." This practice was initiated in the original U.S. model BIT of 1981 and was first seen in the US-Senegal BIT of 1983, where Article II(10) set forth a now-standard requirement[60]:

> Each Party shall make public all laws, regulations, administrative practices and procedures, and adjudicatory decisions that pertain to or affect investments in its territory of nationals or companies of the other Party.

This clause from the U.S. model BIT significantly influenced bilateral treaty negotiations worldwide, which led to the adoption of similar transparency requirements in numerous treaties throughout the 1980s.[61] By the early 2000s, such transparency clauses had become a common feature in IIAs. Thus, by the mid-2010s, they were nearly ubiquitous in new treaties, which indicated a standardization of transparency in treaty texts.[62]

The evolution of transparency in international investment law also extended to arbitral jurisprudence, particularly concerning the FET standard[63] and the customary international minimum standard of treatment.[64] From the early 2000s

[60] Precursors had existed in the earlier practice of signing friendship, commerce and navigation treaties (FCNs), e.g. Article XVII(1) US-Republic of China FCN (1946) and Article XV(1) US-Nicaragua FCN (1956) but were rare. There appear to be no examples of such clauses prior to the negotiations leading up to the Havana Charter, Article 38 of which included the elaborate blueprint for subsequent treaty practice, which reappeared with minimal changes as Article X GATT (1947) and is retained in Article X GATT (1994).

[61] See, e.g. Article XVI(2) Canada-Philippines BIT (earlier Canadian BIT practice had provided for exchange of information between the contracting parties on laws and regulations). A similar provision was later elaborated in the OECD draft Multilateral Agreement on Investment. By contrast, transparency provisions of this type were not common in European BITs until the EU began concluding investment treaties following the Lisbon Treaty. Other states, including Canada, began to include this type of transparency provision from the mid-1990s.

[62] More recently, another dimension of transparency has emerged in international investment law, relating to procedural transparency requirements in ISDS. Unlike substantive transparency requirements that apply to the treatment of international investments on the municipal plane, procedural transparency requirements apply entirely on the international plane. As such, these requirements do not relate to government transparency or public governance transparency in the treatment of foreign investors outside of arbitration and thus fall outside the research questions of the present enquiry.

[63] See further Kläger (2011) 227.

[64] *Metalclad Corporation v United Mexican States*, ICSID Case No. ARB(AF)/97/1, Award, paras. 76, 88, 99 (Aug. 30, 2000) (set aside by a municipal court noting that "[n]o authority was cited or evidence introduced to establish that transparency has become part of customary international law", *Mexico v Metalclad Corporation*, [2001] B.C.S.C. 664, Supreme Court of British Columbia, Reasons for Judgment, para. 68 (May 2, 2001)); Emilio *Agustín Maffezini v Kingdom of Spain*, ICSID Case No. ARB/97/7, Award, para. 83 (Nov. 30, 2000); *S.D. Myers, Inc. v Government of Canada*, UNCITRAL, Partial Award (Separate Opinion by Dr. Bryan Schwartz, concurring except with respect to performance requirements, in the partial award of

onward, arbitral tribunals began to interpret transparency as a critical component of these core standards of protection.[65] Notably, all but one tribunal during this period affirmed this interpretation, which signalled a strong consensus on the importance of transparency.[66]

However, the degree of required transparency has been subject to varying interpretations by different tribunals. In the case of *Tecmed v Mexico*, the tribunal emphasized the need for "total transparency":

> The Arbitral Tribunal considers that this provision of the Agreement, in light of the good faith principle established by international law, requires the Contracting Parties to provide to international investments treatment that does not affect the basic expectations that were taken into account by the foreign investor to make the investment. The foreign investor expects the host state to act in a consistent manner, free from ambiguity and totally transparently in its relations with the foreign investor, so that it may know beforehand any and all rules and regulations that will govern its investments, as well as the goals of the relevant policies and administrative practices or directives, to be able to plan its investment and comply with such regulations.[67]

---

the tribunal), paras. 249–258 (Nov. 12, 2000); *Técnicas Medioambientales Tecmed, S.A. v United Mexican States*, ICSID Case No. ARB(AF)/00/2, Award, para. 154 (May 29, 2003); *Waste Management, Inc. v United Mexican States*, ICSID Case No. ARB(AF)/00/3, Award, para. 98 (Apr. 30, 2004); *MTD Equity Sdn. Bhd. and MTD Chile S.A. v Republic of Chile*, ICSID Case No. ARB/01/7, Award, para. 114 (May 24, 2004); *Occidental Exploration and Production Company v Republic of Ecuador*, UNCITRAL (LCIA Case No. UN3467), Final Award, paras. 184–187 (July 1, 2004); *Saluka Investments BV v Czech Republic*, UNCITRAL, Partial Award, paras. 307, 309, 360 (Mar. 17, 2006); *LG&E Energy Corp., LG&E Capital Corp. and LG&E International Inc. v Argentine Republic*, ICSID Case No. ARB/02/1, Decision on Liability, paras. 127–131, 137 (Oct. 3, 2006); *Champion Trading Company and Ameritrade International, Inc. v Arab Republic of Egypt*, ICSID Case No. ARB/02/9, Award, para. 4.3.2 (Oct. 27, 2006). It should also be noted that occasionally transparency has been analysed indirectly under other principles, such as non-discrimination (*Champion Trading v Egypt*, above), or arbitrariness, *Parkerings-Compagniet AS v Republic of Lithuania*, ICSID Case No. ARB/05/8, Award, para. 295 (Sept. 11, 2007).

[65] *Joseph C. Lemire v Ukraine*, ICSID Case No. ARB/06/18, Decision on Jurisdiction and Liability, paras. 284, 418 (Jan. 14, 2010); *Frontier Petroleum Services, Ltd. v Czech Republic*, UNCITRAL (PCA), Final Award, para. 285 (Nov. 12, 2010); *Ioan Micula and others v Romania*, ICSID Case No. ARB/05/20, Award, paras. 530–533 (Dec. 11, 2013); *Gold Reserve Inc. v Bolivarian Republic of Venezuela*, ICSID Case No. ARB(AF)/09/1, Award, paras. 569–570 (Sept. 22, 2014); *Mamidoil Jetoil Greek Petroleum Products Societe Anonyme S.A. v Republic of Albania*, ICSID Case No. ARB/11/24, paras. 599, 613–617; *William R. Clayton, Bilcon of Delaware and others v Government of Canada*, UNCITRAL (PCA Case No. 2009–04), Award on Jurisdiction and Liability, paras. 442–444 (Mar. 17, 2015), cited favorably by *Mesa Power Group, LLC v Government of Canada*, UNCITRAL (PCA Case No. 2012–17), Award, paras. 501–502 (Mar. 14, 2016); *Crystallex International Corporation v Bolivarian Republic of Venezuela*, ICSID Case No. ARB(AF)/11/2, Award, paras. 543, 545, 579 (Apr. 4, 2016); *Philip Morris Brand Sàrl (Switzerland) and others v Oriental Republic of Uruguay*, ICSID Case No. ARB/10/7, Award, paras. 320, 324, 486 (July 8, 2016).

[66] *Cargill, Incorporated v United Mexican States*, ICSID Case No. ARB(AF)/05/2, Award, para. 290 (Sept. 18, 2009).

[67] *Tecmed v Mexico* para. 154.

Conversely, the tribunal in *Waste Management v Mexico* adopted a more limited view, suggesting that only a "complete lack of transparency" constitutes a violation, especially within administrative processes:

> Taken together, the S.D. Myers, Mondev, ADF and Loewen cases suggest that the minimum standard of treatment of fair and equitable treatment is infringed by conduct attributable to the State and harmful to the claimant if the conduct is arbitrary, grossly unfair, unjust or idiosyncratic, is discriminatory and exposes the claimant to sectional or racial prejudice, or involves a lack of due process leading to an outcome which offends judicial propriety—as might be the case with a manifest failure of natural justice in judicial proceedings or a complete lack of transparency and candour in an administrative process.[68]

This dichotomy in standards—between the broad requirement of "total transparency" and the threshold of "complete lack of transparency"—highlights the main interpretations of transparency within international investment law. The prevailing interpretation often depends on the specific wording of the FET clause in the relevant BITs, with significant implications for the outcomes of arbitration cases and the broader application of transparency standards in international investment law.

6.3.1.3 Scope of Transparency Requirements

Substantive transparency delineates specific responsibilities regarding the dissemination of information by detailing who must disclose, what must be disclosed, to whom, where, how, and when. This examination reveals that the scope of transparency can be more precisely defined within treaty practice than in caselaw, which has led to diverse interpretative approaches regarding the application of transparency across different legal frameworks.

Personal Scope: Who Must Disclose Information? In the context of international investment law, treaties generally create obligations among states by focusing on the treatment that host states must afford foreign investors. Traditionally, transparency requirements are directed at states, not corporations; hence, the obligations typically rest with host states.[69] Caselaw has consistently recognized

---

[68] *Waste Management v Mexico* para. 98.

[69] A question of tentative delimitation is whether express transparency clauses apply to the home state, absent a specific limitation of the applicability to the host states. A literal interpretation would not exclude the application of the clause to home states, yet it could be argued that such an interpretation is devoid of practical significance for several reasons. First, due to the mutuality of treaty obligations, the transparency obligations anyway apply to both contracting states in their respective capacity as host states in relation to the other state's investors. Second, the definition of "investor" and "investment" normally exclude domestic investors and investments. Third, ISDS is normally unavailable to domestic investors. Fourth, transparency clauses normally provide for wide dissemination of information, which makes it difficult to imagine how a domestic investor might be aggrieved, except perhaps in relation to transparency in the administration of the law, but even then only to the extent domestic investors were to enjoy more limited due process rights than foreign investors.

that sudden changes in government policy without public disclosure can breach customary international law.[70] Thus, transparency in treaty terms primarily targets governmental actions rather than corporate behaviours, which are covered under different aspects of governance, like corporate transparency standards.

Material Scope: What Information Must be Disclosed? Transparency obligations under treaties generally fall into three categories: the disclosure of existing laws, the disclosure of prospective laws, and disclosure during the administration of law.[71] First, disclosure involves sharing information about laws, regulations, judicial decisions, administrative rulings, and sometimes international agreements—collectively termed "measures of general application".[72] These obligations are traditionally framed within the context of investment, with phrases like "pertaining to or affecting investments" used to define their scope.[73] The necessity to codify unwritten policies or practices arises when such measures affect investments yet are not formally documented. Questions also persist about whether these transparency obligations extend to customary law and international agreements and how the publication requirements apply to unwritten administrative practices.

Second, transparency requirements extend to the disclosure of forthcoming legislative changes by providing stakeholders the opportunity to review and comment on proposed laws. For instance, an illustrative clause may state,[74]

---

[70] *Jesse Lewis (UK v US)*, Reports of International Arbitral Awards, vol. 11, 85, 92 (UK-US Arb. Trib. 1921).

[71] Occasionally, obligations to combat corruption and other types of requirements related to good governance that do not involve disclosure of information may be categorized together with transparency provisions of the kind just described. However, such obligations do not normally involve disclosure or directly relate to the treatment of investors. They are thus better analyzed as separate categories of obligations.

[72] Treaty provisions normally do not distinguish between different levels of government. Although reference is occasionally made to central government measures, such as Article 26.2(4) TPP, clauses are normally silent on this point, in which case all levels of government would be implicated in line with general rules of interpretation.

[73] It is difficult to imagine that a claim alleging breach of transparency requirements would anyway be arbitrable without a demonstrated link of relevance between the alleged breach and the investment or the subject matter of the treaty. Moreover, it is difficult to imagine what matters might not conceivably be considered to "pertain to or affect" investments, let alone what matters might not be "covered by" an investment treaty or FTA, unless specifically excluded, given the breadth of circumstances that might give rise to "treatment" of an investor.

[74] The reference to Article 10(1)(a) is to "laws, regulations, procedures, and administrative rulings of general application". Cf. Article 11(2) U.S. model BIT (2012). Most treaties qualify the obligation with words such as "to the extent possible" or "the Contracting Parties shall endeavor". Some commentators are quick to characterize any such qualification as rendering the requirement non-binding. However, from a procedural perspective, and particularly with respect to burden of proof, caution is warranted, and attention must be given to the precise formulations used. Proving impossibility is significantly less straightforward than demonstrating a reasonable endeavour to do so. Nevertheless, any type of such a qualification provides a defence, the scope and potency of which is a matter of interpretation.

> To the extent possible, each Party shall:
>
> (a) publish in advance any measure referred to in Article 10(1)(a) that it proposes to adopt; and
> (b) provide interested persons and the other Party a reasonable opportunity to comment on such proposed measures.

Third, administrative transparency mandates that legal procedures be applied impartially and reasonably. For instance, Article 27.3 of the CETA stipulates,

> To administer a measure of general application affecting matters covered by this Agreement in a consistent, impartial and reasonable manner, each Party shall ensure that its administrative proceedings applying measures referred to in Article 27.1 to a particular person, good or service of the other Party in a specific case:
>
> (a) whenever possible, provide reasonable notice to a person of the other Party who is directly affected by a proceeding, including a description of the nature of the proceeding, a statement of the legal authority under which the proceeding is initiated and a general description of the issues in controversy;
> (b) provide a person referred to in subparagraph (a) a reasonable opportunity to present facts and arguments in support of its position prior to any final administrative action, when permitted by time, the nature of the proceeding, and the public interest; and
> (c) are conducted in accordance with its law.

This clause underscores the need for timely and clear communication in administrative processes to ensure that all parties have a fair chance to understand and respond to the proceedings.[75] It is mirrored in the following clause relating to appellate review:

> Each Party shall ensure that, in any tribunals or procedures referred to in paragraph 1, the parties to the proceeding are provided with the right to:
>
> (a) a reasonable opportunity to support or defend their respective positions; and
> (b) a decision based on the evidence and submissions of record or, if required by its law, the record compiled by the administrative authority

The clause requires the contracting states to establish an adjudicatory appeals mechanism with impartial and independent tribunals and to ensure that appellate decisions are implemented.[76]

[75] Note that the duty to give notice applies "whenever possible", which as discussed earlier allows for strict interpretation. Exceptional situations where (advance) notice may not be possible are commonly known in the municipal plane, such as the implementation of freezing orders and other cases where an element of surprise is necessary and appropriate. Note also that not much room is left for third-party participation in the proceedings. The requirement of being "directly affected by a proceeding" does not exclude third-party intervention, but leaves little room for amici curiae. The absence of an obligation to give public notice of the proceedings means that third parties that are not directly affected would not be guaranteed to gain knowledge of the proceedings.

[76] Cf. Article 27.4(2) CETA.

The fundamental due process requirements codified in this clause must be ensured to apply in any adjudicatory proceeding instituted as an appellate review. It guarantees, firstly, that parties to such proceedings are entitled to a "reasonable opportunity to support or defend their respective positions" and, secondly, that the appellate decision be based on the "evidence and submissions of record". While the wording does not spell out that access to the evidence and submissions of record must be granted to the parties to the proceedings, a party must be afforded a reasonable opportunity to support or defend its position, which is impeded when denied access. It is difficult to imagine how a position can be defended without knowing what evidence or submissions to defend against. Therefore, the second subclause is integral to the interpretation of the first subclause.

In recent treaties, a tendency can be detected to limit the material scope of transparency obligations. For example, Article 8.10 of the CETA, mentioned above, limits the concept of FET to a finite number of situations, including a "fundamental breach of due process, including a fundamental breach of transparency, in judicial and administrative proceedings". Similar examples abound in the most recent investment treaties,[77] which prompts the question of how such practices should be interpreted.

Arbitration panels have aligned the material scope of transparency with treaty practices but have also recognized the need for clarity in legal requirements. For instance, in *Metalclad v Mexico*, the tribunal noted,

> All relevant legal requirements for the purpose of initiating, completing and successfully operating investments made, or intended to be made, under the Agreement should be capable of being readily known to all affected investors of another Party. There should be no room for doubt or uncertainty on such matters. Once the authorities of the central government of any Party (whose international responsibility in such matters has been identified in the preceding section) become aware of any scope for misunderstanding or confusion in this connection, it is their duty to ensure that the correct position is promptly determined and clearly stated so that investors can proceed with all appropriate expedition in the confident belief that they are acting in accordance with all relevant laws.[78]

The discussions surrounding the material scope of transparency in international investment law highlight the important role of detailed and accessible legal information in ensuring the FET of investors. The *Metalclad* definition was echoed by the *Tecmed* tribunal, which understood the transparency requirement to ensure

> that [the foreign investor] may know beforehand any and all rules and regulations that will govern its investments, as well as the goals of the relevant policies and administrative practices or directives, to be able to plan its investment and comply with such regulations.[79]

[77] See, e.g. EU-Kazakhstan ECPA (2016), which subjects the transparency chapter to a catalogue of general exceptions modeled on Article XX GATT (1994).

[78] *Metalclad v Mexico* para. 76.

[79] *Tecmed v Mexico* para.154.

Thus, the *Tecmed* tribunal identified transparency with the material scope of the first category of treaty transparency clauses, interpreted broadly to also cover policies, practices, and directives. It made no mention of a duty to clarify. Another aspect was added by the tribunal in *Frontier* v *Czech Republic,* which stated,

> Transparency means that the legal framework for the investor's operations is readily apparent and that any decisions of the host state affecting the investor can be traced to that legal framework.[80]

By emphasizing that transparency covers the legal basis of state decisions, the Frontier tribunal incorporated the principle of legality, which corresponded to the final limb of the treaty clause on administrative transparency, as discussed above. Its inclusion was a further step towards affirming transparency in the administration of law by highlighting the notice requirement of due process (i.e. that an administrative act that adversely affects a person must be preceded by notice, setting forth, among others, the legal basis of the act).

Modal Scope: How, Where, and to Whom Must Information be Disclosed? Treaty texts usually specify the methods by which information should be disclosed, such as publication, notification, or other forms of public availability.[81] The designated platforms for disclosure may include official gazettes or websites, and the intended recipients are often the investors, the home state, or the general public.[82] The method and format of disclosure may vary based on whether the information pertains to existing legal measures, proposed changes, or administrative processes.

Temporal Scope: When Must Information be Disclosed? Effective transparency requires timely disclosure. Treaty norms often mandate that laws and regulations be disclosed "promptly", though the interpretation of prompt can vary.[83] With respect to proposed measures, treaties generally require that these be made public "in advance" of adoption, with a "reasonable opportunity" provided for comment to ensure stakeholders have adequate time to engage with and respond to proposed legal changes. In administrative and adjudicatory settings, the timing of disclosures is crucial, ensuring that all parties have sufficient time to prepare and present their case.

Interim Summary. The integration of these elements into treaty and arbitration practices demonstrates the comprehensive approach required to operationalize transparency in international investment law, which highlights the complexity and the necessity of clear guidelines for the effective implementation of

[80] *Frontier v Czech Republic* para. 285.

[81] See, e.g. Article 10(1) U.S. model BIT (2012), cf. Article 12.3 EU-Korea FTA.

[82] See, e.g. Article 26.2(4) TPP, which is based on Article 11(3) U.S. model BIT (2012), cf. Annex 19–8 CETA. See further, e.g. definition of "interested persons" in Article 281 EU-Ukraine Association Agreement, cf. Article 10 China-Japan-Korea Trilateral Investment Agreement.

[83] See, e.g. *Saluka v Czech Republic* para. 360; *PSEG v Turkey* para. 246; *Siemens v Argentina* para. 308; and *Micula v Romania* para. 872.

transparency standards. The complexity of transparency requirements in arbitration demonstrates the ongoing struggle to maintain legal certainty while accommodating national security interests.

6.3.1.4 Tension Between Transparency and National Security

A central characteristic of the expanded use of foreign investment control mechanisms is that states rely ever more frequently on the notion of ordre public to derogate from the protections guaranteed to investors by the investment treaties.[84] Indeed, investment screening involves Member States discretionarily restricting certain investments by foreign investors as far as the states deem them to constitute a threat to their national security or public order.[85]

The concepts of security and public order are inherently dynamic and indeterminate.[86] Defining these concepts and concretizing the concomitant scope of autonomy granted to the executive has proven to be challenging, so a certain degree of tension with regard to legal certainty appears to be unavoidable.[87] Attempts to shape the concepts have intuitively turned to instances in which risks to security or public order have been deemed intolerable in practice.[88] The viability of such a "bottom-up" "empirical approach" to deriving substance to these concepts is not just questionable. It reaches its limits when the concepts are increasingly given new and expansive interpretations.[89] The situation is aggravated by a lack of caselaw, published decisions, and communicated past practice at the EU and Member State levels.

Against this background, those subject to and affected by an investment screening measure (e.g. foreign investors and target companies) face an uphill struggle to influence the investment screening process. It is challenging for an affected foreign

[84] Nettesheim (2021); Moberg and Hindelang (2020).

[85] Ibid.

[86] Ibid. See also Velten (2020).

[87] The European Court of Justice has upheld the wide scope of the concepts of "public order" and "public security" with the resulting degree of freedom of Member States to invoke those grounds in light of their national needs, although it has determined that these concepts may be relied on only if there is a "genuine and sufficiently serious threat to a fundamental interest of society" and that derogations on the basis of these concepts "must not be misapplied so as, in fact, to serve purely economic ends", see Judgment of 14 March 2000, *Association Eglise de scientologie de Paris and Scientology International Reserves Trust v The Prime Minister*, C-54/99, EU:C:2000:124, para 17.

[88] The Court's casuistic jurisprudence with respect to the concepts of public order and public security is illustrated by Judgment of 14 March 2000, *Association Eglise de scientologie de Paris and Scientology International Reserves Trust* v *The Prime Minister*, C-54/99, EU:C:2000:124, para 21–23; Judgment of 4 June 2002, *Commission v Portugal*, C-387/98, EU:C:2002:326, para 52; Judgment of 4 June 2002, *Commission v France*, C-483/99 EU:C:2002:327, para 47–53; Judgment of 13 May 2003, *Commission v Spain*, Case C-463/00, EU:C:2003:272, para 70.

[89] See the discussion by Nettesheim (2021).

investor to question the assessments of an investment screening authority and demonstrate that the relevant investment does not pose a threat to security or public order.[90]

The situation is not unique. Similar problems arise in other areas, such as merger control and state aid.[91] Nevertheless, what sets investment screening apart is the singular reliance on an abstract standard—the concepts of security and public order—which is not necessarily meant to be concretized over time and given general content in administrative or judicial practice.[92] Indeed, these concepts ensure that investment screening authorities' discretion to act is preserved.[93]

The following section seeks to analyse these questions and examine the scope, if any, of foreign investors' right to be heard by the Commission under the FDI Screening Regulation. The conceptual dynamism and indeterminacy of the concepts of security and public order may arguably become less prejudicial to affected investors if these can effectively influence the screening process by being heard to engage in a quasi-adjudicative dialogue with the Commission in the screening procedure.

6.3.2 Case Study: The Role of the European Commission in Upholding Transparency Under the FDI Screening Regulation

The EU FDI Screening Regulation came into effect on 12 October 2020.[94] In 2023, the Commission evaluated the functioning and effectiveness of the Regulation and presented a report to the European Parliament and the Council.[95] The report

[90] Although the concepts of "public security" and "public order" are to be interpreted strictly and subject to judicial review (*see* Moberg and Hindelang 2020), nevertheless national courts are prone to accord a large degree of deference to the assessments of the executive branch such that the concepts of "public security" and "public order" in practice become self-judging, *see* Hagemeyer-Witzleb (2021).

[91] See e.g. Fritzsche (2010); Kreuschitz and Nehl (2016); Mendes (2016).

[92] Cf. on the "harmonizing effects" of the FDI Screening Regulations, see further Moberg and Hindelang (2020).

[93] The ECJ has consistently held that systems of prior authorization in the form of "golden shares" that are subject to "wide discretionary powers" fail to meet the requirement of proportionality, see Judgment of 4 June 2002, *Commission v France*, C-483/99, EU:C:2002:327, para 51. By contrast, Article 4 of the FDI Screening Regulation enumerates criteria to be taken into consideration in assessing whether an investment constitutes a threat to security or public order. For further discussion, see Zwartkruis and De Jong (2020).

[94] Regulation (EU) 2019/452 of the European Parliament and the Council of 19 March 2019 establishing a framework for the screening of foreign direct investments into the Union.

[95] Cf. Article 15(1) of the Regulation. See European Commission. (2021). Communication from the Commission to the European Parliament and the Council: Advancing European Economic Security: An Introduction to Five New Initiatives (COM/2024/22 final); Commission Staff

recommended amendments to the Regulation and was accompanied by an appropriate legislative proposal.[96] In preparation for the report, the European Commission decided in 2021 to commission a study by the OECD Secretariat to analyze the effectiveness and efficiency of the EU framework for investment screening.[97] In November 2022, the OECD Secretariat released its study, which identified 12 issues that it recommended to be addressed in a future reform of the Regulation.[98]

Information sharing among the Member States and the European Commission was a recurring issue identified in the OECD study.[99] This internal transparency contrasts with external transparency, an issue that the OECD study did not address in its recommendations. Although the study identified different practices of (external) transparency prior to the entry into force of the Regulation,[100] it did not analyze whether such differences persist and how such differences impact the effectiveness and efficiency of the Regulation.

With an understanding of the European Commission's strategic role in FDI screening, it is relevant to dissect the specific elements of procedural transparency as they are applied within the EU framework. The next subsection evaluates the regulatory guidelines and actual practices that govern transparency in EU investment screenings while highlighting the strengths and areas in need of improvement. Thus, the following subsections examine the applicable framework for procedural transparency under the Regulation (6.3.2.1) and outline the composite nature of the investment screening process foreseen under the FDI Screening Regulation and specifically the role of the Commission in that process (6.3.2.2). The section analyzes the scope of application of the right to be heard in EU law in the context of the Commission's role in the investment screening process (6.3.2.3) and examines the material content that the right to be heard as applied to the investment screening process, specifically the duty to notify affected investors of the relevant elements forming part of the Commission's assessment and investigation and the

Working Document Evaluation of Regulation (EU) 2019/452 of the European Parliament and of the Council of 19 March 2019 establishing a framework for the screening of foreign direct investments into the Union Accompanying the document Proposal for a Regulation of the European Parliament and of the Council on the screening of foreign investments in the Union and repealing Regulation (EU) 2019/452 of the European Parliament and of the Council.

[96] Proposal for a REGULATION OF THE EUROPEAN PARLIAMENT AND OF THE COUNCIL on the screening of foreign investments in the Union and repealing Regulation (EU) 2019/452 of the European Parliament and of the Council. Cf. Article 15(2) of the Regulation.

[97] European Commission. (2021). Report from the Commission to the European Parliament and the Council. First Annual Report on the screening of foreign direct investments into the Union. COM/2021/714 final.https://eur-lex.europa.eu/legal-content/EN/TXT/?uri=ELEX%3A52021DC0714qid=1,637,773,254,396.

[98] OECD. (2022). Framework for Screening Foreign Direct Investment into the EU Assessing Effectiveness and Efficiency.https://www.oecd.org/investment/investment-policy/oecd-eu-fdi-screening-assessment.pdf.

[99] Ibid. See issues 9–12.

[100] Ibid. para. 42 at p. 19.

opportunity of affected investors to express their views (6.3.2.4). The section concludes with a reflection on the implications of the legal certainty of foreign investors' exercise of their right to be heard (6.3.2.5).

6.3.2.1 Procedural Transparency in EU Investment Screening

The Regulation contains no detailed provisions for procedural transparency. Although Article 3(2), recalling recital (15), declares that "[r]ules and procedures relating to screening mechanisms, including relevant timeframes, shall be transparent and not discriminate between third countries", no further guidance is provided. Instead, the question of procedural transparency is primarily addressed by the law governing the investment screening procedure (i.e. Member State national law). In addition, at the EU level, procedural transparency applies as a matter of general EU law, notably the fundamental right to good administration, which includes the rights to be heard and to access files.[101] These rights apply to the European Commission[102] and Member States acting within the scope of EU law.[103]

The right to be heard applies whenever an individual measure is taken that affects the person concerned adversely,[104] as well as at every stage of a judicial or administrative proceeding leading to such a decision.[105] The right gives persons concerned by a measure the possibility of communicating their informed opinion and perspective before the measure is adopted. Caselaw has interpreted the purpose of the right to be heard to imply that the person concerned should have the possibility of influencing the decision-making process in question.[106] Having such a possibility is conducive to ensuring that the decision to be adopted at the end of the procedure is not vitiated by material errors and is the outcome of an appropriate balancing of the public interests and the individual interests of the person concerned.[107] Therefore, a person concerned must have had the opportunity to formulate comments on the basis of relevant information. Thus, the right to be

[101] Article 41 of the Charter of Fundamental Rights of the EU (CFR), specifically Article 41(a)-(b). For a comprehensive treatment of the subject, see Mihaescu Evans (2015) 153–192; Azoulai (2000) §§194–334. See also Pohl (2021) 647–661.

[102] Judgment of 11 November 1981, *IBM v Commission*, Case 60/81, EU:C:1981:264, para. 9; Lenaerts et al. (2015) para. 7.161.

[103] In fact, pursuant to Article 51(1) the Member States, when implementing Union law, are also obliged to respect the right. Moreover, as a general principle of law, the right to be heard has been interpreted as being applicable to Member States when they act within the scope of EU law. Mihaescu Evans (2015) 179–180.

[104] An "individual" measure is to be distinguished from a measure of general application. Judgment of 17 March 2011, *AJD Tuna Ltd*, C-221/09, EU:C:2011:153, para. 49–56.

[105] Eckes and Mendes (2011); Mihaescu Evans (2015) 154–156.

[106] Judgment of 2 July 2014, *Psarras v ENISA*, F-63/13, EU:F:2014:177, paras. 34, 35, 41.

[107] Judgment of 14 Sept. 2011, *Marcuccio v Commission*, T-236/02, EU:T:2011:465, para. 115.

heard implies having been provided this information on which to base such comments.

Caselaw affirms that the person concerned must be placed in a position in which they may effectively make known their views (1) on the grounds advanced against them,[108] (2) on the truthfulness and relevance of the facts and circumstances alleged in support of such grounds,[109] including (3) the documents and other evidence obtained by the authority in question to support its claim,[110] and (4) the observations submitted by interested third parties.[111] In other words, the persons concerned must be appropriately informed to make meaningful comments. It is this implied aspect of the right to be heard that provides for and requires procedural transparency.

In principle, the authority taking the relevant measure is under an obligation to disclose to the persons concerned all the information in the file that might be useful for their defence.[112] However, this does not mean that the disclosure of such breadth must be made at the competent authority's initiative. Instead, all that the authority must communicate initially is "sufficiently precise information" to enable the persons concerned to effectively state their point of view.[113] It is then up to the persons concerned to request and obtain further information that is useful to effectively exercise the right to be heard.[114]

Precisely what information needs to be disclosed so that the person concerned has an effective opportunity to be heard is linked to the right to effective judicial protection. Accordingly, the persons concerned must understand the reasons for a decision related to them, either in the document communicating the decision or by requesting and obtaining disclosure, to make it possible to defend their rights in the best possible conditions and to decide, with full knowledge of the relevant facts, whether to challenge the relevant measure.[115] It follows that if the reasons disclosed in the decision are incongruent with the reasons disclosed before hearing the person concerned, the authority evidently did not disclose all the information in advance on which it subsequently based its decision and which might have been useful for the defence.[116]

---

[108] *Commission v Lisrestal,* C-32/95 P, EU:C:1996:402 and Judgment of 21 Sept. 2000, *Mediocurso v Commission*, C-462/98 P, EU:C:2000:480, para. 36.

[109] Judgment of 10 July 1986, *Belgium v Commission*, Case 40/85, EU:C:1986:305, paras. 27–28.

[110] Judgment of 15 Nov. 2011, *Commission and Spain v Government of Gibraltar and the United Kingdom*, C-106/09 P and C/107/09 P, EU:C:2011:732, para. 165.

[111] Ibid.

[112] Judgment of 29 June 1995, *ICI v Commission*, T-36/91, EU:T:1995:118, paras. 69–70, and Judgment of 29 June 1995, *ICI v Commission*, T-37/91, EU:T:1995:119, paras. 49–50.

[113] Judgment of 22 Sept. 2015, *First Islamic Investment Bank v Council*, EU:T:2015:667, para. 79.

[114] Judgment of 6 Sept. 2013, *Bank Melli Iran v Council*, T-35/10 and T-7/11, EU:T:2013:397, para. 84.

[115] Judgment of 4 June 2013, *ZZ*, C-300/11, EU:C:2013:363, para. 53. See also Article 41(2)(c) CFR.

[116] Judgment of 18 July 2013, *Commission v Kadi*, C-584/10 P, C/593/10 P and C/595/10 P, EU: C:2013:518, para. 111.

The right to be heard is further supplemented by the right of access to the file. That right is subject to a confidentiality exception, however, the equivalent of which does not apply to the right to be heard.[117] Although the right to access the file is more circumscribed than the right to be heard, it does not follow that documents that are lawfully withheld on the basis of confidentiality can necessarily be relied on as evidence.[118] Unless other evidence can be adduced to support a particular factual finding, a decision that relies on non-disclosed evidence violates the right to be heard.[119]

6.3.2.2 The European Commission's Investment Screening Role

Under the FDI Screening Regulation, the responsibility for undertaking screening and adopting screening decisions remains with the Member States.[120] The Regulation does not empower the Commission to "authorise", "condition", "prohibit", or "unwind" investment.[121] Rather, the task of the Commission is to issue opinions within the meaning of Article 288 TFEU to Member States with respect to investment planned, completed or undergoing screening in a Member State (a) which the Commission considers likely to affect security or public order in more than one Member State,[122] (b) in relation to which the Commission has relevant information,[123] (c) at the request, or following the consideration, of Member States in certain situations,[124] or (d) which the Commission considers likely to affect projects or programmes of Union interest on the grounds of security or public order.[125]

---

[117] The right of access to the file is limited by the "legitimate interests of confidentiality and of professional and business secrecy", Article 41(2)(b) CFR. On the relation between the right of access to the file and the right to be heard, see Mihaescu Evans (2015) 198–200.

[118] Article 64 of the Rules of Procedure of the General Court.

[119] Judgment of 7 January 2004, *Aalborg Portland v Commission*, C-204/00 P, C-205/00 P, C-211/00 P, C-213/00 P, C-217/00 P and C-219/00 P, EU:C:2004:6, paras. 68, 71, 73–75.

[120] See, e.g. Articles 1(1), 1(3) and 3.

[121] For these elements of the definition of "screening", see Article 2(3) of the FDI Screening Regulation. By contrast, the other elements ("assess" and "investigate") appear to be integral to the process of providing an opinion pursuant to Articles 6(3), 7(2) and 8(1) of the Regulation.

[122] Articles 6(3) and 7(2) of the FDI Screening Regulation.

[123] Ibid.

[124] Articles 6(3), fourth sentence, and 7(3), fourth sentence, of the FDI Screening Regulation provide that the Commission shall issue an opinion where justified, after at least one third of Member States consider that an investment is likely to affect their security or public order. In addition, Articles 6(4) and 7(3) of the Regulation provide that a Member State which duly considers that an investment in its territory is likely to affect its security or public order may request the Commission to issue an opinion, or other Member States to provide comments.

[125] Article 8(1) of the FDI Screening Regulation.

It is then left to the Member States to consider the Commission's opinions before taking action.[126] Procedurally, the Regulation distinguishes between three scenarios.

Scenario 1. First, in the event of an investment undergoing screening in the territory of a Member State, the screening procedure at the EU level is initiated by the Member State undertaking the screening (i.e. the Screening Member State). This Member State shall notify the Commission and the other Member States of the relevant investment as soon as possible. The notification shall include the following information:

1. the ownership structure of the foreign investor and of the undertaking in which the investment is planned or has been completed, including information on the ultimate investor and participation in the capital;
2. the approximate value of the investment;
3. the products, services and business operations of the foreign investor and of the undertaking in which the investment is planned or has been completed;
4. the Member States in which the foreign investor and the undertaking in which the investment is planned or has been completed conduct relevant business operations;
5. the funding of the investment and its source, on the basis of the best information available to the Member State;
6. the date when the investment is planned to be completed or has been completed.[127]

The receipt of this initial notification triggers a fast-paced procedure whereby, within 15 calendar days, the other Member States who may provide comments[128] (i.e. Commenting Member States) and the Commission shall notify the Screening Member State of their intention to provide comments or an opinion.[129] At the same time, the Commenting Member States and the Commission may request additional information.[130] The general rule is then that a Commenting Member State has up to

---

[126] Articles 6(9) and 7(7) of the Regulation provide that the Member State undertaking the screening or the Member State where the investment is planned or has been completed shall give "due consideration" to Commission opinions issued pursuant to Articles 6 and 7, respectively. With respect to opinions issued pursuant to Article 8, the Member State where the investment is planned or has been completed shall take "utmost account" of the opinion and provide an explanation to the Commission if the opinion is not followed.

[127] Articles 6(1) and 9(2) of the FDI Screening Regulation. Article 6(1) also provides that the notification may include a list of Member States whose security or public order the Screening Member State deems likely to be affected, and that, where applicable, the Screening Member State shall endeavour to indicate whether it considers that the foreign direct investment undergoing screening is likely to fall within the scope of EU Merger Regulation.

[128] Comments may be provided by any Member State which considers that an FDI undergoing screening in another Member State is likely to affect its security or public order, or has information relevant for such screening, Article 6(2) of the FDI Screening Regulation.

[129] Article 6(6) of the FDI Screening Regulation. The timeframes for Member States to provide comments and for the Commission to issue an opinion may be derogated from in the exceptional case where the Screening Member State considers that its security or public order requires immediate action, Article 6(8) of the Regulation.

[130] Article 6(6) of the FDI Screening Regulation. Any request for additional information shall be duly justified, limited to information necessary for the Commenting Member States to provide

35 calendar days following the receipt of the initial notification to provide comments unless it has requested additional information, in which case its comments are due no later than 20 calendar days following receipt of the additional information.[131] The timeline applicable to the Commission is, in principle, the same, except that it has another five calendar days to issue an opinion following the comments from the Member States.[132]

Scenario 2. Second, in the event of an investment which is planned or completed in a Member State but not undergoing screening in that Member State, the procedure is different. There is no initial notification, but Commenting Member States and the Commission may provide comments or an opinion within a reasonable period, which may not exceed 15 months after the investment is completed.[133] However, in the likely situation that the Commenting Member States or the Commission requests information from the Member State where the investment is planned or was completed, the comments or opinion shall be provided no later than 35 calendar days following receipt of such information.[134]

In both scenarios, the Commission is empowered to issue an opinion on whether the investment is likely to affect security or public order in more than one Member State or whether the Commission has relevant information in relation to the investment.[135] Moreover, the Commission is required to issue an opinion in two situations: (a) where justified, after at least one-third of Member States consider that FDI is likely to affect their security or public order,[136] and (b) upon the request of a Member State which duly considers that FDI in its territory is likely to affect its security or public order.[137] The Commission's opinion shall be addressed to the Screening Member State or the Member State where the investment is planned or

---

comments or for the Commission to issue an opinion, proportionate to the purpose of the request and not unduly burdensome for the Screening Member State, Article 6(6), second subparagraph, of the Regulation.

[131] Article 6(7), first and second subparagraph, of the FDI Screening Regulation. In the case of a request for additional information, there is no precise outer limit for when the Screening Member State must deliver the requested information. However, Article 9(5) of the Regulation provides that a Screening Member State shall notify the Commission and the Commenting Member States without delay, if, in exceptional circumstances, it is unable, despite its best efforts, to obtain the requested information. The Screening Member State shall then duly justify the reasons for not providing such information and explain the best efforts undertaken to obtain the information requested.

[132] Article 6(7), third subparagraph, of the FDI Screening Regulation.

[133] Article 7(8) of the FDI Screening Regulation.

[134] Article 7(6) of the FDI Screening Regulation.

[135] Articles 6(3), first sentence, and 7(2), first sentence, of the FDI Screening Regulation. The Commission may issue an opinion irrespective of whether other Member States have provided comments. The Commission may also issue an opinion following comments from other Member States.

[136] Articles 6(3), fourth sentence, and 7(2), fourth sentence, of the FDI Screening Regulation.

[137] Articles 6(4) and 7(3) of the FDI Screening Regulation.

has been completed, and the latter Member State shall give "due consideration" to the opinion.[138]

Scenario 3. Third, in the event that the Commission considers an investment likely to affect projects or programmes of Union interest on grounds of security or public order, the procedures described above apply mutatis mutandis with two differences that are notable in the context of this chapter: (a) the opinion shall be sent to all Member States, not only to the Member State to which it is addressed, and (b) the latter Member State shall take "utmost account" of the opinion and provide an explanation to the Commission if the opinion is not followed.[139]

Interim conclusion. Investment screening under the Regulation, which involves the Commission according to each of the three scenarios described above, can be characterized as a composite administrative procedure (i.e. a decision-making process with input from administrative actors from different jurisdictions) where the final decision issued by a Member State is based on procedures involving the more or less formalized input of the various participating authorities.[140] In each scenario, the final screening decision, if any, is taken by a Member State, but with the possible[141] input of other Member States and the Commission.

6.3.2.3 Transparency and the Right to be Heard

At the EU level, the right to be heard is fundamental and a general principle of law.[142] The right generally applies to the adoption of acts of EU bodies and may be invoked in an action for annulment.[143] Can it also apply to the adoption of a screening opinion by the European Commission under Articles 6(3), 7(2) and 8(1) of the FDI Screening Regulation? If a foreign investor adversely affected by a screening opinion has the right to be heard before the Commission issues an opinion, what would that right imply more concretely? On what elements would the investor be heard? Would the investor be given an opportunity to express views on whether the facts of the file are true and relevant, or would the investor also be entitled to support those views with evidence (i.e. counter-evidence) to challenge preliminary risk assessments concerning security or public order? This issue raises

---

[138] Article 6(3), first sentence, 6(7), first sentence, and 6(9) of the FDI Screening Regulation, and, respectively, Article 7(2), first sentence, 7(6), first sentence, and 7(7) of the Regulation.

[139] Article 8(1) and 8(2) of the FDI Screening Regulation.

[140] See Eliantonio (2014) 68.

[141] As discussed above, the comments of other Member States and the opinions of the Commission are facultative in so far as the Member States and the Commission, respectively, enjoy discretion in deciding whether to provide input and with respect to the material content of that input. Note, however, the instances where the Commission is required to issue an opinion.

[142] For a comprehensive treatment of the subject, see Mihaescu Evans (2015) 153–192; Azoulai (2000) §§194–334.

[143] Judgment of 11 November 1981, *IBM v Commission*, Case 60/81, EU:C:1981:264, para. 9; Lenaerts et al. (2015) para. 7.161.

the question of whether the Commission would be obliged to consider the counter-evidence before issuing its opinion.

Audi alteram partem. The principle known as audi alteram partem (i.e. the right to be heard) is of ancient origin and has been received from the Member States' national legal systems as a fundamental right and a general principle of EU law, which is applicable to judicial as well as administrative proceedings.[144] As enshrined in Article 41(2)(a) of the Charter of Fundamental Rights of the EU (CFR), all persons have the right to be heard before any individual measure that would affect them adversely is taken. The right to be heard is vested in "any person" and is incumbent on "the institutions, bodies, offices and agencies of the Union".[145] In principle, the right applies at every stage of a composite administrative procedure.[146]

The right to be heard applies whenever an individual measure is taken that affects the person concerned adversely.[147] A measure may be deemed to affect a person adversely to the extent such person's interests are "significantly affected" or "perceptibly affected" or if the measure is capable of "directly affecting a given legal situation".[148]

Adverse effect. The question of whether an individual measure has an adverse effect can be distinguished from the question of whether the measure is intended to have legal effect. The former concerns the material scope of protection of the right to be heard, whereas the latter concerns the jurisdiction of the EU Courts, namely the existence of a reviewable EU act for purposes of an action for annulment. An opinion by the Commission pursuant to Articles 6(3), 7(2) and 8(1) of the FDI Screening Regulation could significantly affect the interests of the relevant foreign investor, particularly a decision to condition, prohibit or unwind an investment, even though the opinion as such would not be susceptible to annulment. It follows expressly from Article 263 TFEU and generally from EU caselaw that annulment is open only to measures adopted by the institutions, which are intended to have a legally binding effect.[149]

Thus, while the existence of a legally binding effect may be indicative of an adverse effect, the inverse is not necessarily true. In the past, infringement of the right to be heard has been successfully argued in the context of legally non-binding

---

[144] Eckes and Mendes (2011); Mihaescu Evans (2015) 154–156.

[145] In fact, pursuant to Article 51(1) the Member States, when implementing Union law, are also obliged to respect the right. Moreover, as a general principle of law, the right to be heard has been interpreted as being applicable to Member States when they act within the scope of EU law. Mihaescu Evans (2015) 179–180.

[146] Mihaescu Evans (2015) 95. See the discussion below regarding the distinction between "legal effect" and "adverse effect". See also Inghelram (2011) 132–133.

[147] An "individual" measure is to be distinguished from a measure of general application. Judgment of 17 March 2011, *AJD Tuna Ltd*, C-221/09, EU:C:2011:153, para. 49–56.

[148] Judgment of 24 Oct. 1996, *Commission v Lisrestal,* C-32/95 P, EU:C:1996:402, para. 21; see further Mihaescu Evans (2015) 168–175; Bignami (2003).

[149] Judgment of 11 November 1981, *IBM v Commission*, Case 60/81, EU:C:1981:264, para. 9.

EU measures and reviewed directly in actions for damages under Article 340(2) TFEU.[150] Moreover, when a Member State authority adopts the final measure, the validity of an intermediate EU measure may be raised during national proceedings and challenged indirectly before the EU Courts through a reference for a preliminary ruling pursuant to Article 267 TFEU.[151]

In summary, one can conclude that a foreign investor who is involved in an investment that is planned, completed, or undergoing screening in a Member State and who is liable to be adversely affected by an opinion by the Commission under the FDI Screening Regulation is entitled to a fair hearing by the Commission before it issues the opinion. A separate (but linked) question, which falls outside the scope of this chapter, is how effective the remedies that are available to the investor in the case of an infringement of the right to be heard at the interim stage are.[152]

6.3.2.4 The Material Content of the Right to be Heard

Once applicable, the right to be heard gives persons concerned by an adverse measure the possibility to communicate their informed opinion and perspective before the measure is adopted. The purpose of the right to be heard has been interpreted in caselaw to imply, in substance, that the persons concerned should have the possibility of influencing the decision-making process in question,[153] which is conducive to ensuring that material errors do not vitiate the decision to be adopted and that it is the outcome of an appropriate balancing of the public interests and the individual interests of the persons concerned.[154] Hence, the persons concerned must have had the opportunity to formulate their communication on the basis of relevant information, as further discussed below. Thus, the right to be heard can be conceptualized for analytical purposes as consisting of two constituent sub-rights: the right to obtain information (i.e. the notification of relevant elements) and the right to impart information (i.e. the opportunity to express views).

Notification of relevant elements. The right to be heard requires the competent authority to ensure that the persons concerned are placed in a position in which they may effectively make known their views on the grounds advanced against

[150] Judgment of 8 July 2008, *Franchet and Byk v Commission,* T-48/05, EU:T:2008:257, para. 398; see also Judgment of 20 May 2010, *Commission v Violetti,* T-261/09 P, EU:T:2010:215, para. 59.

[151] See further Eliantonio (2014) 81–82.

[152] The opinion is not legally binding and cannot (normally) be annulled. Although such an infringement may contaminate the final Member State act and could result in a preliminary question of the validity of the opinion, it should be recalled that access to the EU Courts via the preliminary reference procedure is not available to applicants as of right.

[153] Judgment of 2 July 2014, *Psarras v ENISA*, F-63/13, EU:F:2014:177, paras. 34, 35, 41.

[154] Judgment of 14 Sept. 2011, *Marcuccio v Commission*, T-236/02, EU:T:2011:465, para. 115.

them[155] and the truthfulness and relevance of the facts and circumstances alleged in support of such grounds,[156] including the documents and other evidence obtained by the competent authority in question to support its claim,[157] as well as observations submitted by interested third parties.[158] In other words, the persons concerned must be appropriately informed to make meaningful comments.

Variable material scope. The material scope of the notice requirement is dynamic. There is no fixed set of information that must be conveyed. In principle, the competent authority is obliged to disclose to the persons concerned all the information in the file that may be useful for their defence.[159] However, it does not mean that disclosure of such breadth must be made spontaneously (i.e. at the competent authority's initiative). Rather, all the authority must communicate initially is "sufficiently precise information" to enable the persons concerned to effectively state their points of view.[160] Subsequently, the onus shifts to the persons concerned to request and obtain further information.[161]

Elements of a notice. A notice may set forth a summary of the elements on which the proposed measure is to be based. In the context of an impending opinion under the FDI Screening Regulation, it may require a summary of (a) information referred to in Article 9(2) of the Regulation, (b) information requested pursuant to Article 6(6) or 7(5) of the Regulation, and (c) other information available to the Commission that is relevant to the investment that is planned, completed, or undergoing screening.

Regarding the level of detail of this summary, a connection can be made between the right to be heard and the right to effective judicial protection. The latter requires that the persons concerned must be able to ascertain ex-post facto the reasons upon which the decision taken related to them is based, either by reading the decision or by requesting and obtaining disclosure of those reasons to make it possible to defend their rights in the best possible conditions and to decide, with full knowledge of the relevant facts, whether to challenge the relevant measure.[162] It follows that if the reasons disclosed ex-post facto were incongruent with the reasons disclosed ex-ante facto (i.e. before the hearing), then the competent authority evidently did not disclose all the information on which it based its

---

[155] *Commission v Lisrestal*, C-32/95 P, EU:C:1996:402 and Judgment of 21 Sept. 2000, *Mediocurso v Commission*, C-462/98 P, EU:C:2000:480, para. 36.

[156] Judgment of 10 July 1986, *Belgium v Commission*, Case 40/85, EU:C:1986:305, paras. 27–28.

[157] Judgment of 15 Nov. 2011, *Commission and Spain v Government of Gibraltar and the United Kingdom*, C-106/09 P and C/107/09 P, EU:C:2011:732, para. 165.

[158] Ibid.

[159] Judgment of 29 June 1995, *ICI v Commission*, T-36/91, EU:T:1995:118, paras. 69–70, and Judgment of 29 June 1995, *ICI v Commission*, T-37/91, EU:T:1995:119, paras. 49–50.

[160] Judgment of 22 Sept. 2015, *First Islamic Investment Bank v Council*, EU:T:2015:667, para. 79.

[161] Judgment of 6 Sept. 2013, *Bank Melli Iran v Council*, T-35/10 and T-7/11, EU:T:2013:397, para. 84.

[162] Judgment of 4 June 2013, *ZZ*, C-300/11, EU:C:2013:363, para. 53.

decision and which may have been useful for the defence. A requirement for such congruence is therefore implied.

This link was first explicitly recognized in *Commission* v *Kadi*, where the competent authority was required to disclose to the person concerned the evidence against that person which was available to the authority and was relied upon by it as the basis of its decision

> so that that individual is in a position to defend his rights in the best possible conditions and to decide, with full knowledge of the relevant facts, whether there is any point in bringing an action before the Courts of the European Union.[163]

Congruence of reasons. The need for congruence of reasons stated before and after the measure is adopted also means that certain de minimis information must be reflected in the notice, which follows since the right to effective judicial protection requires that the decision be adequately motivated to permit—as part of a review of the lawfulness of the grounds of the measure—that the measure is taken on a sufficiently solid factual basis[164]:

> That entails a verification of the factual allegations in the summary of reasons underpinning that decision [. . .], with the consequence that judicial review cannot be restricted to an assessment of the cogency in the abstract of the reasons relied on, but must concern whether those reasons, or, at the very least, one of those reasons, deemed sufficient in itself to support that decision, is substantiated.[165]

Therefore, congruence between the notice and the statement of reasons requires that this "floor" of minimum information also be reflected in the notice.

Similarly, one can argue for a form of a "ceiling" in terms of what the notification of elements must contain. Here, the right to be heard transitions into the right of access to the file, which is separately protected under Article 41(2)(b) CFR. This right is subject to a confidentiality exception; however, the equivalent of this does not apply to the right to be heard.[166] Although the right to access the file is thus more circumscribed than the right to be heard, it does not follow that documents that are lawfully withheld under Article 41(2)(b) of the CFR can be relied on as evidence.[167] Unless other evidence can be adduced to support a particular factual finding, a finding that relies on non-disclosed evidence is impossible to sustain.[168]

Applied to the context of investment screening, the Commission would be able to invoke its legitimate interests of confidentiality and professional secrecy to deny

---

[163] Judgment of 18 July 2013, *Commission v Kadi*, C-584/10 P, C/593/10 P and C/595/10 P, EU:C:2013:518, para. 111.

[164] Ibid., para. 119.

[165] Ibid.

[166] The right of access to the file is limited by the "legitimate interests of confidentiality and of professional and business secrecy", Article 41(2)(b) CFR. On the relation between the right of access to the file and the right to be heard, see Mihaescu Evans (2015) 198–200.

[167] Article 64 of the Rules of Procedure of the General Court.

[168] Judgment of 7 January 2004, *Aalborg Portland v Commission*, C-204/00 P, C-205/00 P, C-211/00 P, C-213/00 P, C-217/00 P and C-219/00 P, EU:C:2004:6, paras. 68, 71, 73–75.

an affected investor access to documents which either the Commission would not rely upon in its opinion or are unnecessary to support its conclusions in light of other available evidence to which the investor has access.

Finally, the material scope of factual disclosure must enable the persons concerned to comment on the "truthfulness and relevance" of the facts.[169] Thus, it is insufficient to enable the persons concerned to comment solely on the veracity of alleged facts. It is also necessary that they be in a position to communicate a point of view on the relevance of the facts.[170] Even if the truthfulness of the facts is not contested, the legal assessment of the facts may be disputed; it may be contested that the facts satisfy the applicable legal criteria required to produce the legal effects of the measure in question.[171] Therefore, the affected investor must be in a position to understand if and how the facts alleged by the Commission correspond to applicable legal requirements, notably the criteria laid down in Article 4 of the FDI Screening Regulation. The reference to "truthfulness and relevance" is a reminder that the person concerned must, in principle, be in a position to challenge the factual conclusions (i.e. cause) and the legal reasoning on which the competent authority proposes to base an impending measure (i.e. effect).

Other requirements applicable to the notice. Moving beyond the level of information to be disclosed, the notice requirement of the right to be heard also means that the affected investor must be informed in time,[172] effectively[173] and personally.[174] The timeliness requirement has two dimensions: (1) the point in time when information is disclosed and (2) the point in time when comments are due. It is clear that the information may not be disclosed so late that the investor does not have enough time to review and comment on the full file of disclosed information.[175] Indeed, if the comment period ran right up to the date of adoption of the opinion, there would not be a reasonable period for the competent authority to carefully examine the comments.

---

[169] Judgment of 25 October 2011, *Solvay v Commission,* C-109/10 P, EU:C:2011:686, para. 53.

[170] Judgment of 21 Nov. 1991, *Technische Universität München v Hauptzollamt München-Mitte,* C-269/90, EU:C:1991:438, para. 25.

[171] Eckes and Mendes (2011).

[172] Judgment of 14 July 1972, *Cassella v Commission*, Case 55/69, EU:C:1972:76, paras. 13–15.

[173] Judgment of 18 December 1992, *Cimenteries CBR v Commission*, T-10/92, T-11/92, T-12/92 and T-15/92, EU:T:1992:123, para. 38, and Judgment of 1 April 1993, *BPB Industries and British Gypsum v Commission*, T-65/89, EU:T:1993:31, paras. 29–30.

[174] Judgment of 2 Oct. 2003, *ARBED v Commission*, C-176/99 P, EU:C:2003:524, paras. 19–25. Note that, in cases where a surprise effect is essential, the hearing, and therefore also the date by which the relevant information must be disclosed, may be postponed to after the imposition of the adversely affecting measure. Such was the case in the Kadi case (n. 116). However, pursuant to Article 52(1) CFR, such an exception, which goes against the wording of Article 41(2)(a) ("before any individual measure … is taken"), "must be provided for by law and respect the essence" of the right to be heard.

[175] The time period within which to review the file would reasonably not begin to run until the file was complete.

Opportunity to express views. Once properly informed, an affected investor should be in a position to exercise its right to be heard and may provide any comments it sees fit or may choose to abstain from providing any comments. In principle, there is no particular form that a hearing must adhere to. It need not be a meeting; any opportunity to provide oral or written observations might qualify as a hearing.[176]

Scope of comments. The material scope of the comments that the person concerned is entitled to make is a reflection of the notice requirement, which the person concerned should have had the opportunity to participate in delimiting in the process of requesting and obtaining disclosure. It may potentially involve making use of any information in the file that the person concerned finds useful for defence or that may concern the factual and legal grounds of the measure.

The right to be heard includes the right of the persons concerned to present their cases, including facts and arguments in support of their position, including counter-evidence.[177] Moreover, the right to be heard requires the competent authority to receive the comments made by the persons concerned and to examine, carefully and impartially, whether the alleged reasons are well founded in the light of those comments and any exculpatory evidence provided with those comments.[178]

6.3.2.5 The Transparency-Due Process Conundrum

An unavoidable tension exists between preserving the autonomy of Member States to define their needs for security and public order and guaranteeing legal certainty. In the end, EU Courts must determine, case by case, whether Member States have acted within the limits of that autonomy. Hence, casuism is here to stay.

Under such circumstances, what is interchangeably referred to as participation rights or procedural rights, viz., the enabling of "individuals to influence a specific administrative determination before a final decision is taken",[179] are essential to avoid arbitrary use and abuse of discretion. Of these, the principle of audi alteram partem, or the right to be heard, is perhaps the most fundamental.

Although the concepts of security and public order cannot be concretized in a generally applicable manner without encroaching on the autonomy of the Member States, their application may be crystallized as to the facts of a specific case. Through the disclosure of the facts and legal analysis on which the

---

[176] Azoulai (2000) § 310.

[177] Judgment of 17 Sep. 1998, *Primex Produkte v Commission*, Case T-50/96, EU:T:1998:223, para. 63; Judgment of 9 Nov. 1995, *France-Aviation v Commission*, T-346/94, EU:T:1995:187, para. 32; Judgment of 21 Nov. 1991, *Technische Universität München v Hauptzollamt München-Mitte*, C-269/90, EU:C:1991:438, para. 25.

[178] Judgment of 21 Nov. 1991, *Technische Universität München v Hauptzollamt München-Mitte*, C-269/90, EU:C:1991:438, para. 14, and Judgment of 22 Nov. 2007, *Spain v Commission*, C-525/04 P, EU:C:2007:698, para. 58.

[179] Bignami (2003).

Commission intends to rely in rendering an opinion under the cooperation mechanisms of the FDI Screening Regulation, affected investors can attain a level of certainty as to the factors that will determine or influence the final screening decision.

The present discussion has provided a bird's-eye view outlining the applicability and application of the right to be heard in the context of an intermediate EU measure in a composite screening procedure. It has sketched the active role that an affected investor may play in the screening process. The principal shortcoming of relying on the right to be heard in intermediate-stage proceedings has been highlighted: opinions are incapable of annulment with the effect that the remedies available to investors in case of an infringement of the right to be heard are limited to direct actions for damages and questions of validity raised in national proceedings and reviewed by the EU judiciary through the preliminary reference procedure. Nevertheless, the right to be heard constitutes an essential tool whereby affected investors may seek to influence the screening process and obtain a degree of legal certainty.

6.3.3 *Balancing Confidentiality and Transparency in National Security Screenings: Blueprint for a Vicarious Transparency Mechanism*

If the EU's fundamental right to good administration, which incorporates elements of procedural transparency, is not observed at the Member State level, the Regulation guarantees that the investor concerned has a right to recourse.[180] Although this right does not clearly imply the right to judicial recourse,[181] the system of preliminary rulings assures that the EU judiciary would be involved in matters concerning the interpretation and application of EU law.[182]

In the readily imaginable case that a national screening authority in the screening procedure withheld sensitive information from the file on which a screening decision exclusively relied, would an aggrieved investor fare better before the EU Courts? The chances are slim, partly because the European Court of Justice has never developed a strict requirement that the basis on which the person concerned has a right to be heard must be meaningful, in the basic sense of being practically worthwhile to pursue.

Between the limits developed in caselaw, there is still the possibility that an authority presents incomplete information to the person concerned, which withholds information the person concerned does not know. Even where the existence of undisclosed information is known, the authority need not disclose it if it

[180] Article 3(5) of the Regulation.

[181] Verellen (2021) 22–23; Hagemeyer-Witzleb (2021) 798–800.

[182] Article 267 TFEU. See also Eliantonio (2014) 81–82.

successfully argues that it has disclosed other information that equally supports the same finding as the non-disclosed information.[183] Moreover, the Court has never developed a strict requirement that the authority should disclose its reasoning as to the relevance of facts invoked, except insofar as the relevance relates to different legal measures or effects.[184] Hence, how the authority reasons that the facts are meant to satisfy different legal requirements (i.e. the authority's legal arguments) is not something that the Court's caselaw has clearly affirmed as part of the right to be heard, apart from the oft-mentioned lofty wording that the right comprises the "truth and relevance" of facts.

Therefore, in practice, the EU protection of the rights to be heard and access to the file does not constitute an insuperable impediment to Member States' non-disclosure of sensitive confidential information. To the corresponding extent, EU law does not require that the right to be heard must serve a meaningful purpose in the case at hand. If there is no meaningful right to be heard, is there any point in seeking judicial recourse? EU caselaw on preparatory acts demonstrates that there are classes of cases where seeking redress before courts does not make sense.[185] The situation is indeed similar in the United States, where the *Ralls* case confirmed that procedural transparency (due process) only applies to the non-classified information in the file.[186]

The conclusion that it is not meaningful to challenge a screening decision before courts because of the lack of a meaningful right to be heard is further supported by another argument: that it could, in fact, not be otherwise. If procedural transparency were required, the Member State undertaking the screening would face a dilemma: either to disclose sensitive information that would be injurious to its security or public order or to intentionally violate the investor's fundamental rights. Only by excluding sensitive information from the scope of the right could the dilemma be overcome. Moreover, even if procedural transparency were required, it would not guarantee a meaningful remedy. If the screening decision was annulled, the screening authority could just continue to make the same decision again.

If the right to be heard and the right to access the file cannot provide meaningful procedural transparency, could other devices be conceived that would achieve the same aim? One possibility is that sensitive information is disclosed to a trusted third party who attests to its "truthfulness and relevance". This third party would supervise the good administration of the legal framework in question and ensure that the risks of poor procedural transparency—including overreach, factual

---

[183] See *Aalborg Portland v Commission* (n. 119).

[184] Judgment of 21 Nov. 1991, *Technische Universität München v Hauptzollamt München-Mitte*, C-269/90, EU:C:1991:438, para. 25.

[185] See, e.g. Judgment of 8 July 2008, *Franchet and Byk v Commission*, T-48/05, EU:T:2008:257, para. 398; judgment of 20 May 2010, *Commission v Violetti*, T-261/09 P, EU:T:2010:215, para. 59.

[186] *Ralls Corp. v CFIUS*, 758 F.3d 296, 305–06 (D.C. Cir. 2014). See also Eichensehr and Hwang (2023).

mistakes, and abuse—were avoided. The obvious third party is the European Commission.

Certainly, procedural transparency directed towards someone other than the party concerned cannot ensure as effectively that material errors do not vitiate the screening decision and that it appropriately balances the public interests and the individual interests of the person concerned. Only the investor would be able to address any potential error on the basis of undisclosed information and properly express its interests. Therefore, a third-party transparency mechanism would never safeguard procedural transparency to a degree equivalent to the right to be heard.

Nevertheless, a third-party transparency mechanism may provide some level of protection compared to today's absence thereof, similar to the advantage of search warrant proceedings over warrantless searches. In search warrant proceedings, the suspect of a crime is not involved. Instead, a judge or magistrate determines the existence of probable cause based on information provided by law enforcement.[187] Compared to proceedings where the suspect is involved, search warrant proceedings provide no procedural rights to the suspect. However, they are nevertheless vastly superior to warrantless searches and provide a minimum of protection of the interests of the suspect.

If the European Commission, or, better, a special board of review or audit group set up for the purpose, reviewed or audited the file of the Member State screening authority, it could effectively prevent the risk of overreach and abuse while obtaining a sense of the nature and gravity of the undisclosed, sensitive information pertaining to the investor or the investment. While it would not prevent factual errors, it would certainly reduce their likelihood. Furthermore, the Secretariat of an FTA could also be considered for this role, acting as a 'trusted third party' to ensure that the investment screening processes are fair and transparent. This broader application would not only benefit the European context but could also be adapted to other international agreements, promoting a more consistent and reliable investment environment globally.

At what stage would such a review or audit occur? It is submitted that, given the timeframes for screening, a diligent investigation of the file would be better conducted after the screening decision was made. Indeed, the purpose of preventing overreach and abuse could be equally or better served by ex-post audits than as part of the already time-stretched screening process.

What screening decisions would be audited? It seems intuitive that the investors concerned would be well placed to identify the screening decisions in need of an audit. Indeed, the audit could be understood as a form of administrative recourse, as per Article 3(5) of the Regulation, even if it is not an adjudicatory process. As such, it would be for an aggrieved investor to request an audit, and only such screenings as the request would cover would be audited. It is also conceivable that the board of review should be given the authority to initiate an audit.

[187] Similarly, see further Böse (2021); Robertson (2016); Bignami (2003).

Would the board of review's findings be binding? The risk-mitigating purpose of a third-party transparency mechanism does not require the board to have the power to issue binding rulings. In any event, such powers would be hard to reconcile with the Member States' exclusive competence in the area of their national security.[188] It would be perfectly sufficient if the board reported its findings to the European Commission, which could then initiate discussions with the Member State concerned in an effort to prevent overreach or abuse or to seek clarifications concerning the relevant information regarding the investor or investment.

What would be the composition of the board of review? Given the collective nature of the cooperation mechanisms under the Regulation, it would seem that representatives of the Member States and the European Commission ought to comprise the board's membership. This composition would institutionalize existing collaborative structures and keep the proceedings sufficiently privileged and secure. It would also promote the broader, ongoing dialogue among the Member States and the Commission as to the functioning of the investment screening framework.

Investment screening decisions can result in significant government interference with the property rights of investors. Normally, such decisions would require meticulous observance of transparency on behalf of the government. Investment screening is special, however, insofar as it is motivated by the screening State's vital security interests, which prevail over many other important interests, which is notably so with respect to procedural transparency.

The examination of the FDI Screening Regulation highlights a essential tension between the necessity for national security and the principles of transparency and procedural fairness. This analysis concludes that while the EU framework aims to safeguard essential interests, it simultaneously imposes limitations on transparency that may hinder investors' ability to effectively challenge or understand decisions affecting their investments. Similarly, the European Commission could further develop the suggestion regarding a board of review, as this was a key insight that could also apply beyond its scope. For instance, the Secretariat of an FTA could take on the role of a 'trusted third party' to ensure procedural fairness and transparency in investment screenings. This approach could harmonize practices and enhance the legitimacy of the investment screening processes across different jurisdictions.

This lack of transparency, although inherent in the nature of national security considerations, presents significant risks and challenges. For investors, the ambiguity and opacity of the screening process can make pursuing legal remedies seem futile when fundamental procedural safeguards are perceived as inadequate or

---

[188] Article 4(2) TEU; Directive 2009/81, recital 1 to the preamble; Case C-300/11 *ZZ v Secretary of State for the Home Department*, ECLI:EU:C:2013:363, para 35.

ineffectual. This situation can adversely affect the Member States conducting the screenings by undermining the legitimacy and perceived fairness of their actions. Furthermore, the potential misuse of screening mechanisms for purposes other than security threatens the integrity of the system and risks systemic degradation and the erosion of trust among economic actors.

Despite these challenges, the current regulatory framework does not provide a robust means for ensuring meaningful procedural transparency at either the administrative or judicial stages. As such, investors are left with limited recourse and insufficient remedies, which compound the perception of an imbalanced and potentially unjust system.

In response to these deficiencies, the European Commission could play an instrumental role in mitigating these risks by being empowered to audit screening decisions made by Member States. Such audits, conducted post-decision, could serve as a form of checks and balances, ensuring that decisions are made based on justifiable grounds and are not disproportionately influenced by non-security considerations.

Proposed is the establishment of a review mechanism akin to non-adjudicatory review models found elsewhere in EU governance—such as the European Ombudsman or the Administrative Boards of Review of the European Central Bank and the European Securities and Markets Authority. These models provide valuable blueprints for creating a mechanism that can oversee and evaluate state actions in a manner that respects the confidentiality required for national security and the need for procedural fairness. Additionally, the Secretariat of an FTA could potentially assume the role of a 'trusted third party', thereby extending this review mechanism's application beyond the European Commission. This could facilitate a more uniform approach to investment screenings across different FTAs, enhancing both procedural transparency and investor confidence.

This mechanism could offer a retrospective evaluation of screening decisions and proactively guide Member States by providing recommendations to harmonize practices and enhance transparency without compromising security objectives. This mechanism would ideally involve a diverse panel of experts capable of balancing security interests with investment freedoms to foster a more predictable and stable investment environment across the EU.

In conclusion, while the current state of procedural transparency in investment screening poses distinct challenges, there are mechanisms that can strengthen the system. By integrating a review mechanism that draws on successful models of non-adjudicatory oversight, the European Commission can help ensure that the dual imperatives of protecting national security and upholding the rights of investors are more harmoniously balanced. This approach can rectify current shortcomings and anticipate future challenges to pave the way for a more resilient and equitable investment screening framework.

6.3.4 Summary

The intrinsic tension between maintaining adequate transparency and protecting national security interests was a recurrent theme. Transparency is fundamental to ensuring that investment screenings are fair, predictable, justifiable, and ultimately legitimate. Nevertheless, the protective cloak of national security often necessitates a departure from full disclosure, which leads to a challenging balancing act. As states seek to shield sensitive information under the guise of security, the resultant opacity can stymie investors' ability to fully understand or challenge the decisions that affect their investments.

The case study of the European Commission's role under the FDI Screening Regulation illustrated the potential and the limitations of existing frameworks. While the Commission provides a layer of oversight, its recommendations and opinions do not bind Member States, which limits their practical impact. However, the Commission's role is pivotal in fostering a cooperative environment where Member States can share information and best practices to enhance the collective capacity to manage foreign investments more transparently and effectively.

Our exploration into the procedural rights afforded to investors revealed significant gaps, particularly in the implementation of the right to be heard. Despite legal provisions ensuring this right, practical challenges abound, from the timeliness and completeness of the information provided to investors to the actual consideration of their input in the decision-making process. These gaps undermine the effectiveness of procedural safeguards and impact investor confidence and the overall investment climate.

In light of these findings, several forward-looking solutions aimed at reconciling the need for security with the principles of fairness and transparency are proposed. Enhancing transparency in national security screenings does not necessarily require a diminution of security. Instead, innovative mechanisms, such as the introduction of a third-party review system or more robust interstate consultations within frameworks like the European Union, could provide meaningful checks without compromising sensitive state interests.

Policy reforms should focus on clarifying the scope and application of transparency measures within national security contexts by defining the thresholds of information disclosure and establishing clearer criteria for exceptions. Additionally, strengthening the procedural rights of investors by ensuring more substantial compliance with the right to be heard could mitigate some of the current criticisms of the FDI screening processes.

The critical need for ongoing reform and dialogue among all stakeholders involved in international investment arbitration is underscored. By striving for greater transparency and more robust procedural safeguards, we can aspire to create a more equitable and predictable investment screening environment that respects the security imperatives of states and the rights of investors.

6.4 Conclusion

This chapter examined the relationship between the sovereign right of states to regulate investments for national security and the principles of fairness and transparency that govern international investment law.

This exploration underscored a significant legal tension. While states possess an inherent authority to regulate economic activities within their territories, especially for national security purposes, this right must coexist with the obligations imposed by IIAs. These agreements demand that any regulatory actions be transparent, non-discriminatory, and respect the property and procedural rights of investors.

In dissecting the EU's regulatory approach, particularly through the FDI Screening Regulation, this chapter highlighted the fragile balance states must maintain. On one side, there is a compelling need to shield sensitive information on national security grounds; on the other side, an equally imperative requirement exists to ensure that the processes governing investment screenings are transparent and equitable. This balance is important for upholding legal standards and maintaining investor confidence and the integrity of the regulatory environment.

The complexities of this legal field are magnified by the practical challenges associated with implementing the FDI Screening Regulation. The regulation aims to provide a framework for the EU and its Member States to screen foreign investments effectively without compromising the Union's open investment environment. However, the effectiveness of this regulation is often hampered by ambiguities in its application and the diverse interpretations by Member States, which can lead to inconsistencies and potential biases in the screening process.

Moreover, the procedural rights of investors, particularly the right to be heard and to access relevant information, are pivotal to ensuring that investment screenings are conducted fairly. However, these rights are not always sufficiently safeguarded in practice, which leads to situations where investors may feel side-lined in the decision-making processes that directly affect their investments.

As a result, this chapter proposed enhanced roles for supranational bodies such as the European Commission to address these challenges and mitigate the risks associated with opaque regulatory practices. By empowering the Commission to audit and review Member States' screening decisions, a more harmonized and transparent approach could be established. Such measures could reinforce the legal framework and enhance the overall accountability and consistency of investment screenings across the EU.

In conclusion, while the EU strives to protect its essential security interests, it must also commit to the principles of transparency and fairness. Strengthening the procedural mechanisms within the FDI Screening Regulation can serve as a significant step towards achieving a balanced and equitable investment environment. This commitment can uphold the rights of investors while preserving the credibility of the EU's regulatory framework.

References

Azoulai L (2000) Les Garanties Procédurales en Droit Communautaire: recherches sur la Procédure et le Bon Gouvernement. EUI

Banisar D (2006) Freedom of information around the world 2006: a global survey of access to government information laws. Privacy International

Bignami F (2004) Three generations of participation rights before the European Commission. Law Contemp Probl 68(1):61–83

Bjorklund A (2010) The national treatment obligation. In: Yannaca-Small K (ed) Arbitration under international investment agreements: a guide to key issues. Oxford University Press, pp 411–444

Bonnitcha J, Skovgaard Poulsen LN, Waibel M (2017) The political economy of the investment treaty regime. Oxford University Press

Böse M (2021) Judicial protection in international and EU law. In: Böse M, Bröcker M, Schneider A (eds) Judicial protection in transnational criminal proceedings. Springer, pp 395–436

Brandeis LD (1914) Other people's money and how the bankers use it. Frederick A. Stokes

Cassese S (2005) Global standards for national administrative procedure. Law Contemp Probl 68(3):109–126

Chesney RM (2009) National security fact deference. Va Law Rev 95:1361

Della Cananea G (2010) Minimum standards of procedural justice in administrative adjudication. In: Schill S (ed) International investment law and comparative public law. Oxford University Press, pp 39–74

Dolzer R, Schreuer C (2012) Principles of international investment law, 2nd edn. Oxford University Press

Dolzer R, Kriebaum U, Schreuer C (2022) Principles of international investment law 3rd edn. Oxford University Press

Eckes C, Mendes J (2011) The right to be heard in composite administrative procedures: lost in between protection? Eur Law Rev 36(5):651–670

Eichensehr KE, Hwang C (2023) National security creep in corporate transactions. Colum Law Rev 123(2):549–614

Eliantonio M (2014) Judicial review in an integrated administration: the case of 'composite procedures'. Rev Eur Adm Law 7(2):65–102

European Commission. (2021) Report from the Commission to the European Parliament and the Council. First Annual report on the screening of Foreign direct investments into the Union. COM/2021/714 final

Fisher E (2010) Transparency and administrative law: a critical evaluation. Curr Leg Probl 63:272–314

Fritzsche A (2010) Discretion, scope of judicial review, and institutional balance in European law. Common Mark Law Rev 47(2):361–403

Hagemeyer-Witzleb TM (2021) Access to legal redress in an EU investment screening mechanism. In: Hindelang S, Moberg A (eds) YSEC yearbook of socio-economic constitutions 2020: a common European law on investment screening (CELIS). Springer, pp 795–833

Harlow C (2006) Global administrative law: the quest for principles and values. Eur J Int Law 17(1):187–214

Henckels C (2015) Proportionality and deference in investor-state arbitration: balancing investment protection and regulatory autonomy. Cambridge University Press

Inghelram JFH (2011) Legal and institutional aspects of the European Anti-Fraud Office (OLAF): an analysis with a look forward to a European public prosecutor's office. Europa Law Publishing, Groningen

Jacob M, Schill SW (2015) Fair and equitable treatment: content, practice, method. In: Bungenberg M, Griebel J, Hobe S, Reinisch A, Kim Y-I (eds) International investment law: a handbook. C. H. Beck/Hart/Nomos, pp 700–763

Katselas AT (2012) Do investment treaties prescribe a deferential standard of review? Mich J Int Law 34:87–150
Kläger R (2011) 'Fair and equitable treatment' in international investment law. Cambridge University Press
Kriebaum U (2007) Regulatory takings: balancing the interests of the investor and the state. J World Invest Trade 8:717–744
Kriebaum U (2015) Expropriation. In: Bungenberg M, Griebel J, Hobe S, Reinisch A, Kim Y-I (eds) International investment law: a handbook. C. H. Beck, pp 959–1030
Lenaerts K, Maselis I, Gutman K (2015) EU procedural law. Oxford University Press
Levmore S (1989) Parliamentary law, majority decision-making, and the voting paradox. Va Law Rev 75:971
Lockwood TJ (1967) A history of royal commissions. Osgoode Hall Law J 5(2):172–197
Mendes J (2016) Discretion, care, and public interests in the EU administration: probing the limits of law. Common Mark Law Rev 53(2):419–452
Metcalfe DJ (2014) The history of government transparency. In: Ala'i P, Vaughn RG (eds) Research handbook on transparency. Edward Elgar Publishing
Michener G, Bersch K (2013) Identifying transparency. Inf Polity 18(3):233–242
Mihaescu Evans BC (2015) The right to good administration at the crossroads of various sources of fundamental rights in the EU integrated administrative system. Nomos
Mitchell A, Munro J, Voon T (2019) Importing WTO general exceptions into international investment agreements: proportionality, myths, and risks. In: Sachs LE, Johnson L, Coleman J (eds) Yearbook on international investment law and policy 2017. Oxford University Press, pp 305–355
Moberg A, Hindelang S (2020) The art of casting political dissent in law: the EU's framework for the screening of foreign direct investment. Common Mark Law Rev 57(5):1427–1460
Kreuschitz V, Nehl HP (2016) Direct actions and judicial review before the Union Courts. In: Hofmann HCH, Micheau C (eds) State aid law of the European Union. Oxford University Press, pp 406–449
Nettesheim M (2021) Screening for what threat: preserving "public order and security", securing reciprocity in international trade, or supporting certain social, environmental, or industrial policies? In: Hindelang S, Moberg A (eds) YSEC yearbook of socio-economic constitutions 2020: a common European law on investment screening (CELIS). Springer, pp 481–504
Newcombe AP, Paradell L (2009) Law and practice of investment treaties: standards of treatment. Kluwer Law International BV
OECD (2005) Managing conflicts of interest in the public sector: a toolkit. OECD Publishing
OECD (2022) Framework for screening Foreign direct investment into the EU assessing effectiveness and efficiency
Palombino FM (2018) Fair and equitable treatment and the fabric of general principles. T.M.C. Asser Press & Springer
Paparinskis M (2013) The international minimum standard and fair and equitable treatment. Oxford University Press
Patnode D (2006) A history of parliamentary procedure, 4th edn. Parliamentarians International
Piotrowski SJ, Borry E (2010) An analytic framework for open meetings and transparency. Public Adm Manag 15(1):138
Pohl JH (2017) Substantive transparency requirements in international investment law. Rev Inst Colomb Derecho Trib 54(77):179–212
Pohl JH (2018) Openness in international investment law: too much of a good thing? Univ Bologna Law Rev 3(2):219–231
Pohl JH (2021) The right to be heard in composite investment screening procedures under Regulation 2019/452. In: Barrett G, Rageade J-P, Wallis D, Weil H (eds) The future of legal Europe: will we trust in it? pp 647–661. Springer
Reinisch A (2015) National treatment. In: Bungenberg M, Griebel J, Hobe S, Reinisch A, Kim Y-I (eds) International investment law: a Handbook. C. H. Beck, pp 846–869

Robertson VH (2016) The Spar cases in Austria: shaping the legal framework for digital evidence gathering during competition dawn raids. J Eur Compet Law Pract 7(3):205–211
Salacuse JW (2013) The three laws of international investment: national, contractual, and international frameworks for foreign capital. Oxford University Press
Schauer F (2011) Transparency in three dimensions. Univ Ill Law Rev 2011:1339–1357
Schefer KN (2016) International investment law: text, cases, and materials, 2nd edn. Edward Elgar Publishing
Schill SW (2012) Deference in investment treaty arbitration: re-conceptualizing the standard of review. J Int Disp Settl 3(3):577–607
Schudson M (2015) The rise of the right to know: politics and the culture of transparency, 1945–1975. Harvard University Press
Van den Bossche P, Zdouc W (2017) The law and policy of the World Trade Organization: text, Cases, and materials, 4th edn. Cambridge University Press
van Harten G (2013) Sovereign choices and sovereign constraints: judicial Restraint in investment treaty arbitration. Oxford University Press
Vaughn RG (2014) The associations of judicial transparency with administrative transparency. In: Ala'i P, Vaughn RG (eds) Research handbook on transparency. Edward Elgar Publishing, pp 247–250
Velten J (2020). The investment screening regulation and its screening ground "security or public order": how the WTO law understanding undermines the regulation's objectives. Graduate Institute of International and Development Studies, Centre for Trade and Economic Integration, Geneva. CTEI Working Paper 2020–01
Verellen T (2021) When integration by stealth meets public security: the EU foreign direct investment screening regulation. Leg Issues Econ Integr 48(1):19–42
Vidigal G, Schill SW (2021) International economic law and the securitization of policy objectives: risks of a Schmittean exception. Leg Issues Econ Integr 48(2):109–118
Waldeck J (1972) Legal nature of Parliamentary procedure. Clev St Law Rev 21:85
Yannaca-Small K (2010) Fair and equitable treatment standard. In: Yannaca-Small K (ed) Arbitration under international investment agreements: a guide to key issues. Oxford University Press, pp 385–410
Zwartkruis W, De Jong B (2020) The EU regulation on screening of foreign direct investment: a game changer? Eur Bus Law Rev 31(3):447–474

Chapter 7
Conclusion

Abstract This chapter synthesizes the findings of the dissertation and evaluates the role of international arbitration in disputes arising from national security screening of foreign investments. Drawing on doctrinal analysis of international investment agreements, arbitration awards, and judicial decisions, the chapter assesses how arbitral tribunals navigate the tension between protecting investor rights and respecting the sovereign authority of states to safeguard national security. The analysis demonstrates that while international investment agreements provide substantial protections—such as guarantees against unfair treatment, discrimination, and uncompensated expropriation—the invocation of national security exceptions can significantly limit these protections. Arbitral tribunals generally recognize national security as a legitimate state interest but vary in the degree of deference granted to state assessments of security risks. The research finds that tribunals in adjacent national-security and emergency cases have often applied principles such as proportionality, necessity, and procedural fairness when evaluating such measures. Although arbitration provides a neutral and structured forum for resolving these disputes, the inherently political nature of national security introduces challenges for consistency and predictability. The chapter concludes that arbitration remains a viable mechanism for balancing investor protection and state sovereignty, while highlighting the need for clearer treaty drafting and more consistent jurisprudential approaches to national security exceptions in international investment law.

The interplay between national security considerations and the protections afforded to foreign investors under international law presents a complex and evolving legal terrain. This dissertation examines the role of arbitration in resolving disputes arising from national security screenings of foreign investments. This subject has become increasingly relevant in today's globalized economic environment. Against the backdrop of rising geopolitical tensions and growing instances where national security is invoked to scrutinize or even block foreign investments, this research

J. H. Pohl, *Arbitration of Disputes related to National Security Screening of Foreign Investments*, EYIEL Monographs - Studies in European and International Economic Law 50,
https://doi.org/10.1007/978-3-032-26342-1_7

aims to illuminate the intricate balance arbitration seeks to maintain between upholding state sovereignty and ensuring investor protection.

Central to this exploration were several guiding research questions that probed the depths of legal frameworks, arbitration practices, and the broader implications of these interactions for international investment law. Therefore, this conclusion synthesizes the comprehensive findings from the dissertation and summarizes how each element contributes to our understanding of the dynamic between national security imperatives and international legal obligations. By addressing the scope and efficacy of arbitration in this context, the study seeks to enhance scholarly knowledge and offer practical insights into managing conflicts that arise at the intersection of national security and global investment.

7.1 Methodology

This dissertation employed a doctrinal research methodology, a foundational approach in legal academic studies that is particularly suited to exploring complex intersections of international law. By systematically analyzing IIAs, arbitration awards, and judicial decisions, this study sought to elucidate how national security considerations are integrated and managed within the framework of international arbitration.

Primary sources formed the cornerstone of the research, including a variety of bilateral and multilateral investment treaties that embody provisions for arbitration involving national security exceptions. These documents provided the legal basis for understanding the rights and obligations of states and investors, and they offered insights into how these principles are applied in practice. Key arbitration awards and decisions where national security has been a significant factor were scrutinized to identify how arbitrators interpret and balance the competing demands of protecting national security and upholding investor rights.

Secondary sources, including scholarly articles, legal commentaries, and previous jurisprudential analyses, supported the primary data by offering theoretical contexts and comparative insights. These resources helped frame the issues within broader legal and geopolitical debates and provided a multifaceted understanding of the arbitration process and its outcomes. Extensive use of legal databases such as Westlaw, LexisNexis, and JSTOR ensured a comprehensive coverage of relevant literature and caselaw, which was crucial for a thorough doctrinal analysis.

The analytical approach involved a critical evaluation of how arbitration tribunals navigate the tensions between state sovereignty in national security matters and the enforcement of IIAs. This analysis included an examination of the interpretation of treaty provisions concerning national security, the application of legal standards across different cases, and the extent to which arbitral tribunals defer to state authority in determining what constitutes a national security threat.

This methodological framework allowed for a detailed and systematic exploration of the selected topic to ensure that the findings were grounded in solid legal doctrine while also being responsive to the complexities presented by the relationship between national security and international investment law.

7.2 Results and Answers to Research Questions

The investigation into the arbitration of disputes related to national security screenings of foreign investments yielded comprehensive findings across several key dimensions:

What is the degree of protection promised to foreign investors under international investment agreements in the context of national security screenings? IIAs typically offer substantial protections to foreign investors, which include guarantees against unfair and inequitable treatment, expropriation without compensation, and promises of full protection and security. However, the research identified that when these protections intersect with national security exceptions, tension arises and manifests in the form of restrictive measures imposed by host states under the banner of national security, which can significantly undermine these promised protections. The analysis of cases such as the domestic judicial analogue *Ralls* highlighted scenarios where host states utilized national security as a defence, which often resulted in a restrictive interpretation of investor protections. This collision between investment guarantees and national security measures poses considerable challenges to the predictability and reliability of international investment law as a protective mechanism for foreign investments.

To what extent is it legitimate for investors to expect that their protection under international law will be subjugated to a host state's national security interests? The legitimacy of subjugating investor protections to national security interests varies across cases. While national security is a recognized defence, its application is inconsistent. Tribunals in non-screening related but analogous cases like in *CMS Gas Transmission Company v. Argentina* scrutinize the proportionality and necessity of national security measures. The findings show that while national security is a legitimate defence, its invocation must be justified by genuine and substantial threats to the state's security.

What constitutes a manageable level of national security risk for a host state regarding foreign investment, and how should these risks be evaluated? Evaluating national security risks involves assessing the thresholds and criteria used by states, heavily influenced by geopolitical contexts. These variations impact the arbitration process, where determinations of what constitutes a national security risk are crucial. The dissertation found that arbitral tribunals often defer to the assessments provided by host states. However, this deference varies depending on the tribunal's perception of the state's transparency and the rationality of the security measures implemented. This deference was evident in illustrative cases like *Continental Casualty v The Republic of Argentina*, where the tribunal upheld the state's economic security measures despite significant investor losses.

According to what criteria and which procedures should the opposing interests of host states and foreign investors be weighed in arbitration? Balancing opposing interests involves examining the proportionality of the state's measures against the national security threat. Tribunals aim to respect state sovereignty while ensuring that national security is not a cover for unjustifiable measures against foreign investors. Procedural fairness and a thorough examination of both parties' arguments are crucial. This balanced approach is seen in cases like *Continental Casualty v Argentina*, where the tribunal sought to respect both state sovereignty and investor rights.

Can international arbitration effectively and fairly resolve disputes arising from national security screenings of foreign investments? The dissertation concluded that arbitration is a viable means of resolving such disputes but has limitations. The process provides a neutral ground, yet the political nature of national security can complicate proceedings. Despite these challenges, arbitration remains a viable mechanism for producing legitimate outcomes, as seen in various cases where tribunals have successfully navigated the complexities of national security and investor protection.

Therefore, the results of this research painted a detailed picture of the challenges and opportunities within the arbitration of disputes involving national security screenings. They highlighted the delicate balance that must be maintained between protecting investors and respecting the sovereign rights of states, which is crucial for the stability and fairness of the international investment system.

7.3 Discussion

The findings from this dissertation offer substantial insights into the dynamic relationship between national security considerations and international arbitration and contribute to theoretical and practical aspects of international investment law. This section discusses the conceptual contributions, jurisprudential insights, methodological rigour, implications for policy and practice, and recommendations for further research based on the study's results.

7.3.1 Conceptual Contributions

The research significantly advances our understanding of how arbitration can address tensions between national security and foreign investment. By dissecting cases where national security arguments are pivotal, the study develops a framework for analyzing similar disputes in the future. This framework helps to understand the thresholds that states must meet to justify national security measures under international law and the extent to which these measures may impact investor rights. Conceptually, the dissertation enriches the discourse on the balance of power between states and foreign investors by emphasizing the role of international arbitration in mediating these powers within the confines of legal structures.

7.3.2 Jurisprudential Insights

The study provides critical insights into the evolving jurisprudence around national security exceptions in international arbitration. It highlights how arbitral tribunals are increasingly required to interpret intricate and often vague national security clauses in investment treaties. The analysis outlines a trend towards a more cautious approach by tribunals, which reflects a deeper appreciation of the geopolitical contexts that influence national security decisions. The findings illustrate the challenges tribunals face in ensuring that national security is not used as a blanket justification for violating investor rights to contribute to a more refined understanding of legal standards and practices in this area.

7.3.3 Methodological Rigor

The methodological approach adopted in this dissertation underscores its academic rigour and the reliability of its conclusions. By employing a comprehensive doctrinal analysis supported by a diverse range of primary and secondary sources, the research offers a robust examination of the legal principles at play. This methodological rigour enhances the credibility of the findings and sets a benchmark for future studies in the field. It demonstrates the importance of a thorough and systematic approach to legal research, especially when dealing with the complexities of international law and arbitration.

7.3.4 Implications for Policy and Practice

The findings of this study have significant implications for policymakers and practitioners involved in drafting IIAs and arbitrating disputes. The insights into how national security considerations are handled in arbitration can inform the development of clearer and more precise treaty language that better balances state security interests with investor protections. For practitioners, understanding the nuances of arbitral decision-making in cases involving national security can improve the strategies employed in representing both states and investors. Moreover, the study's revelations about the inconsistent application of national security exceptions suggest a need for more standardized procedures in international arbitration.

7.3.5 Recommendations for Further Research

Given the complexities uncovered in this research, further studies are recommended to continue exploring the interface between national security and international arbitration. Future research can focus on comparative analyses across different legal systems and their treatment of national security in foreign investments. Additionally, empirical studies examining the outcomes of arbitration cases involving national security measures can provide deeper insights into the trends and patterns in arbitral decision-making. Such studies can be invaluable in developing a more comprehensive understanding of the practical implications of arbitration on international relations and investment security.

This discussion underscores the dissertation's contribution to an improved understanding of a critical area of international law. The exploration of arbitration's role in mediating disputes involving national security and foreign investments fills a significant gap in the literature and provides a foundation for ongoing academic and practical advancements in this field.

7.4 Conclusion

This dissertation systematically explored the challenging intersection between national security measures and the protections guaranteed to foreign investors, with a particular focus on the role of arbitration in resolving disputes arising from national security screenings. The findings illuminated the complexities inherent in balancing state security imperatives with the principles of international investment law to provide a better understanding of the arbitration process as a critical mechanism in this context.

The study demonstrated that while arbitration offers a viable platform for resolving disputes involving national security, the process is fraught with challenges. Arbitral tribunals frequently grapple with the dual demands of respecting state sovereignty in enforcing national security measures and upholding the legal rights of foreign investors. This delicate balance is often influenced by the broad and sometimes vague definitions of national security provided in international agreements, which can lead to inconsistent interpretations and outcomes. Through rigorous doctrinal analysis, this research contributed to the broader discourse on international arbitration and highlighted the need for clearer guidelines and more precise treaty language that delineate the boundaries of national security exceptions. The findings suggest that a more standardized approach can enhance the predictability and fairness of arbitral decisions to strengthen the global investment climate.

As international investment continues to intersect with critical issues of national security, the insights from this dissertation offer valuable guidance for policymakers, legal practitioners, and scholars. They underscore the importance of continuous dialogue and adaptation in treaty-making and arbitral practice to accommodate the evolving domain of global security and economic relations.

In conclusion, this dissertation advances our understanding of the intersection between national security and international investment law while underscoring the vital role that arbitration can play in this field. It calls for ongoing research and policy refinement to ensure that arbitration remains an effective and equitable tool for resolving disputes that touch on the sensitive nexus of national security and foreign investment.

7.5 Propositions

1. The phenomenon of weaponized investments, where foreign direct investments are strategically used by states to achieve geopolitical objectives, poses significant challenges to national security and necessitates the implementation of stringent investment screening mechanisms by host states.
2. Investment screening mechanisms are increasingly being used by states as a tool to mitigate geoeconomic risks posed by foreign investments, particularly those that may threaten national security.
3. The application of security exception clauses in investment treaties allows states to deviate from their treaty obligations to safeguard national security, reflecting a balance between state sovereignty and international legal commitments.
4. The inherent right of states to regulate for national security purposes must be balanced against the protections afforded to foreign investors under international investment treaties, particularly in terms of non-discrimination and fair and equitable treatment standards.

5. The jurisdictional complexities associated with sovereign investors in international investment law highlight the need for clear treaty definitions to guide arbitral tribunals in distinguishing between commercial and governmental activities of sovereign investors.
6. The necessity defence under customary international law can be invoked by states to justify measures taken for national security that would otherwise breach investment treaty obligations, although its application requires a high threshold of proving grave and imminent peril.
7. Arbitral deference to national security considerations can undermine the process of judicialization in international investment law and, by extension, weaken the rules-based order that underpins global investment governance.
8. International legal frameworks must adapt to the evolving landscape of geoeconomic risks and national security concerns, influencing the development of more robust and transparent investment screening mechanisms worldwide.
9. Enhancing transparency in the investment screening process is essential to ensure procedural justice and maintain investor confidence in international arbitration systems.
10. The awareness and management of geoeconomic risks have become central to state behavior towards inbound FDI, reflecting a shift from purely economic considerations to strategic geopolitical calculations.
11. National security screening mechanisms have the potential to become instruments of lawfare and geolegal rivalry, where states use legal tools strategically to achieve geopolitical objectives, thereby complicating international investment relations.

The manufacturer's authorised representative in the EU is Springer
Nature Customer Service Centre GmbH, Europaplatz 3, 69115 Heidelberg,
Germany. If you have any concerns regarding our products, please
contact ProductSafety@springernature.com

Printed and bound by CPI Group (UK) Ltd, Croydon, CR0 4YY
05/10/2026
02228023-0005